How They Did It

Billion Dollar Insights from the Heart of America

First published 2010 by RedFlash
Press, a division of RedFlash and
InterimCEO, Inc.

Design by Lee Blair

Printed in the United States of America

15 14 13 12 11 10
1 2 3 4 5 6 7 8

ISBN: 978-0-615-38543-3

This book is available at special
discount when purchased in quantity.
For details contact: info@redflash.com
or the address below.

RedFlash Press
1450 Techny Road
Northbrook, IL 60062

Phone: +1(847) 849-2800

www.redflash.com

www.howtheydiditbook.com

Interviews began on September 8, 2008, when 21 founders gathered at the Four Seasons hotel in Chicago to multi-author *How They Did It*.

dedication

This book is dedicated to Dick Heise, without whose support I could not have launched my first company, Online Access. There is no finer example of a gracious investor and entrepreneur's champion.

If there are modern day versions of the Medicis, patrons of the arts in Renaissance Italy, those princes would be Rich Heise and Eric Lefkofsky, whose masterful ability to launch and grow companies gave an opportunity to one of their shareholders to pursue his dream of creating and publishing this book.

About this Book

This is a book of quotes: thoughts, ideas, and inspiration from 45 of the most successful living company founders to come out of the American heartland. The intention here is a quick jolt of inspiration.

For those readers who enjoy a deeper dive, there is a second book lurking in the margins: advice and insights shared by the founders in interviews conducted over the course of 2008 to 2010. The interviews were edited, excerpted, and approved by the founders. Handwritten quotes were submitted by the founders themselves.

Robert Jordan

Would the company be a billion dollar success? I didn't know, but could I create value? Absolutely. Could I create a good business? Absolutely. And can I help solve a need in the market? Help patients? Absolutely. So I believed and I still do. There's a need. I can fill it. I can solve this.

Jeff Aronin

Jeff Aronin

Ovation Pharmaceuticals
Illinois

Let's talk about the goat farm for starters.
We developed a drug using genetically modified goats to help people whose blood doesn't clot. We insert a strand of human DNA a protein that creates blood clotting—into a goat embryo's DNA. As the baby goat matures, it can produce this enzyme in its milk. We have a fully FDA-regulated goat farm that produces the ingredient used to make the drug. It's the first transgenic drug ever developed in the world.

The world thinks it understands entrepreneurs, but it's not that easy, is it?
It's very difficult to get the same

perspective as an entrepreneur if you haven't been one. I would think it would be very difficult to write about it.

Don't get me started. So many CEOs were suggested for this book who didn't start any companies, and our sole focus was, and is, about great company founders.
I put it in three categories. First there's family business. Family business has its own set of challenges and can be very tough. But you're not an entrepreneur if you didn't start it. Second, there's the professional manager who's hired to come run something. I don't care if it's Day Five of the company's existence. It's still different than being an entrepreneur. It doesn't mean you can't become one, and I'm not saying one is better

or worse. It's just different. And then there's being an entrepreneur. That's what I'm passionate about.

Passion drove you to start Ovation, which you ultimately sold to Lundbeck for $900 million. What's different about an entrepreneur?
It's a unique set of skills. The ability to say, "I'm going to bet it all on this." When I started there was nobody to make coffee or take out the garbage. Coming from a Fortune 500 environment, you're giving something up. I believe once you've been an entrepreneur, you can't do anything else. I mean, there's nothing like building and growing.

You're the definition of showing moxie at a young age. While you were in college you took a girlfriend

with asthma to the hospital, ended up chatting with the docs, who referred you to pharmaceutical reps because they thought you'd be good at it.
I cold-called the reps and said "I don't want anything from you. Just let me drive with you one day. I want to learn more about what you do."

That had to have worked.
The rep told the manager, "You gotta hire this guy. He really cares about this, he's passionate." So the rep convinced the manager to hire me. They weren't even recruiting on campus.

That's a great lesson for a new college grad.
I needed to differentiate myself. I had already done a summer job selling cable door-to-door. The cable company

When you're in a small company it's going to get rocky, and you just better be ready for it.

– Jeff Aronin

2

Jeff Aronin

had full-time people selling, and I did it three to four hours a night at the end of school. I was the number one sales guy in the country against the full-time people for three months out of the summer.

You discovered some secret way to sell cable services?
I was just more personable and I worked a lot harder. I didn't go home until I hit a certain number. I liked the whole thing and I started to see how business worked.

Sales aptitude led you to pharma and fast promotion—you became a manager at 23.
I loved science, I loved medicine. It was a good place to start. I was with a Fortune 500 company, Carter-Wallace. But they didn't innovate and invest in

new growth, which ended up hurting them. I started in sales and quickly became a manager.

How does one advance in pharma?
Everybody wants the big brands, everybody wants to be in on the blockbuster drugs, even if you're #11 on a team.

That's not for an entrepreneur.
You made your name working on the big brands. But I didn't want to be the 12th man on the big team, so I took on smaller brands and grew them.

You were the champion for an underdog brand. Then came an opportunity to head up marketing at an underdog company.
Thanks to great mentors, an opportunity came along, to help out a

struggling company, American Health. We were able to grow the business and ultimately sell the company. Some venture guys who'd seen what I did brought me in to run another pharma company called MedCare Health.

How did MedCare Health do?
We had some great success, some failures. I learned that the things I could control I did very well. Then there were the things I could not control. The lesson was to try to eliminate or minimize those things. One thing that really struck me was that I had not chosen that company's mission, even though people were betting on me.

So you left to start Ovation. One in a thousand drugs gets approved. It takes 10 years and $800 million to

get a drug approved, and then only 40 percent of all approved drugs ever make back the money that was invested in them. What was your reasoning in leaving to start a new company?
The industry was consolidating in 2000. Searle was acquired by Pharmacia Upjohn. Pharmacia Upjohn was acquired by Pfizer. So some drugs that were once important to Pharmacia or Searle were no longer important to Pfizer. These were the drugs I had a history of working on. Trust me, if you have a disease that's a small disease state, you could care less that it's considered small. To you it's big. These smaller disease states were being overlooked.

Why?
Pfizer has over $50 billion in revenue.

I was demanding. Our hires had to be very talented. When you're starting and growing, there are no trees to hide behind. Everyone sees what you do. Now we're big; we're $2 billion in revenue at Lundbeck. We're complex. Somebody could hide a little bit. In the early days you couldn't.

Jeff Aronin

They need to grow double digit earnings, and it can't be done with a drug that only does $100 million in revenue. The math doesn't work. They have to focus on billion-dollar drugs and, thank God, they do. But there is a need for companies to invest in drugs for things like epilepsy and Huntington's disease.

For you, it was about these diseases that were being overlooked.
Epilepsy, for example, is considered a small disease state. There are a lot of people with it, but the revenue is small compared to other diseases. I had worked with the doctors and the families, and I had seen what happens. It may not seem like a terrible disease until you see a baby having a hundred spasms a day or a young girl who has

to have a surgery where they literally take off the top of her head to map the brain and figure out where her seizures are coming from. There are drugs that should have been available.

It was a business challenge and yet emotional. What did you do?
I said, this is wrong, because there are drugs that will work. They're sitting on shelves, maybe only in phase one or phase two, but we have the ability to develop these drugs and improve the lives of people with these diseases. It wasn't the research. Research is hard and risky, but the expensive part is in drug development—testing it in patients—because sometimes it works, sometimes it doesn't. It's long and it's hard. And then getting it commercialized. That was where I was going to focus.

You left a CEO's corner office at a public company, $300 million revenue, to become an army of one. Sometimes spouses have issues with this kind of career shift.
My wife knew I had opportunities with big pharma companies and she said, "You're doing what?" I said, "Listen." This was November of 2000. Her birthday was in April. She said, "Just do me a favor. Evaluate this at my birthday." She was nervous but she believed in me. I said, "All right. I'll do that. By the way, I'm putting all our savings in it."

She missed that line?
To be quite honest, I don't ever remember thinking, what do I do if this doesn't work? There weren't many options. I didn't come from a wealthy

background, so it wasn't like there was a safety net.

But you must have had a drug in development. Something you took with you?
No.

This is all about confidence. How does someone starting a company get confidence?
I learned teamwork from sports. You can be a leader without being the best at everything. Like in basketball—you don't need to be the best outside shooter or the big guy. You can play a role, and being a leader is a role that I was good at. Working with others, giving people credit. Give and take. Knowing how to make hard decisions. I learned how to believe in myself and my team.

I'm not saying it wasn't scary. It's a little bit of levitating early on. When you call on a senior VP or CEO you don't say, 'I started this new company.' You say, 'I'm CEO of a new company and what we're doing is this and I'd like to come by.' They have to believe that you can actually get a deal done.

Jeff Aronin

Jeff Aronin

So you wrote a business plan for Ovation. What about investors?
I did an angel round for one reason. Not for the money but because I wanted to get some smart, talented people vested in the deal.

At the end of 2000? The market was imploding.
Right. Dot com bubble. In '99, being young helped you raise money. In 2001, the worst thing you could do was not have gray hair. So I had to surround myself with people with gray hair. I went to people I knew who knew pharma, ex-CEOs of pharma companies who had credibility, and got them to be investors and to serve on my advisory board, and I raised a few million dollars.

Did your advisors really help?
I built a great advisory board. Since I wasn't a public company, I told them that there was basically no risk. All I wanted them to do was advise me. And I listened. I really cared about what they said. But I also called them with my wish list, the products I wanted to acquire.

You're a believer in advisory boards. What about other resources?
I called the senior partner at a law firm and told him I wanted him to be behind me on this. Not only did they do a lot of the early work for very little money, they invested. I started with the best of the best: Deloitte for accounting and Katten Muchin for legal. It was amazing because I had nothing at the beginning other than my vision and my word that I would work hard.

Plenty of start-ups don't make it. What was the secret sauce at Ovation?
From Day One we have been very good with data. We have the ability to tear apart information—enormous amounts of data—better than most. We're very focused on what the market is gonna look like in five years, what the need will be, what else is out there, what's coming.

How did you raise money?
I figured out who does what. I just focused on six or seven private equity funds and five or six venture guys. It took awhile. The market had blown up. I had credibility from my advisory board and early investors and we were able to raise $150 million with nothing more than an idea.

You used a funding concept popularized by the GTCR fund, but for drug acquisition.
GTCR had never done a pharma deal before. They said, "You knew exactly what the products and the models were. You looked like a big company, and you only had three people."

And with only $47 million from GTCR's war chest, you got to a good size.
Before we sold we had 22 drugs in 87 countries around the world. We were about to be a billion dollars in revenue within three years.

Any thoughts on hiring?
I was demanding. Our hires had to be very talented. When you're starting and growing, there are no trees to hide behind. Everyone sees what you

You can be a leader w/out being the best at everything. like in basketball— you don't need to be the best outside shooter or the big guy. you can play a role, and being a leader is a role I was good at. Working with others, giving people credit. Give and take. knowing how to make hard decisions.

— Jeff Aronin

do. Now we're big. We're $2 billion in revenue. We're complex. Somebody could hide a little bit. In the early days you couldn't.

You gave equity to every employee. Why?
We all had to be pulling in the same direction. We really were aligned. And people who are owners make incredibly rational decisions.

But you also paid less upfront salaries.
It was one of my rules. Lower base, bigger bonus. And you get equity. People took a risk because they saw the upside. And they saw that there were other great people and they wanted to be a part of that. The final thing was that we were making the world better by getting drugs developed that would help patients and you actually could make a difference individually.

This is a great example of sticking to what you know. You were expert in diseases of the central nervous system, so you focused all of Ovation's energies around that.
We did buy a couple drugs that drug companies were losing money on, that they didn't know how to manufacture or market well. We figured out a way to improve distribution, grow the market, and find the patients who had those diseases.

Was the company ever in doubt of surviving?
No, but we had a lot of tough times. The FDA came back with bad news, and I had managers who started saying, "the sky is falling." So we moved some people out, and they kick themselves now. The rest of the team looked at each other and said, "We're in for another year of really rough times, and we're gonna make it. We believe in this."

The FDA approves about 25 new chemical entities a year, and in just a sixth-month window, Ovation will have four drugs approved. More power to you, Jeff. And congratulations on the Humanitarian of the Year award from the Illinois Holocaust Museum and Education Center.
Thanks. I want to focus on what I'm most thankful for—the people who left their companies when they were climbing high. They believed in me and came to work at Ovation. They are the real stars. I also believe we have an obligation in the industry to keep developing drugs and improve the lives of patients. We have that ability.

I had this idea with the few dollars that I had. I bought a van that was going to be a lab on wheels. To make a long story short, I was the courier but I never once used the lab in the back because I got so busy. Who the heck had time to do that stuff at the back of the van?

Bonnie Baskin

Bonnie Baskin

ViroMed Laboratories, AppTec Laboratory Services

Minnesota

Your career was inspired by a famous book, Rachel Carson's *Silent Spring*.
I read her book and, as a result, I decided I wanted to become a marine biologist. When it came time to apply to schools, I applied and went to University of Miami. They have a very good school of marine biology and oceanography. First semester, this was in 1966, I took my first course in marine biology. We had to go out on Biscayne Bay in these little boats with a little cabin. I got seasick. I was just incapacitated and I made a decision that marine biology was probably not

in my future and that while I really was interested in science, I wanted to be involved in something that was landlocked.

Seasickness was motivating.
That was it for me. I think there must have been a fairy godmother when I made that decision as I ended up majoring in microbiology.

And that led to a PhD.
At that time the University of Miami was quite the play school and, quite frankly, I had a wonderful time. You hear of people who are driven and focused and know exactly what they want. Frankly, I had no idea what I wanted. All I knew is that I didn't want to work. I was offered the possibility of going to graduate school there and getting a masters in microbiology.

They offered me a full ride, and I thought, well, I've got nothing better to do, so I'll do it. I was there for about a year, and then they said, "We'd love for you to go straight on for a PhD, and we'll also get you a teaching assistantship and take care of your tuition." I figured, why not? I got my PhD in microbiology in 1975.

You have such an interesting story, Bonnie. You didn't want to work coming out of college. You were invited to attend graduate school, then went on to complete your PhD. You won a post-doctoral scholarship at NIH, then found yourself in a lab at the University of Minnesota. Whatever motivated you to start a company?
I was really going to be a researcher

and that was going to be my career. I wound up leaving the University. The person that I worked for was not very sympathetic or flexible with respect to a woman who had two very small boys. I left and found myself without a job. I had to think about what I was going to do. I had to take care of my kids and myself.

And then came the spark of an idea?
I had an idea about the possibility of opening a private clinical virology laboratory. They didn't exist at that time. This was pre-AIDS, pre-hepatitis C. I knew the FDA was going to be approving the first antiviral drug against herpes simplex in the beginning of '82, so I thought, well, maybe there will be a need for doctors to do diagnostic testing. There's a

There are so many people I've met who are very talented, but they become paralyzed when faced with problems. These are difficult problems and they just can't figure a way out. I think, really to be successful, you have to be able to continually see that glass half full, and not ever, ever give up.

Bonnie Baskin

reason to do it because there's a therapy.

You created companies that ultimately sold for a total of $203 million but how did you initially get funding?
There was no way in the world I could go to a bank. I had never had a job before. I had no idea what it was like to write a business plan. But I had a $50,000 loan from my family.

What was your next step?
I started talking to people at the various hospitals and colleges around Minnesota and said, "Look, if I open up this lab, do you think you would send me some samples, and, by the way, how many would you send?"

You may have had an academic background, Bonnie, but the savviest salesperson couldn't have said it better.
I was just trying to see if I could make this business somewhat sustainable. I was able to forecast numbers that showed that I had a chance of success.

Did you have help?
I talked to two women that I worked with at the university who were wonderful laboratorians. They committed to leave their jobs and work with me to open up ViroMed.

Were you hiring the best or proving something in a male culture?
Both.

What was the lab's competitive advantage?
One of the problems with viruses is that they don't live very long outside the body. So a lot of times, you can take a specimen and get a negative result, but it's not that the virus wasn't there, it just died before the testing could begin. So I had this idea with the few dollars that I had. I bought a van that was going to be the courier van, and I remodeled the back of it to be a mobile lab. By putting a little incubator in there I could keep the viruses alive until the sample could be processed in the lab.

A lab on wheels?
Right. The plan was you'd go to the hospital, pick up the sample, and immediately, in the back of the van, put it in the special food that it

needed, and keep it that way under the conditions that it liked to grow. At the end of the day, you would bring everything back to the lab and process it.

Everyone liked that plan?
It was well received because it gave the physician the opportunity for much better results.

And the van worked okay?
I used the van to pick up the samples, but I never once used the lab in back because I got so busy. Who the heck had time to do that stuff at the back of the van?

I have to introduce you to Dick Costolo (see *Dick Costolo, page 23*)—he also does stand-up comedy. So you found out that you could pick it up fast enough so that the virus

My timing was perfect. We became very busy. There wasn't anybody else who was really doing this virus work because most hospital labs did not have the expertise.

Bonnie Baskin

Bonnie Baskin

didn't die before you got it back to the lab?
Right. The lab opened in February of 1982. My timing was perfect. That was about the time when *Newsweek* and *Time* put the STD epidemic, herpes, and chlamydia on their covers. We became very busy. There wasn't anybody else who was really doing this virus work because most hospital labs did not have the expertise or the safe environments required.

Just not equipped.
Nobody knew that much about viruses. And there was concern about contagion. At the time you were just starting to hear about AIDS and the HIV virus.

ViroMed is also a great example of someone who was in, shall we say, retail, and then discovers an entirely

new business in wholesale?
These viruses only grow in living cells, and many of them grow in monkey kidney cells. They have to be fresh from a monkey's kidney, and they only last for one week.

So every week you had to get fresh cells?
Yes, and they were very expensive. There was a minimum amount of cells per order, and there was no way in the world I could use all of them. Most of the cells would be wasted and that would bring up my cost of doing the test to a prohibitive point. It was a dilemma for me. However, I was able to solve the problem as I knew someone starting a virus lab just like mine, for one of the hospitals in St. Paul. It dawned on me that he was going to run into the same

problem. So I called him and said, "Hey, how 'bout this. I'll buy the cells from these guys on the East Coast. I'll prepare them and sell you what you need, and I'll keep the rest." And he said, "Yeah." It was a win-win.

That opened up a completely new line of business for you.
There are other cells needed for a virus lab, so I started making all of his cells for him. Then I thought maybe I should make them for other labs, too. I wound up having the largest cell culture business in the country and I sold to just about every laboratory that needed these kinds of cells. I sold about 150,000 units a week.

A single mom, zero to 350 employees. Now that's entrepreneurship.

I had them coming and going. Either they would send us the patient samples and we would do the work, or I would sell them the raw materials for them to do the work. The joy of it is the building of the business and its strategy, and taking something that you have and repackaging it, and adding to it, to be able to find another opportunity to grow. I can do operations but I don't especially like it.

You then repackaged all that expertise for the medical device industry. You acquired an Atlanta company for that?
Again, a small woman-owned company—I always called the founder my "steel magnolia." She had created a very high quality lab focused on services for the medical

The joy is the building of the business and its strategy, and taking something that you have, repackaging it and adding to it, to be able to find another opportunity to grow —

Bonnie Baskin

device industry. I wanted to add those services to our testing portfolio.

Then another acquisition in New Jersey.
New Jersey was a disaster. I bought the company from the investors—I got it for pennies on the dollar. It cost me way over a dollar to get it working, but it really was the beginning of this whole idea of our industrial group – a continuum of testing services for both medical device and biologic therapeutics.

You not only made that work, but pushed forward at exactly the right time to sell the company.
I was following these large, clinical, publicly traded labs and their valuations were really high. I contacted an investment banker at Piper Jaffray to sell the clinical diagnostic virology division of ViroMed. I didn't want to sell the new industrial part because it was just starting and wasn't profitable yet, and why should I sell it when I couldn't get full value for it?

You sold the clinical lab portion of ViroMed in 2000, at $26 million revenue, to Laboratory Corporation of America for $40 million. Congratulations.
It was a nice sale. Then I took the piece that I didn't sell and spun it out and that became AppTec.

AppTec had $12 million in revenue, operating losses and 130 employees. What was your game plan?
I wanted to try something else, and I really wanted to create a company that was significantly larger than ViroMed.

In order to do this the way we wanted to do it, I had to raise a significant amount of money because we needed to build a new facility.

You raised venture capital, then grew AppTec to $70 million revenue. How did you know it was time to call Piper Jaffray again?
I had no desire to be a public CEO. I had too many friends who were public CEOs and it didn't look like a lot of fun to me. We had a sexy company, really starting to hit its stride. We heard about this company, WuXi PharmaTech, that JP Morgan was taking public. It was a Wall Street darling at the time of the IPO. We all thought it would be an interesting company because they were looking to be global and have a presence in the

US. We sold it to them for $163 million in January '08.

Congratulations again, Bonnie. That sale completed right before the biggest economic crash since the Great Depression. With your timing you should do a hedge fund. There was no board of directors at ViroMed. Your father owned a successful chemical company. Was he like a board member or a mentor?
Without question. And I learned a lot from him. He is a very caring person and he was a wonderful employer. And I learned from him the right way to treat people, whether it be a customer or somebody who works for you. Everybody at both my companies has always had equity positions in the company. One of the original

I divide people into categories—either you see the glass half empty or you see the glass half full. And it speaks to the crises you go through. You have to have the perspective and the personality that, when these bumps, mountains or doglegs happen, you don't focus on everything that's wrong. You continue to be optimistic and to move forward to solve the problems. There are always lessons learned and you wind up doing the post-mortem over and over again in your head as to what happened. But the most important aspect is to solve the problem, not to let the problem bog you down.

Bonnie Baskin

Bonnie Baskin

women who started with me from the University, worked with me through both companies all the way. I have good people who have worked for me for 20 plus years. I learned all of that from him. The right way to do things, the right way to engage people, and that you can't build businesses by yourself.

What's the biggest crisis you've faced?
We decided to bid to do all of the HIV testing for the US Navy, Marines, and Coast Guard. It was a big Department of Defense contract throughout the world. We knew how to do the testing, but there was an IT component, so that once the testing was done, the results could be transmitted back to the Navy. We found a company outside of

Washington that had worked with the government. We partnered with them and we won the contract. It was 60 days from the time we were awarded the contract to the time the first samples came in. We were prepared on the laboratory side – we had built out all the required robotic equipment to perform high volume testing. The computer company also said they were ready. Ten days before the first samples were going to arrive, we found out that there was no software package—they never did it.

You mean they were faking it?
Yes, perhaps. You know, they ran into problems. They didn't tell us that they didn't have the staff. There was nothing. We had maybe 80,000 specimens a day that would be coming in from all over the world.

What did you do?
We cancelled the contract with them. Then we negotiated with another company that ultimately did it, but there were months in between. I had the commander of the Southern fleet calling at 3 a.m. screaming at me. We ended up taking over a whole floor of our building for data entry. Then we hired people to work all night long. Everything was done manually.

What's the key to success?
I divide people into categories—either you see the glass half empty or you see the glass half full. And it speaks to the crises you go through. You have to be prepared. You have to have the perspective and the personality that, when these bumps, mountains or doglegs happen, you don't focus on everything that's wrong, but rather you

continue to be optimistic and to move forward to solve the problems. There are always lessons learned and you wind up doing the post-mortem over and over again in your head as to what happened. But the most important aspect is to solve the problem, not to let the problem bog you down, and continue to move.

So I stood up, whistled, gave a time out signal and said, "Ladies and gentlemen, let me solve the dilemma for you. I'm going to quit and do this myself, so thank you all very much. I appreciate your time today and hope you'll be a customer someday." And I walked out of the boardroom, cleaned out my desk, and went home.

David Becker

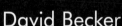

David Becker

First Internet Bank, re:Member Data Services, Virtual Financial Services
Indiana

Your first company was re:Member Data Services (RDS), which you sold to OSI for $24 million. Then you sold your second company, Virtual Financial Services (VIFI), to Digital Insight, now part of Intuit, for $52 million. While all that was happening you started the first de novo virtual bank anywhere in the world, appropriately called First Internet Bank, which now has $500 million in assets.
I started First Internet in 1999 as an online, real-time Internet bank using the software products I created.

I was at the Museum of Science and Industry in Chicago recently and I could have sworn I saw your bank's name on the permanent exhibit of the history of the Internet. Are you listed on the timeline?
Yep. And also on Google's Top 100 list.

How did you come to start RDS? I think you derived some insights from a prior decision on which college to attend.
When I was in high school my parents didn't have funding to send me to college. In fact, nobody on either side of my family had ever been to college. I got an appointment to the Coast Guard Academy. I didn't have political connections. I was just one of 10,000 kids across the country who applied, made the cut when they narrowed it down to four, and was finally granted

admission. I decided instead on DePauw University in Greencastle, Indiana, and graduated with a degree in political science.

You won out over 10,000 applicants and declined—why?
The Vietnam War was on, and I knew I'd probably tell the first guy who told me to scrub the deck with a toothbrush where to put it, and I'd wind up on the first boat to Vietnam. So at the last second I jumped over to DePauw.

After graduation you went to GE. Why didn't you stay there?
I moved up through the channels pretty quickly, but seniority in our division was north of 20 years, and I was told to pay my dues. After three years in there was no place else for me to go.

"Pay your dues" went over like, say, being told to scrub the deck with a toothbrush.
So I got a job as a consultant with the Indiana Credit Union League. In 1979 deregulation came along for financial institutions. The credit union industry lacked software programs and services to utilize their new powers. I complained until the chairman of the league told me to either shut up and support the services they had or find an alternative.

What did you find?
I spent six months researching computer services across the US. I created a business plan, found a product that I felt really met the needs of the industry, and presented the plan to the board of directors.

You're very hesitant to fire your first employees, but a lot of times the company outgrows their abilities or takes on a different direction.

David Becker

David Becker

What was the board's decision?
It wasn't really even a discussion of whether or not it was a good idea, just what committee should review it. So I stood up, whistled, gave a time out signal and said, "Ladies and gentlemen, let me solve the dilemma for you. I'm going to quit and do this myself, so thank you all very much. I appreciate your time today and hope you'll be a customer someday." And I walked out of the boardroom, cleaned out my desk, and went home.

'Atta boy! What next?
I called the software seller in Michigan I had recommended and told him things were going south, and that I'd like to buy computer time from him because I couldn't buy the software until I got a customer base. I drove to Grand Rapids and we struck a deal that

night at dinner. Next day I went to my lawyer and formed the company.

You took a big leap, because you didn't have the league as your customer, and you didn't know upfront that the Michigan company would sell to you.
The board's indecisiveness just frustrated me. In the end, more than half of the board members in the room became customers of mine.

Pretty good for no computer science background.
I still to this day cannot write a line of code if my life depended on it. But I can drink as much coffee as a programmer.

So now you had a corporation on paper. How did you grow the business?

I put a map of Indiana on the wall, and figured I could go 150 miles out from Indianapolis, to make a call or do whatever I needed to do, and get back in time to finish up the daily workload for the other clients I already had. My goal was 45 institutions in three years and we landed 40 of the 45.

Then came your next startup, OneBridge, 13 years later.
It does real-time credit and debit card processing for 30 financial institutions coast to coast. I'm listed as the CEO and have a president that runs it. We issue a contact-less credit card containing a RFID chip, where you just tap it at the terminal and it processes the transaction. We're an innovator and leader in the credit/debit card processing world.

More recently, you formed DyKnow.
DyKnow launched eight years ago. It's real-time software for capturing everything that goes on in the classroom. We have two products, Vision and Monitor. Vision captures what the professors or instructors are doing in the classroom. If they are doing a PowerPoint, for example, the student no longer has to take notes. It's all captured on a computer device.

What's the benefit for the student?
The student can replay the notes and annotations and everything that was shared by other students and faculty in the classroom, so you actually get to think about what went on instead of playing human copying machine.

What is Monitor?
In the K-12 arena it allows the instructor

*Delegate, delegate, delegate, which is
phenomenally tough to do
when it's your vision, your idea, your baby.*

David Becker

to see a thumbnail of the student's computer device in the classroom so they can tell if students are sitting there playing games or doing something they shouldn't. They can actually take control of the machine and lock it into the classroom arena.

Teachers must love it.
Without question. And because of their age and tenure, most K-12 teachers honestly feel that the students are smarter with technology than they are. This capability gives them the feeling they have control of the class and can track what's going on. Another great feature kind of looks like a traffic light. On the instructor's terminal, if all of the students understand what's being taught and they are staying with the instructor, the screen shows 100

percent green. If students start to get lost, they can hit a yellow button and it will show a certain percentage of yellow, and if they're completely lost, they just hit red. So without having to call attention to themselves, students can get the help they need. The teacher can say, "Based on what I'm seeing here on my screen, you're a bit lost. Let me back up and go over this again."

Retail Inventory Control System (RICS) is a more recent acquisition and proves once again the dangers of boredom for an entrepreneur. I have to introduce you to Jim Dolan (see Jim Dolan, page 32).
I was laid up for nine months from a pretty serious motorcycle accident and got bored to tears, so I started

throwing out some feelers. I had been introduced years before to Charlie McQuinn and his company, Retail Inventory Control System. Low and behold, Charlie surfaced, and we connected and pretty much negotiated a deal while I was laid up in bed.

Why did you buy RICS?
It was a nice little lifestyle business in Des Moines selling point-of-sale inventory control systems primarily to retailers, especially in footwear and athletic apparel. We flipped it into software as a service, built a web play, and now sell it by the slice.

How is it going?
We've got over 400 stores around the world live on the system now.

Why would a store choose RICS?
Small retail owners essentially never go on vacation, because they are afraid they can't keep track of the store while they're gone. In an online real-time environment with our software's dashboard components, an owner can look into a store from any PC anywhere in the world and see sales for the day, sales by product, sales by salesperson, and sales by store. They can track buying history and run specials, internal gift card programs, or frequent buyer programs. Ultimately, what we're working on at RICS is total integration, so a mom-and-pop operation or a five-store chain can have the same level of IT infrastructure and capability as the big players without spending millions of dollars on software.

You have to do certain things at certain times in your life, or the opportunity goes away.

Bill DeVille

David Becker

How do you keep hitting home runs with these companies?
There's a common base between the different firms with real-time interactivity. And I would always seed the next company with two or three key employees from my existing firm. I was very confident in their abilities.

What is the biggest crisis you have faced?
I've bootstrap financed all my companies. It was tough in the Midwest, particularly in the '80s and '90s, because as an information technology company we had no hard assets. It was a frustrating game.

What's most important for someone starting a company right now?
I used to bounce stuff off my grandfather, who had a seventh-grade education but ran 800 head of cattle in the Badlands of North Dakota, then came back to Wisconsin and got into eggs, real estate, and all kinds of things. He had two pieces of advice for me. He said, "You're young enough that if it doesn't work you can file bankruptcy and start all over again. Don't worry about it." And, "No matter how bad it gets, they can't eat ya."

No, they can't.
There have been times I felt like people were taking some big chunks out of me, but the bottom line message is to keep focused, stay with it, and, ultimately, survive. They can't do anything to you personally so you can always rebound, recover, and keep moving.

So many entrepreneurs freeze up, especially in a crisis.
You have to love what you're doing. It's not about the money, and it's not even about the product and the service. I guarantee you there's not an entrepreneur in the world who doesn't know every crack in the bedroom ceiling, every spot on the wall. Most successful ones have a piece of paper by the bedside. They wake up in the middle of the night thinking about things and scratch it out, write it down.

Any thoughts on hiring? RDS went from a solo operation to 150 employees and VIFI went from zero to 200 employees in five years.
Hire to your weaknesses, not your strengths. And delegate, delegate, delegate, which is phenomenally tough to do when it's your vision, your idea, your baby. But if you surround yourself with great folks, it gets a lot easier.

You have grown three Inc. 500 companies. What's the biggest mistake company founders make?
You're very hesitant to fire your first employees, but a lot of times the company outgrows their abilities or takes on a different direction. I tell everyone that the only constant around here is change.

Anything you would change if you could do it all over again?
I would try to strike more of a balance. I've been so focused on businesses over the years. It was tough to step away to take a vacation, but when I did I was reenergized and could recharge the batteries.

People think if you study long enough, you'll get clear direction to go ahead. That's never going to happen. You just have to have enough confidence in yourself to move forward.

Al Berning

Al Berning

Pemstar
Minnesota

You started Pemstar in '94 with IBM colleagues when IBM decided to move disk drives to Asia.
IBM was doing some major restructuring and we started looking at ways we could keep the team intact and pursue new opportunities.

So you left—
Seven of us. All senior managers. It was a team that quickly turned into several hundred.

All because the disk-drive industry was changing radically.
The entire industry had migrated launch and production to Asia. We had an outstanding launch and production team in Rochester, Minnesota, that wanted to continue living and working there.

Your role was founding chairman and CEO?
I organized the original business plan with the six other senior managers and quickly put the team together. We concluded we could create a new company that focused on outsourced design and manufacturing services.

Was IBM the first customer?
IBM was one of the first three customers.

How hard was it to raise money?
We quickly raised money, found a manufacturing and development lab location, and started setting up the business.

How much money did you raise along the way?
In the first round, including equity and a line of credit, we raised $4 million. We did two initial founder/angel rounds and then a couple mezzanine rounds. We did the IPO in 2000 and then two follow-on rounds.

But at the time of the IPO, wasn't the whole market declining fast?
It was declining, which we considered a positive. The stock price stayed in a normal, more realistic range.

You defied an incredible down-market to achieve your IPO, and then severe market declines following the tragedy of 9/11.
It was a tough market and we had the added challenge that a large percentage of our business involved designing and manufacturing optical components. When that market collapsed, we were faced with doing our own restructuring and redirection into new markets.

How did you do that?
Fortunately, we had already started. We just needed to speed up the transition to the new markets.

Eventually you sold Pemstar in 2007 for $300 million. For a big-company guy, your team proved to be very nimble.
We were fortunate our team had the precision-assembly and design skills required for several high-growth markets and the ability to quickly shift from one market to another.

Ultimately, you don't sell customers the physical product, you sell them the outcome and benefits of that product.

Viresh Bhatia

Al Berning

But you didn't know that upfront.
IBM was never in the business of contract manufacturing. What worked out very well for us was that we mapped the skills and expertise our team had within IBM and then looked outside the specific disk-drive industry for areas that fit our skills and where we could provide a competitive advantage. There were several nice fits using our technology expertise—including optical components, medical devices, and military electronics.

You knew you could do a good job building medical devices?
Right. One of our best examples was the Given Imaging capsule.

Oh, I love that company.
It's a micro camera that you swallow, and it goes through your digestive track. We worked with the company to design the product for high-volume manufacturing capability, built automation modules to assemble the product, set up the facility, and worked with them in Israel to manufacture the product. We set up another manufacturing facility in Ireland that also used precision-assembly and robots.

You picked a great industry.
There were a lot of products like that in the medical industry, where the traditional contract manufacturing industry didn't have the skills on board to tackle the engineering and automation required for the projects. The manufacturing by itself is important, but what led to most of the projects was our ability to either design or co-design the product so it would fit a cost-competitive, high-quality, and often automated manufacturing process.

What spurred you on to start your own company?
I'm from an extended family of people who ran their own businesses or agribusiness operations, so I was comfortable with the entrepreneurial part of it.

You took the plunge.
It was relatively steady progress, and the '90s were a good time to start almost any company. We recognized it wouldn't last forever so we diversified and made sure we had backup revenue streams. Everyone faced the same industry downturn and upheaval post 9/11.

At the time Northern Telecom was a juggernaut. It appeared to be unstoppable and was one of the leaders in optical infrastructure, but eventually it went bust. Contract manufacturing is not necessarily a recipe for hitting a home run.
We were pleased with our results. We chose the right time to merge with Benchmark, which was larger than us but had similar values and focused on product design and engineering.

So what was the key?
It was a combination of things that came together at the same time, especially the change in favor of outsourcing, which started in the '80s and accelerated through the '90s. We concluded that outsourcing was going to be the predominant way that most electronic products would be

AT THE START OF THE COMPANY THERE HAS TO BE SOMETHING EXPLOSIVE. THERE HAS TO BE SOME EXPLOSIVE EVENT OR CAPABILITY THAT GIVES YOU THE INITIAL ENERGY — ESCAPE VELOCITY — THAT TAKES YOU TO THE NEXT LEVEL

VIRESH BHATIA

manufactured, and that part turned out to be very true.

This was not just a case of a rising tide lifts all boats.
A rising tide, but even with that it's a competitive business, and if you didn't pick the right industries, and match it with the right skills, it wasn't a guarantee that you would do well. There were several similar-sized companies that either went bankrupt or dissolved in that same timeframe.

What mistakes did they make?
Overextending themselves, picking the wrong markets, like those that overlapped with larger contract manufacturers. As smaller players, they didn't have a competitive edge.

You would not compete with someone like Flextronics?
Exactly. Our plan was not to go head-to-head with Flextronics by building motherboards for PCs. We didn't do that.

You stayed for the duration of Pemstar and ultimately led negotiations to sell the company. At the time of the sale your revenue was $860 million and you employed 8,000 people. Did you know from the get-go how big Pemstar would become?
We knew we had to become a $500 million-plus company within 10 years to take on big projects.

Many successful founders could not conceive, at least initially, how they would get to half a billion.
Obviously many great companies are

started by people who don't have Fortune 500 experience. You take advantage of your skills and expertise.

And now you are leading Hardcore Computer.
The company is based on our patented total liquid submersion cooling technology. All the electronics are cooled by direct contact submersion in our dielectric cooling liquid. We launched in the high-performance PC and gaming space, which is the ultimate, aggressive early adopter. Since the initial launch we've expanded into universities, design centers, and medical institutions.

How did you get into this?
The two founders came up with the technology and filed the initial

patents. They approached me after the Pemstar/Benchmark merger.

How's it going?
We've had a lot of media coverage—several hundred articles in various languages around the world. The idea was to get out there, get a name in the tech press, learn and mature the technology, and then move into business markets—first with the work station and then with the server. We're in the process of launching the Liquid Blade server and have received great response and an industry award. It can save up to 80 percent of the energy cost to cool a data center.

Any advice for someone launching a company?
Just do it. People think if you study long enough, you'll get clear direction

Entrepreneurs get so excited about the product or the technology, but they forget about perception and image.

Viresh Bhatia

Viresh Bhatia

to go ahead. That's never going to happen. You just have to have enough confidence in yourself to move forward.

InstallShield
Illinois

You have a classic background for a tech company founder—a degree in computer science. Did you immediately start a company upon graduation?
My entrepreneurial career started right after I finished at Northwestern University. I'd always been interested in business and starting my own company.

How did you know what you wanted to do?
I met someone at Northwestern and we decided that we would find the next great idea in computer science and start implementing it.

What did you find?
The idea happened to be a geographic information system—a mapping system. We were really fascinated by the idea of putting two addresses into a computer and getting directions from one address to the other address.

That was not easy in 1988.
It predates the Internet and the computer power available today. We wrote the computer algorithms and it worked. We entered two addresses, my address and my partner's home address, and let the computer run all night long. The next morning when we came in, it had directions printed on the screen accurately—something you can do in your car today in a matter of seconds.

Where'd you go with that?
We did that for about three years but recognized that nobody is going to wait overnight for information. Back then computers didn't have the horsepower that was needed. Shipping geographic data on floppy disks would have taken about 400 floppy disks just for the city of Chicago.

Not a sustainable business.
So we transformed the company into doing some software development tools for Microsoft Windows, which was just emerging in 1990.

That was a good move.
That was a lucky transformation. The Windows market space started growing fairly rapidly and we grew with it.

A LOT OF CUSTOMERS THOUGHT WE WERE AS BIG AS THE BIG GUYS, WHEREAS WE WERE SITTING IN A 10 FOOT BY 10 FOOT ROOM, JUST TWO GUYS.

VIRESH BHATIA

But how did you get to InstallShield, which became a worldwide standard?
We did a bunch of other things, some worked and some didn't, but the company kept growing on the basis of the software development tools we were selling.

But eventually InstallShield became a runaway success story and sold for $80 million.
The inspiration to create InstallShield was almost accidental. A layout artist suggested that we needed an even number of products to make our print advertising look attractive. We had five products, so we needed to create the sixth one. InstallShield was it. I think the inspiration to improve and create new products came from listening to customers very closely.

That's it? Good listening?
Well, typically customers told us they wanted things that would improve productivity or cut costs. Ultimately that's what it boils down to, that's what you can sell to customers. You don't sell them the physical product, you sell them the outcome of that product, the benefits of that product.

What caused InstallShield to become the de facto standard? Was it Microsoft support, your marketing, or was it something else?
It wasn't Microsoft. We barely had any relationship with Microsoft internally or externally, but many people thought that we were part of Microsoft. Our relationship was to the extent that they made the operating system and we had to fit neatly inside it. We never got a single penny from Microsoft.

Did they give you other kinds of support?
They didn't give us any freebies, nothing.

Okay, I give up. What's the secret?
The key was marketing. It wasn't the technology. I will tell you today that our technology was not revolutionary. There were many competitors but you can't name a single one.

My impression of you is that of a techie, but I'm going to have to rethink that.
I think this is a great lesson for entrepreneurs. Typically, at that time small companies would put small ads in the back of computer magazines promoting their products. When our company was just two people—myself and my co-founder—we decided to put a full-page, four-color ad right next to Microsoft and Lotus and other big companies.

And that created a perception about InstallShield?
That was a pivotal change because a lot of customers thought we were as big as the big guys, whereas we were sitting in a 10 foot by 10 foot room, just two guys.

Let me get this straight. You created something that's on virtually every single PC on the planet—all from that?
Image perception makes a big difference. That's one of the things I tell entrepreneurs today. Fine, focus on products, focus on customers and all that good stuff—that's necessary. But

IF I COULD HAVE CUT TURNOVER IN HALF, I PROBABLY WOULD HAVE TRIPLED THE AMOUNT of MONEY THE COMPANY MADE IN ALL THOSE YEARS.

JOE PISCOPO

Viresh Bhatia

the image that you project is also key. Don't forget that.

Believe me I won't.
Entrepreneurs get so excited about the product or the technology of the business—of the new gizmo that they have invented—but they forget about perception and image.

Entrepreneurs tend to think that if their new technology is better than anything else then that's all they'll need to succeed.
Philippe Kahn, founder of Borland Software, said that at the start of the company there has to be something explosive. There has to be some explosive event or capability or something that gives you the initial energy—escape velocity—that takes you to the next level.

Any more advice for entrepreneurs?
You can't figure out what drives the business until you get inside it. The best founders discover the key issues when they are actually in the business, when they are actually doing it. And they're listening to the customer, listening and observing the problems firsthand. Think, plan, but take action. Many entrepreneurs forget about the amount of time—I call it the Runway—available to them to succeed or fail.

We consistently hear that retaining good people is key.
What it boils down to is making sure that employees have passion for the company and the environment, the products, and whatever you're trying to do. All the other stuff falls in place relatively easily.

You sold your company to Macrovision in 2004. Why sell? Why then?
I had run the company from 1990 to 2004, and it was the right time to figure out where to take the company next. When they made us an offer, it was just the right time for the investors, for me, and in the marketplace.

Mike Blair

Cyborg Systems
Illinois

In the Internet age, we take for granted how relatively easy it is to start a technology-related company. Not so easy in 1974?
Back in 1974 there really wasn't much of a software industry, let alone the Internet.

And going off on your own wasn't exactly a career path then.
My first job out of college was with International Harvester. They put me into their training program for data processing and had us design a payroll system for the factory plants. I got excited about all the system automation that was taking place.

You start looking at ways to get little bits of revenue here and there, and before you know it, you're running around in circles.

Mike Blair

But that wasn't enough to jump-start Cyborg?
I went to a consulting company that was kind of trying to create software but really wasn't. They were just taking a consulting project at one company and changing it a little bit for the next. So I started thinking that there's got to be a way to make a product that's really designed to be a package.

How was your timing?
The timing was perfect because the software industry was just getting started. Anybody back then that built a product that really was a package was going to do well. Starting here in Chicago became an advantage.

Why?
Because we couldn't find anyone who would loan us money. Venture funds didn't really exist for the industry and banks didn't know what we were doing. It forced us to build a business and grow organically, and be very focused on making a profit, positive cash flow, etc.

Lack of funding forced a discipline on you.
It may have been a plus. We certainly didn't have a lot of money to try crazy things or experiment. Our target customers were organizations with at least a few thousand employees, so it was easy to find out who our prospects were and fairly easy to get in touch with them through trade organizations and so forth. That's how we got it going.

Your strategy evolved from planning for many products to focusing on one product across the globe?
We had a business plan put together and we were going to sell four products a year for five years. The first year we sold 11 companies on the first product, and then 30 more companies. So we decided to stay in the human resource area and started growing markets outside the US to Canada, then to the UK, Africa, Asia, and South America.

Was that the secret ingredient—focus?
I think it's so easy at the beginning to think you can do all these things to move ahead. You start looking at ways to get little bits of revenue here and there and, before you know it, you're running around in circles. We chose to stay focused on a particular application area.

That sounds good but how did you actually do it?
We spent a lot of time understanding what value we were bringing to our customers, like British Airways. We'd talk to different customer drivers, usually the CFO or director of human resources, trying to understand why they bought from us, why they used our product. Out of that we could build our strategy—which markets we'd attack, what our messages would be. Otherwise you could end up where you believe your own marketing hype and you're out telling people how great you are, but in reality nobody cares.

What about hiring in the heartland?
We were able to find talented people who didn't job jump. I had friends out in the Valley who said guys would get mad and, at lunch, they'd go across

I KEEP STARTING COMPANIES BECAUSE OF ALL THE REGRETS I HAVE ABOUT THE 50 THINGS I DID WRONG ON THE PREVIOUS ONE.

Dick Costolo

Mike Blair

the street to another company and get a 20 percent salary increase. We had employees with us for 25 to 30 years and they were good, talented people.

Was there ever a crisis?
I think we went through five technology waves and we missed one of the five.

How bad was the miss?
We committed to and spent $20 million on building object-oriented technology and then saw it all go up in smoke—it was replaced by Java. You had to be near the leading edge, but you didn't have to be on the bleeding edge. That was a crisis as to how to regroup—how to get everybody back to re-engineering a product that we spent a fortune on and never really got to market.

How did you get past that?
I just shut it down. I wrote it off and started over once we clearly saw that it had been a mistake. If anything, I probably waited too long because I had this huge investment and I was thinking, maybe somehow this will actually make it. Maybe it's not as bad as it appears.

What's the secret to hiring good people?
We focused on getting people who had an entrepreneurial spirit and who understood what we were trying to do and bought into what was going on.

Then you got bigger and that changed.
As you get bigger and you've got offices around the globe, you've got to have processes and procedures. We

went through ISO 9000 certification. We were the first application software company to do it. Then all those seat-of-the-pants wild people are no longer what you want.

That's not an easy transition.
We had to rehire in certain key positions and, in some cases, we took people who were good entrepreneurial types and let them run a small part of the business. We didn't have much success in getting them to become structured, procedurally oriented people.

And you resisted the urge to hire family members?
I asked my dad for advice on this because he was an entrepreneur who had built his own construction company. He told us not to spend any

time with friends or relatives early on. He was right. We didn't hire any relatives until we were large enough that they would not be reporting to me. They were hired through the normal vetting process. You can do it at that point.

Investors are your friends when things are going great. You gotta be smart enough to realize that if things head south, they're not necessarily going to be your friends anymore.

Dick Costolo

Dick Costolo

FeedBurner
Illinois

Congratulations, Dick, you are the only comedian to make the list of champion tech company founders in the book. Seriously.
My degree's in computer science, but I didn't take any of my job offers. I came to Chicago and went over to The Second City. I took improv classes and performed with Steve Carroll and others.

That sounds like fun, but that's not the career track that led to Google.
Second City has one main stage and four touring companies. I ended up passing on auditions. I couldn't survive on a $120 stipend or whatever they paid touring around during the week

so I took a job at Accenture while still performing at the Annoyance Theatre and in some other one-man shows I wrote.

But you had some epiphany around technology or owning your own company?
We started using the Web in 1993 to build a training program for an application at Andersen. Andersen was a big Lotus Notes shop; Lotus Notes was the accepted future for networks there. When we showed them this application training we had developed for the Web, there was a general reaction of: "You guys are idiots; Notes is a solid infrastructure. You can't build anything on this; it's not a platform."

I guess you didn't like hearing that.
We thought everything would head

toward the Web. We left Accenture and started a consulting company building websites. That got acquired in 1996.

Did you stay with the buyer?
The buyer was bought in a roll-up, so we went out in 1998 and started another company doing wireless alerts. Spyonit.com was our second company, same three founders. We sold that. We had a great exit.

You sold Spyonit to a public company, 724 Solutions, for $54 million.
Our sale closed on September 12, 2000. That date became important because we had a one-year lock-up on our stock that expired September 12, 2001—the day after the tragedy of 9/11. Remember, the stock markets

didn't open on September 12th, 2001. When the markets finally reopened, our stock had lost 85 percent of its value. I remember my wife saying, "You know you can't go around and complain; now would not be a good time to whine about financial losses."

Luckily you had the skills to press on. Is that what led to FeedBurner?
We left there and started FeedBurner in 2003. The idea was just, "There's a thing that no one's doing that somebody should do," not "We gotta do this because I care deeply about this." We started FeedBurner because more and more content was being syndicated. People were going less and less to NYT.com in the morning and more to different places—to Google news or wherever—and their

I tell young entrepreneurs that our business model was like going to the eye doctor. Better like this or like this? A or B? B or C? Oh, C's doing better than B. Let's do more C.

Dick Costolo

Dick Costolo

thinking was, "I want to aggregate all my content and get it in one place." We thought that we should start a company that sits between publishers and subscribers and acts as a clearinghouse for content. Content moves around where it needs to go— that's FeedBurner.

How did you know that the opportunity was there? A lot of people look at the world and they don't see those unmet needs. You saw it.
In our previous company we were doing a lot of work with wireless alerts. We saw that these content feeds were a great way to distribute information because it didn't really matter whether the end point was a website, mobile phone or whatever; it was always in the same format.

But so many great Internet ideas never make any money. How did you solve that problem?
We went to publishers and said, "Look, this is going to be the way that more and more of your content is going to be distributed, and you don't understand this technology. We'll manage the content distribution for you for free, but we want 35 percent of the ad revenue in syndication." It was an easy thing for them to sign up for. At the time they weren't making any money from syndication. The hypothesis was: if that's the way most of the content gets distributed, then that's where the ads will go. This, of course, ended up happening to a significant enough extent that our dominant market share was strategically attractive to a lot of companies.

You were in Chicago, not Silicon Valley. Was there anything about location that helped, or was it just serendipity?
Well, Warren Buffett always says that being in Nebraska kept him from being at the bar in Manhattan with all these other guys talking about what a lousy stock XYZ is. He can sit back and see a good value without all the subjective shop talk. We were able to sit here in Chicago and say, "Here's the thing that none of those guys are talking about and it's going to be important."

How did you feel about having five VC funds at the table and maybe losing control?
That never bothered me. Investors are your friends when things are going great. You gotta be smart enough to

realize that if things head south, they're not necessarily going to be your friends anymore.

You mastered a hard reality.
You read these stories about entrepreneurs who raise a bunch of money from VCs and then are horrified to discover that their co-founder is getting kicked out of the company because he or she is not meeting revenue numbers. They think, "these aren't the same people we raised money from." I think we were always smart enough to know that if things go well, the relationship will be fine; if they don't, these guys will demand that we bring someone else in to run it. I just worked on the assumption that we'll try to figure it out and do it ourselves and not lose the board's

EXECUTION IS EVERYTHING. EVEN IF YOU START A BUSINESS WITH THE WRONG IDEA OR TOO MANY COMPETITORS, YOU CAN OUT-EXECUTE ALL THE OTHER IDEAS IN THE RIGHT MARKET.

Dick Costolo

confidence. We had New York, Silicon Valley and Midwest VCs in. I liked having those guys around just for their perspective.

You had a home run launching, growing and ultimately selling FeedBurner to Google. Is there anything you'd do differently?
I keep starting companies because of all the regrets I have about the 50 things I did wrong on the previous one.

Wow. Most of these home run hitters say they have no regrets.
A great example: I still don't like the way we interviewed or hired at FeedBurner, and I would revise that process in another company in order to really nail it down. Another example you already know: we sold our second

company with a one-year restrictive stock lock; we won't do that again.

Any advice for someone starting a company right now?
Execution is everything. Even if you start a business with the wrong idea or too many competitors, you can out-execute all the better ideas in the right market.

How do entrepreneurs screw things up?
I run into young entrepreneurs who have an idea about what their business model should be and they just stick to it, irrespective of what the evidence indicates. I tell them that at FeedBurner it was like going to the eye doctor. Better like this or like this? A or B? B or C? Oh, C's better than B; let's do more C.

Execute, but with flexibility?
What I mean by execution is the ability to do what you're setting out to do and then being able to zig when the market zags. For lots of start-ups, the market head-fakes them in one direction and they stay down that rigid path.

Three home runs, Dick. How do new ideas come to you? While you're just tootling along with your current company?
No. I don't like thinking about new ideas when I'm working on something else because I find it too distracting.

That's a mental discipline not shared by most other entrepreneurs.
Otherwise you short-change both the thing you're supposed to be working on and the new idea, because you can't devote any time to it. So we've

come to the conclusion—let's not even think about those things until we can go out and do something. Of course you see opportunities and you think, well, that's stupid. That should be changed. But those end up not even being the things we go and do anyway.

Definitely not a scattershot approach.
We didn't initially have the idea for Spyonit. It was more like, this other company got rolled up; let's go do something else. When we left 724 Solutions, we had no idea what we were going to do. We got an office for three months and then came up with the idea for FeedBurner. Another reason I end up leaving and starting other companies is just because it's more fun working for yourself.

People get caught up in just going through the motions in their career, and then later regret that they didn't do things. Especially in difficult economic times, I think a lot of people try to play it safe. I just decided that I was willing to take the risk and live with the consequences.

Bill DeVille

John Croghan

You moved in 2010 from Google to COO at Twitter. How long will you stay?
As long as it takes!

Are you lucky or good?
Just like I can think of my 50 mistakes, I can think of the 50 places we got lucky; for example, competitors misstepping, instead of us purposefully out-executing them. You put yourself in a position to be successful and you hope you're lucky.

Extended Care Information Network
Illinois

You and Dr. Phil Sheridan co-founded Extended Care Information Network. Why start a company?
As a practicing physician and geriatric specialist, I wanted to innovate for the elderly. In a hospital setting, when a loved one is sick or has a broken hip and, instead of coming home, suddenly needs a nursing home, it's a crisis for both the patient and the family. The idea behind ECIN was to use an Internet database to quickly find an available, appropriate nursing home bed that matches the needs of the patient and the family. Basically it's a Sabre system (airline computer

reservation system) for nursing home placement.

You and your co-founders eventually sold the company to Allscripts for $100 million. How important was the elderly market for them?
The fastest growing population in the US is 85 and older. Serving the needs of this population is very important for a healthcare software company like Allscripts.

That probably wasn't obvious when you started in 1994?
Our eventual exit sale to Allscripts in 2007 was not obvious in '94. What was obvious was that getting a patient from hospital to nursing home was a hugely inefficient process. So Dr. Sheridan and I went back and forth on this idea.

We had a business plan and a board of directors.

Was your background as a doctor a plus or a minus?
Both a plus and a minus. Plus: Being a doctor caring for the elderly allowed me to recognize the tremendous problem of discharge planning of seniors from the hospital into nursing homes. Minus: I was a physician and vision guy with no business background and I was initially sort of naïve in the software development world. I set out to develop a software application but didn't know what "source code" was. We hired a consultant to help us write the software. It was never discussed in the contract ahead of time who would own the source code, so when

I had all these people that supposedly knew better than me telling me to focus. Be one thing. Do one thing. And scale up doing one thing. But I'd been through a highly regulated industry and seen how, with the stroke of a pen, the rules of the game change. So I was an advocate for diversification.

Bill DeVille

J. William DeVille

Health Personnel Options
Ohio

that question inevitably arose as the prototype was being developed, the relationship with that consultant blew up into a legal squabble that almost put us out of business.

Did you fund it yourselves?
We initially funded with seed money from friends and family. We then found a great angel, Tasso Coin, who had a great track record representing a group of individual investors. We put together a wonderful board and our investors hung in there with us. With the Internet craze in '99, we were able to secure $6 million in venture capital funding with William Blair & Co. At that time Glen Tullman joined our board (*see Glen Tullman, page 147*) and we went from a regional effort to a national one. Tullman brought in Jeff Surges—an

incredible leader and a one-of-a-kind, driven, great sales guy (*see Jeff Surges, page 141*)—as our CEO.

What made your business successful?
I reviewed our business plan from '95 a few months ago and it turns out that we actually did what we set out to do. We stuck with the plan and sticking with the plan was important.

That can be rare in technology businesses.
We had to stick to the plan and be tenacious because in hindsight we were ahead of the market. It took us 10 years.

You spent 18 years in what could be described as a normal corporate career before your breakout moment as an entrepreneur.
I started in the executive recruiting business when I was in college and ended up staying with it. After 18 years in a business where we were convincing people to change jobs and relocate to other parts of the country, it occurred to me that I'd never done either of those two things, and if I was going to do it, I needed to get going while I was still young enough to start over if, for any reason, I failed. I'd seen other friends and family members start businesses and have great success,

and I decided that I wanted to take that same career track.

Good rationale, but how did you actually set out and do it?
I got introduced to a guy who was a finance type of person, who'd had some entrepreneurial experience and was interested in the staffing industry. The two of us collaborated on a business plan and raised some venture capital. We started our company with an acquisition of a kind of mom-and-pop healthcare staffing business.

The VC gave you the money just like that?
My partner had a long-standing relationship with them and I had a credible background for operating in my industry. Investors are always looking for investment-worthy

a lot of people go through life trying to avoid failure, and they never accomplish success.

Bill DeVille

J. William DeVille

management. They said, "Go find the deal. We want to be there with you. We like you guys and we want to do this." It was inspiring. The fact that somebody would be willing to take a flier on a couple of guys with suits and a business plan, you know—

Neither of you had started a company or hit a home run before that?
No. We both had meaningful success in our careers, but neither of us had demonstrated a huge return for venture capital investors before. Personally, I'd never gone out and done anything that was home run worthy, in terms of the business world, so it was kind of an amazing experience to be honest with you.

Why healthcare, why personnel?
I saw a kind of mega trend in American business to increase its reliance on and strategic use of contract labor. And I knew that the valuations of those kinds of businesses were substantially higher than the valuations of the business that I'd come from, which was executive search. Also, I saw that the aging population and Baby Boomers were going to increase the demand for healthcare and exacerbate what already was a shortage of qualified healthcare professionals. My executive search company was predominantly healthcare. We were one of the top 10 US boutique healthcare executive search companies by the time I left the firm. So I had a good healthcare background.

You gave up the glamour of dealing with chief executives for contract labor.
I thought at the time, I'll take the less glamorous business line and build a business that's got a lot of value.

How right you were. You raised a total of $5.5 million, built the company, and sold it to On Assignment for $150 million. One of your investors told me your company was one of the top five investments they'd ever made.
I think it was actually one of the top two. They had one deal that was better than ours, which sort of irritates me on a certain level.

Ah, well, you deal with the pain.
The other thing was that the industry was highly fragmented. Lots of mom-and-pop companies and very limited numbers of good-sized businesses, I mean over $100 million. If we couldn't become the industry leader, we thought we could put together a strong number two.

What did you focus on?
We looked at rehabilitation therapy because it was among the hotter sectors and had good bill rates, good pay rates, and good margins. And there was already a company in that sector that did an IPO at $60 million in sales. We thought we could draft right behind these guys. The end game was to create a diversified healthcare staffing business, but the starting point, because you have to start somewhere, was rehabilitation therapy.

In the first round, you need to get enough capital to see your way through potentially difficult times. Everything isn't going to go well in the first couple of years, and you need to get to cash flow positive. You need to have enough capital to be able to do that and then a little more. You don't want to be going back for a second round of capital when everything isn't going well.

Bill DeVille

My wife Sharon is an OT.
That's great!

You chose rehab therapy but then the Balanced Budget Act of 1997 eliminated $80 billion in Medicare spending...
Which put the top four nursing home chains into chapter 11 and evaporated the demand for rehabilitation therapy.

Wow. How did you recover from that?
We accelerated the acquisition of a company that had no therapy exposure whatsoever. That was fortuitous because when the revised Medicare reimbursement rules were implemented, it was Armageddon. The company we had hoped to draft behind went from about $100 million down to $30 million in a 12-month period.

Many entrepreneurs think only of organic growth. Initially you grew by acquisition.
We started by acquiring several small therapy staffing businesses. We had three therapy acquisitions prior to acquiring Health Personnel Options, which was at about $10 million revenue in staffing in nursing, allied travel, per diem allied, and permanent placement. The others were small. We bought a million and a half dollar business, a two-million dollar business, and a half-a-million dollar book of business without buying the infrastructure.

In total you made five acquisitions that brought in $16 million in revenue. And then you grew them organically. And dramatically. Any advice for entrepreneurs?

Two things: first of all, I did not do all of this alone. Doing what we did really does "take a village." I had a great partner and a supportive investor. We chose a good niche that had a bright future and we surrounded ourselves with excellent people. Second, I had all these people that supposedly knew better than me telling me to focus. Be one thing. Do one thing. Scale up doing one thing. But I'd been through a highly regulated industry and seen how, with the stroke of a pen, the rules of the game change. So I was an advocate for diversification.

Up to a point. You stayed broadly in healthcare.
Right. The other thing we believed was the saying, "a rising tide lifts all boats." We got into healthcare because we

thought the demographics were a rising tide. Go find that rising tide.

So you had a plan —
I heard some research about whether a founder should write a business plan and implement it in a disciplined, rigorous way or adapt the plan after the business gets started. The research showed that the people who had big success were those who changed plans after they got started. It turns out that the value is not the plan but the planning.

It's not the plan.
You can't be in love with the plan. You can't be so wedded to it that you don't react to market changes, opportunities, and serious threats. Had we stuck to what a lot of business

It turns out that the value is not the plan, but the planning. You can't be in love with the plan. You can't be so wedded to it that you don't react to market changes, opportunities, and serious threats.

Bill DeVille

J. William DeVille

advisers told us to do, we would have died.

And it's about survival?
I think some people get confused about what the primary goal should be for their company. They think the goal of every company is to maximize profits. I think that the number one goal of every company is to survive, and the second objective may be to maximize profits.

One thing that fascinates me is that you could take over a business someone else had worked hard at and then grow it tenfold. How did you do that?
There were some really valuable things that the previous owner had done that I thought he had not capitalized on.

Strike staffing, for example?
They signed contracts to send 300 nurses out to a particular hospital when the nurses would go on strike. To mobilize 300 nurses to staff a hospital on a moment's notice, you must have all their documents ready in advance. You have to do credentialing and licensing and background checks and drug tests. And you have to build your database. The previous owner had done that, so what they had was a very powerful database of nurses willing to drop everything and run off to whatever crises would occur in the United States.

How were you able to utilize them?
We had a flu epidemic in California at one of our largest accounts. They said, "We need any qualified nurses you can get out here right now." They told

us they were even willing to accept them on short, two- to four-week assignments. We told them it would be expensive. They said, "That's fine. Just get us the nurses." We did it, and had a big boom in sales. We thought, you know, if these guys like this service, maybe we can build a business around it. We pioneered a service line called Rapid Response Travel Nursing, which is short-term travel assignments for staffing crises. And that Rapid Response niche we created fueled our growth like crazy.

In your industry everyone took for granted that the standard service was a 13-week stint for the nurse. So that was the problem.
The competition all offered the same inflexible solution for clients and their

nurse employees. We found a big problem in the market and we solved it. I think if you want to succeed in business, you have to find a big problem that your customer has and solve it for them.

So many industries are like that—a disruptive solution wins.
All the real estate agents charge six percent, for example. And you say, why six percent? Well, because that's the way it's always been done. Look at Federal Express. It's a pretty big jump from a 44-cent stamp to a $14 overnight package. You really better need that package to get there tomorrow to justify that price.

Could you give me a Mercedes convertible—please?
To develop a continuous supply of

When you think you're done, always do just one more thing.

Jim Dolan

candidates, we needed to build our database. So we gave away a brand-new, convertible red Mercedes.

How did it work?
We used Internet recruiting aggressively. Everybody that applied to our company and did all of our paperwork got an entry into the contest. Everybody that worked for us got another entry, and everybody that extended their assignment got another entry. If they referred us a candidate, they got an entry.

That's a great, bold approach.
It was a big, splashy campaign and a big, audacious thing to do, especially for a company of our size. It got a lot of visibility. Traffic to our website was huge.

Any thoughts for company founders on raising money?
I think in the first round, you need to get enough capital to see your way through potentially difficult times. Everything isn't going to go well in the first couple of years, and you need to get to cash-flow positive. You need to have enough capital to be able to do that and then a little more. You don't want to be going back for a second round of capital when everything isn't going well.

And if you do that right—
In the second round, keep the amount of capital raised as low as possible to minimize dilution and maximize ownership for the founders. As I said, that is not prudent for the first round.

Why did you stay after you sold?
I felt an obligation. Also, I'd never worked for a publicly traded company before. I thought it would be good for my career and professional development and that I needed to take this adventure.

How did you like it?
I learned that I didn't like publicly traded companies or managing to the quarterly reports. I didn't like the fact that my income was public to the world, including my internal staff. I didn't like telling my competitors what my business plans were, what my margins were, and all the things that I was doing. And the worst thing was, I didn't like the fact that I couldn't tell anybody how things were going when they would ask me.

So you became an entrepreneur again and started Health Carousel.
Yes. It's staffing in nursing and allied healthcare, places I know about. But we started with a focus on international supply. America has occupational shortages, and there's a fundamental inability to solve them, at least in the near term.

You are bringing nurses to the US on scholarship work-study programs.
Our scholarship program is one of our featured services. We offer a variety of conventional staffing and recruiting programs, but we are especially proud of our scholarship program because we are helping to solve the nursing shortage by preparing the next generation of nurse educators. Qualifying nurses come to the US to go to school, get a master's degree,

> *The problem is boredom.
> If I'm bored, I may break something just for the fun of fixing it. That's kind of rough on the people who actually work in the company, you know?*
>
> Jim Dolan

Jim Dolan

and then return to their home country to teach and help alleviate their own shortage. It is also an ethical international nursing program—our version of social entrepreneurship. It's really a different approach and it's about sustainability for the nursing profession. It's a whole different business model than conventional nurse staffing solutions.

**The Dolan Company (DM)
Minnesota**

Things have gone well.
Recently, yes. We went public in 2007, and it's been a roller coaster ride. Not the best time in the world to go public. We're doing well now, but there were some bad days last year.

How did a career in journalism turn into launching companies?
I had a number of little businesses that I started and was fiddling around with when I was a little kid.

Like what?
Fireworks taught me the time value of money, for instance.

Fireworks. You are speaking figuratively?

I bought a large quantity of cherry bombs and didn't use them all on the Fourth of July. I found them around the Christmas holidays and was getting ready to do the stupid kid thing, blow them up, and someone offered me a dollar for one of them. I had paid a quarter. And the light bulb went on.

You gotta love those "a-ha!" moments.
I sold them all for a dollar each. The following year I took all of my savings and bought fireworks when they were on sale. I put them away for six months and sold them at an even bigger markup. This rolled forward over several years until finally some law enforcement people came calling because I was ordering such large quantities of explosives. They didn't know I was a kid.

Fast forward. How did you come to work for Rupert Murdoch?
I went to work in a very competitive newspaper market in San Antonio, Texas. I was happy in the newsroom and love journalism to this day. Rupert Murdoch bought the company. A lot of employees didn't survive when he first came in. I was one of the survivors, largely because I was physically not there. I was running the state capitol bureau.

But eventually you arrived on the corporate side of things?
I wound up getting transferred to Australia, then back to the US. Rupert's theory, which I agree with, is that if you're making a product, you should also be involved with selling it. That way if you're making it wrong, you'll know it and you can fix it more quickly.

We did 13 rounds of private equity before we went public. And it's funny because the first half of the battle of raising private equity is proving that you've actually got a good idea or something that will work, but the last part of it is proving what you're not. People try to peg you into predetermined slots that they're thinking about when they listen to you pitch.

Jim Dolan

So I had circulation responsibilities at the same time I was running the newsroom in San Antonio. Eventually I was with Murdoch in the New York corporate office.

What a great education.
It was a real eye-opener because Rupert is one of these people who has an attitude that anything is possible. He's creative and finds a way around obstacles and looks at things a little differently than everybody else. Every single thing he does is with an approach. So many people get trapped in their own way of thinking and in traditional thinking. Rupert is not one of those guys.

You left the newspaper business to run an electronic information company in Chicago, and from there went to an investment bank.
I went to work on Wall Street for a few years to sharpen my deal-making skills and learn more about finance. I didn't have time to take courses but I went to Northwestern University and got the core summaries of textbooks and just read the books myself.

When you took the entrepreneurial plunge, you had help from Cherry Tree Ventures in Minneapolis.
We jokingly called it the Let's Find Jim a Job Company. It was Cherry Tree and me for eight months. We looked at all kinds of things centered around media because that was what my experience was, thanks to Murdoch.

Dolan Media Company was born. What did you acquire?
We were looking at a pretty wide range of things. That flexibility allowed us to start with the newspaper group in '92. We're still in the newspaper business—we're in 21 markets now—and that's been a very good growth engine for us, but along the way we felt free to pursue public records, which we built into something very large, then sold off to Lexis-Nexis. We got into telemarketing briefly, but didn't like that too much so we sold that. We're in legal services now. We've never once in a boardroom had anyone say, "That's not our mission or that's not our business plan or that's not what we signed up for."

What is the mission?
There's been an understanding from the beginning with all our investors that they're signing up to join a management team that knows how to make money. We went public in 2007, so that narrowed the scope to some extent because you've got to tell the Street what you are intending. But even today we don't feel constrained very much. If we find something really interesting, I'm sure we'd have no trouble with our board saying, "Let's try it."

That sounds unique among winning companies.
The only key question for us is, do we know how to do it and can we make whatever it is better by our involvement? It's not that we're going to start a Dairy Queen franchise or a lumber mill or something like that, but those starting questions give us plenty of latitude to have fun and make money at the same time.

I had some early entrepreneurial efforts that didn't go so well and I tried to learn from the mistakes. One of the things I did was to hire an industrial psychologist to basically do a study of me, for me.

Jim Dolan

Jim Dolan

Is the common rallying point around media or—
I don't think there is a common rallying point.

You're the common rallying point.
I suppose so.

But what is the secret sauce? There's something that caused all this success.
The first thing we did was to target about 600 business newspapers around the country. There was not much aggregation, but there were some common threads. Most of them had public records in the back. And when we began talking to subscribers in our focus groups, they all said they bought the newspapers partly because they wanted to know about property transactions, divorces, new

corporations, and things like that. We thought, there's a business here.

How did you capitalize on that?
We were the largest public records gathering company in the US until 2003. That's not media, that's a business service. Our investment strategy early on was to resell the contents of the newspapers, but we wound up making newspapers its own division.

No one had ever asked the subscribers why they subscribed?
No. And, oddly enough, that had never been done in the previous newspapers we bought either.

No one asked?
The first newspaper we bought was 107 years old and had a 94 percent

renewal rate, which is extraordinarily high in media. So one of the first things I did was to call up and ask why. I didn't want to have a third party learn about it and then regurgitate it to us. I made the staffers who worked on the newspaper come in and do the work early and then take a couple of hours at the end of the day. We carved up our subscriber lists and everybody made calls from a script I put together.

What did you ask?
Why do you read this newspaper? And I mean, precisely, what do you read first? How do you use what you read? Things like that. I called some subscribers a second time and asked: If we had this, if we had that, how would you use it? And I've learned the hard way: never ask people what they

would pay in the future because they will never tell you the truth.

Good to know.
What we've done is to listen to customers and work backward from what they tell us. We see if we can understand a way that's better than what they've been getting. Faster, better, cheaper are the three legs of most success stories. In the case of public records, we could do all three.

Other companies were already collecting public records.
We concentrated on getting courthouse records much faster. We took a technology leap to get records sent electronically to our clients and embedded in their systems in a useful way, and we could charge a lot more for it. We eventually found a way to

Just like you learn more from bad times than from good, you learn more from complaints than from compliments. I always discount compliments I get from customers because I think a lot of times they're just being nice. The complaints—those are real.

Jim Dolan

charge by the time slice, so we could charge more if they got the records by noon.

The previous owner did not see the assets.
It was a process of working backward. We didn't hear, "Gee, if you only had this, I would pay for it," but they certainly had problems they were willing to talk about very openly. I still hear people in all walks of life talk about the problems they have, but no one seems to be listening to their complaints. If they did, they'd hear business opportunities.

That's the genius in it, isn't it?
Right. Just like you learn more from bad times than from good, you learn more from complaints than from compliments. I always discount

compliments I get from customers because I think a lot of times they're just being nice. The complaints—those are real.

You took a company manually gathering public records from nine counties in Minnesota and expanded it to 10,000 courthouses delivering to every large financial institution and every credit bureau.
In five years, we had about 92 percent of the national market for public records used for credit purposes.

Before you showed up—
Actually, we made the market more rational and more efficient. The core of the business was gathering data about bankruptcies, tax liens, money judgments, births, deaths, divorces, marriages—anything that would affect

credit. There were several thousand little mom-and-pop companies gathering these things manually from courthouses across the country and it took them an average of three months to get the information into the hands of decision-makers.

Three months?
That's what everybody accepted and it had been that way for years. No one gave it a thought.

How did you get to 10,000 courthouses?
We hired stringers to go into courthouses and we got pretty good at it. Here's a strange little fact. The ideal public records gatherer is a retired junior high or high school teacher, preferably math or English. They don't put up with crap from anybody. They

are meticulous and you can count on them. Eventually, of course, more and more courthouses went electronic.

What inspired you to start a company?
If you know how to do something better you should be allowed to try. I had some early entrepreneurial efforts that didn't go so well and I tried to learn from the mistakes. One of the things I did was to hire an industrial psychologist to basically do a study of me for me.

Kind of like Walt Whitman's poem, "Song of Myself."
Teams do better than solo acts in almost all situations. And I have strengths and weaknesses. I'm not a Renaissance person by any means. I needed to have an objective

I've learned the hard way: Never ask people what they would pay in the future because they will never tell you the truth.

Jim Dolan

Jim Dolan

understanding of what it would take to balance out me.

Balancing out the entrepreneur— that's a good way of looking at it.
The problem is boredom. If I'm bored, I may break something just for the fun of fixing it. That's kind of rough on the people who actually work in the company, you know?

Yes.
There are people who are equally happy keeping things running smoothly and tweaking them. I have a lot of those people here now and it's really great. There are also people who like going in and unwinding things and saying, "Kill that, kill that, kill that." Honing in on things. I don't find that to be much fun. I've got

some people who are really good at that. It's a matter of balancing out the team around me so that we are much stronger as a team than we'd ever be if each of us stood alone.

Has your Minnesota location helped you?
Lots of the founding families here in the Twin Cities sold out like families often do, but they didn't leave. The money stayed here and it drives all kinds of things. It supports investment banks and a private equity industry that far exceeds what you would expect in a city of this size. So the expertise is here for the asking—it's in the elevator with you when you go up every morning.

How was the process of raising money?
We did 13 rounds of private equity before we went public. And it's funny because the first half of the battle of raising private equity is proving that you've actually got a good idea or something that will work, but the last part of it is proving what you're not. People try to peg you into predetermined slots that they're thinking about when they listen to you pitch.

What kind of slots?
The first hurdle is, "Is this just a Minnesota thing?" Then we do it in two more states—my third acquisition was in Oklahoma. So there were people in New York saying, "We're not sure this thing really has legs beyond these three states." Then

it was Maryland, then Oregon. At some point, they run out of negatives, because we are coast-to-coast now, we're everywhere. They've stopped trying to pick holes in it based on silly, geographic things. Had we started this in New York, I would've had none of that, because people are assuming that if you can make it there, you can make it anywhere. That silly old song, you know?

Sure. You know Stephen Shank (see Steve Shank, page 118)
Steve was in the next office at Cherry Tree. Both of us had come from high-powered jobs and suddenly we're solo guys in a VC office. We each had an idea and some hope.

I still hear people in all walks of life talk about the problems they have, but no one seems to be listening. If they did, they'd hear business opportunities.

Jim Dolan

Advice for entrepreneurs?
I made a ton of mistakes, but I tried to learn from all of them. One of the things I learned from Rupert was: you don't bury mistakes, you learn from them. Every time I made a mistake at News Corp, it was dragged out, dissected, discussed, and fully digested, rather than hidden.

That's good, if painful.
Another thing, you're always selling. I'm selling you right now. I think I'm making the sale, but I guess we'll see when the book comes out. Everyone is selling all the time in all directions. And if you don't understand that, then you're failing at selling.

You're doing fine. What else?
When you think you're done, always do just one more thing. My investment banker friend Janet Muir would say, "Let's think of one more thing we can do. One more call we can make. One more thing we can put together. Let's just do one more thing." It was annoying. We were all tired. But when I look back, I realize how much that contributed to the quality and quantity of stuff we got done.

That's a big one. How have you used that advice?
Every time we did private equity financing, we worked our asses off to get a lot more meetings, phone calls and pitches out there than we ever thought we needed. If you don't work hard to develop more choices, you're gonna get squeezed someday. It's inevitable.

You are describing a big rookie mistake. They get one investor who's going to give them money, and that's deadly.
Always have a hot standby.

What's that?
Here's my real-life example. I was financing a company and this very well-known investor agreed to invest. We had a glorious time, we liked each other, and we signed the paperwork. The sun was streaming through the windows and we hugged and pledged undying loyalty. And then about two days before closing, his bankers called my bankers and announced a new deal that was a lot less attractive. This call was at 10 o'clock in the morning and they said I had until noon to accept it.

What did you do?
All along Janet had been having meetings, making pitches, and talking to people, and we had several "standbys." We called them all, wound up exchanging term sheets by fax, and signed one by noon that day. We never called the investor back. It was a ton of work to keep all those people in the loop but, boy, did it pay off.

> If we find something really interesting, I'm sure our board would say, 'Let's try it.' The only key question for us is, do we know how to do it and can we make whatever it is better by our involvement?

Jim Dolan

> You're always selling. I'm selling you right now. I think I'm making the sale, but I guess we'll see when the book comes out. Everyone is selling all the time in all directions. And if you don't understand that, then you're failing at selling.

Jim Dolan

Mike Domek

TicketsNow
Illinois

So many entrepreneurs have multiple focuses, or maybe it's a lack of focus. That's not true for you.
I have done one thing since I left school. I left college to start TicketsNow.

Why did you do that?
I wanted to put together a business that would connect buyers and sellers of event tickets because this was a passion I'd had since childhood.

You and Joe Mansueto (see Joe Mansueto, page 82) are similar in that you both started businesses in your apartments and went on to build multi-hundred million dollar enterprises.
I started in my one-bedroom apartment with a music-on-hold adapter from RadioShack, a two-line telephone and a pretend computer. When people called, we'd hit the keyboard and pretend we were typing so we sounded professional.

Was it originally conceived as an online service?
It started out as a concierge type service. We grew that completely offline for four or five years and generated enough capital to take the company online.

That was 1999, when you launched TicketsNow.
It was one of those things that started with the first buyer and we just kept reinvesting the capital within the company.

You hit the Internet bubble bursting right at that point.
The crash of 2000 was great for us because ad rates plummeted and we were able to buy up space on Yahoo. Then I met a guy who had started a company called Google, and we began advertising with them. We were one of their first advertisers.

It's inspiring to hear about succeeding in a downturn!
We just kept reinvesting in our successes. We went online at about $8 million in gross ticket sales and by the time we sold the company to Ticketmaster in 2008, we hit $300 million.

And you didn't need a PhD to appreciate ticket sales.
My inspiration is a passion for live entertainment and sporting events. I loved the feeling I had as a kid, walking into Wrigley Field in Chicago, seeing the perfect field out there, you know, the green grass. I wanted to do something in that industry—even if it was just parking cars—and be a part of it somehow.

Turning that into a business was the challenge.
In college, I'd always look in the newspapers to see who was selling what tickets for how much. One day I found a deal to sell. Jonathon Brandmeier, a Chicago radio personality, was doing concerts at Poplar Creek. I remembered seeing a listing for somebody that had some

The opportunity I saw was, let everybody else take all the inventory risk.

Mike Domek

tickets for sale and another listing for somebody that wanted them. I called the one guy and found out he was selling them for $30 each. Then I called the other guy—he was willing to pay $35. That was like, "Oh, my God."

From that to $300 million is not intuitive. What was the secret sauce? How did you do it?
The secret sauce was molding the business into a scalable opportunity, getting it online and getting our first order. For seven years I watched people answer phones and give out the same information saying, "okay, thanks," and 1 out of 10 would order. But on the Internet, the information was there and people were doing it all themselves.

The Internet was the missing ingredient?
When we got our first web order we thought, "wow, that guy didn't call us, he didn't ask any questions, he just went on the Internet." We had all the information there and he just placed an order. For me that was the "eureka!" moment. That was when I realized this thing can be scalable.

But you didn't stop there.
Then the secret sauce was really figuring out what to spend on the Internet—knowing how much to spend and how much you'd get back.

It sounds more like art than science.
We screwed up like everybody else online. We overspent for banner ads. Everybody wanted to be at the top of Yahoo because it was cool, but at the end of the day everyone overpaid for it.

You ended up correcting for that as you went along.
We had to learn what every keyword on every search engine and every ad placement was worth to us. By the time we figured that out, rates fell through the floor and we went back to Yahoo and Google with these enormous insertion orders that were just way out of our league. If I had been wrong, I would've been bankrupt, but I went with what the data was telling me.

Ticket brokering is an old business. How did you know, with all the other players around at the time, that you guys had the business plan that was going to be different—and better?
Nobody else was thinking this way. The competition wanted to just do their thing and they thought we were

a little nuts for trying to do this. The opportunity I saw was, let everybody else take all the inventory risk. Let's not take any inventory risk. Let's just take all of their tickets and put them in one place.

So the challenge was to get access to other brokers' inventory?
The only question that the brokers really asked of us was, "Is this Internet thing going to stick around? Are people comfortable buying online?" Those are the things we were betting on. There was no cost to brokers. In fact, they got extra sales because of it. And we made it easy for them to upload their tickets. They said, "Sure, whatever. We think you're nuts but it doesn't cost us anything so we'll try it."

We just kept reinvesting in our successes.

Mike Domek

Nobody else was thinking this way. The competition wanted to just do their thing and they thought we were a little nuts.

Mike Domek

Mike Domek

Talk about having to fire people.
We had been growing from $35 million in revenue to 55 to 100 to 142 to 200, and I always wanted to be prepared for that growth. I kept expecting that growth knowing full well that sometime the 100 percent growth would go down to 20 percent growth. When the exponential growth slowed down to, you know, considerable growth, we had to do one downsizing. That hit me hard emotionally, but it was something we had to do. Everybody understood it, nobody liked it, myself included. That was the one crisis— managing it and getting through it. That was a tough time.

Launching in the Midwest: Was that a plus or a minus?
We built the company to 200-plus employees before I ever issued stock options to anyone. That wasn't the driver for them. Midwest people are hardworking. They have strong values and an enormous sense of pride. On the West Coast, the driver for getting people to come to the company might be, what do I get in equity?

How did your staff feel about selling to Ticketmaster?
Half the people in the company came up to me after the transaction and thanked me. The reason they came to the company was because they wanted to be a part of something great, something big. And they could see that that was my goal.

You didn't start out with the idea to eventually sell your company?
My goal wasn't to build a company and sell it. It was to create something great, something big. Ultimately, we did the transaction because it fit with my goal for the company, which was to have it grow and become the biggest thing that it could. In the hands of Ticketmaster, the world's largest ticketing brand, I gotta think it's going to continue to thrive and even accelerate.

Did you have friends and family in the company?
At the beginning, I had a lot of friends who were graduating from college and were unemployed, so they'd work for nothing and help me out. One guy lost his license so he lived with me and basically worked for free. It was the perfect arrangement at the time. It's funny because, as they found real jobs, it forced me to say, "Okay, let's make a real business out of this," and we moved out of my apartment and into my first office.

Sometimes the early risk, even though in hindsight it was small, feels big.
It was a huge risk—a 400 square foot office! I bought a phone system from some guy in the paper. I met him in the McDonald's parking lot and paid him cash.

It's not easy to have friends and family as employees, is it?
It was completely successful. It didn't work with some of them but it was a clean break. The reason it worked with others was because we were able to successfully separate work from friendship and family. And they understood that, at work, I'm the boss

Our competitors had executives from Amazon and Apple, but I built the company with just a couple of regular guys like myself.

Mike Domek

Tony Faras

and this is what goes. Outside of work we're all the same.

How do you make an environment that will nurture the next entrepreneur, the next TicketsNow?
The thing we need to do is to keep creating opportunities where we live. Talent will follow opportunity. When I went out and recruited our CFO, the company was going from $35 to $100 million in revenue in two years. I actually pulled in a CFO from Silicon Valley to Chicago and it wasn't because I was charming or persuasive. It was because there was a phenomenal opportunity, not even in Chicago, but way out in Crystal Lake, Illinois.

Do you have any advice for someone starting out right now with just an idea?
I believe you need to start with a passion, not an exit strategy.

What would you do differently?
I wouldn't change my experience for the world.

MGI Pharma
Minnesota

Congratulations on the sale, Tony.
It's been quite a ride for my co-founder Frank Pass and me, starting a company from zero and eventually selling for $3.9 billion to Eisai.

You were in good company from the start. Future Nobel Prize winner Mike Bishop, who won for discovering the nature of the cancer gene, and Herb Boyer, founding scientist at Genentech, were both at UCSF with you.
I certainly picked the right place to do my post-doctoral work. Mike Bishop had an extremely active lab in cancer research and Herb Boyer was just down the hall from us trying to find

enzymes that could cut up DNA—the foundation for gene splicing as we know it today.

You could have had a nice life working at Genentech.
We had the opportunity to work with Herb Boyer and Bob Swanson at Genentech early on when they were considering animal healthcare. They were also thinking of going into veterinary medicine products because those didn't require the lengthy FDA review process for human products. We decided to do it on our own and it probably was a good thing, because I think Genentech got out of that area when they saw their human pharmaceuticals moving quickly to success.

I didn't find it difficult to be able to distinguish between somebody who was really good and somebody who was really mediocre. When you see truly bright people, it amazes you.

Tony Faras

Tony Faras

Before you moved to the University of Minnesota Medical School and started MGI, you had a faculty position at the University of Michigan, my alma mater.
Go blue!

Then you and Frank Pass started the company and focused on viruses, which cannot be cultured in tissue like influenza.
We decided to use a gene-splicing technology to isolate the genes that would produce a vaccine, and by developing that technology, we realized we had something of commercial interest. That's what started us moving into a business plan to develop veterinary pharmaceuticals.

Luckily your first product worked and produced revenue, and animal products were orders of magnitude less expensive to create and commercialize.
It was really interesting to take a product from the lab right up through production and commercialization. But what we found was that, despite the fact that the products worked, the amount of revenue we could generate was always limited because farmers were becoming more tightly bound to the ups and downs of the agricultural market, the profit margins weren't that terrific, and farmers were less willing to spend money on veterinary medicine products if they thought they could get by without them.

That prompted your move into human pharmaceuticals?
We realized that large revenues were going to come from human pharmaceutical markets.

Hard to see upfront or did you know that going in?
It's very clear now, but it wasn't back then. We were developing products and had sales, but once we could see that the sales weren't going to be as profitable as we hoped, we expanded and also got into plant genetics.

Did MGI face any kind of crisis?
There were continuous highs and lows in biotech. It was a scary ride. I remember standing at the window of the lab one day thinking we might be able to make one more payroll and that was going to be it.

Oh boy. But the market did help you?
When Genentech's IPO came out, it was sky high and running like crazy. Then it came down, then it jumped up, and biotech's been up and down like that ever since our first large infusion of capital. Our first big win after venture capital funding was American Cyanamid coming in and buying a piece of the company. That allowed us to expand into the areas we wanted to, including plant genetics.

Things worked in your favor and you were able to raise over $100 million from a variety of sources, including private rounds of funding and your own IPO.
It was a great thing. But I remember going on a trip with my family—my first trip after working 16 hours a day to get this thing going. We had the IPO all set and it was just a matter of closing it out, so I took off in a Volkswagen camper and went up into the Canadian Rockies. This was pre-

The biggest mistake company founders make is their inability to let go of control. Many founders think they need to be in control even when the company has evolved beyond them. You need to know your limitations and, if necessary, find people who are more adept at running the company and taking it to the next level.

Tony Faras

cell phones, so I remember stopping at telephone booths along the way for updates because the biotech market was starting to sour. It was one of the rollercoaster rides coming down and our original pricing had to be cut dramatically to complete the IPO.

Shakespeare's line, to not "lose the name of action"?
It was close. There were a lot of times when it could have gone the other way, and once you start losing your personnel, you start losing everything. We had worked very hard to get top quality scientists and did not want to lose them.

Frank Pass managed the business and you led the science and recruitment of scientists. Was there a point when you both realized

things were going to be okay, that you were going to make it?
We believed we could do it and could see it moving in the right direction, but we were never that confident. If you get too confident you might reduce the drive required to be successful.

You were always on guard?
There was always a fear that something could go wrong. It could be anything from fundraising to research and development. It could be approval of the product or acceptance of the product in the marketplace. There are all kinds of things that can happen that you can't predict. And even though you might know your thing works beautifully, you don't know if it's going to generate the amount of revenue and profit that you need or whether something will happen during

production. Our concerns always kept us from stepping back from it.

What's the best decision the company ever made?
The home run for the company was making the decision to go into human pharmaceuticals. More to the point, it was hiring great people that allowed us to move into human pharma, and my good friend Chuck Muscoplat was a big part of that.

Lots of biotech companies made that decision and never developed any secret sauce.
Our philosophy was, let's keep moving and develop more revenue. Musicians will tell you, you become great for three reasons—practice, practice, practice. This company was ultimately successful for three reasons—work, work, work.

No secret sauce?
There was no secret ingredient or secret patent. There were obviously patents, but the strategy wasn't to go against the big guys, but to develop a group of drugs that larger pharmaceuticals weren't interested in. And with a sales force, you can get enough attention to start generating profits. With those profits, you continue to develop and acquire additional human pharmaceuticals and the bottom line starts moving up because you have multiple drugs that are all working. We didn't have one huge revenue-generating drug.

Go for singles, not home runs.
Right. In the animal healthcare area, we tried for a home run. We sent researchers to Argentina to develop a foot-and-mouth virus vaccine, an

We knew what we wanted to do, but we had no bloody idea what technology would allow us to do it.

Gian Fulgoni

Tony Faras

alternative to producing the vaccine by traditional means.

That's huge.
It turned out to be costly to get the vaccine to remote farms, and that's why foot-and-mouth disease is still an issue in those areas. You just can't get the vaccine to all of the animals.

Is the pharma industry likes sports—you sign the most outstanding player and you're all set? You get Michael Jordan and everything's good?
Yes, and we recruited several of those stars right off the bat. In general I didn't find it difficult to be able to distinguish between somebody who was really good and somebody who was just mediocre.

Just intuition?
The experiences that I had with my previous mentors and collaborators were invaluable in developing the kind of intuition that you're talking about. When you see truly bright people, it amazes you. I mean, there are not that many out there. There are many smart people but not so many truly bright people. Mike Bishop, for instance, was a truly bright person.

What's the biggest mistake company founders make?
Their inability to let go of control. Many founders think they need to be in control even when the company has evolved beyond them. You need to know your limitations and, if necessary, find people who are more adept at running the company and taking it to the next level.

The issue of having majority control of the company—
We never had it to begin with.

So you knew you could be fired.
You are never in control. If you own 51 percent of the company and you're unsuccessful, you no longer have a company. If you have 49 percent and you're successful, you're doing what you want to do because you're successful and people are supporting you.

Gian Fulgoni

comScore (SCOR)
Illinois

How does a physics major end up an entrepreneur?
I think most scientists are inherently curious and like discovering and doing new things—and that's certainly been a characteristic of the information businesses I've been involved in building. I went to one of the top science schools in the UK and found that there was a lot of competition in the physics program. But in the UK, you can't easily change your major; you have to finish what you started, or start all over again. So it was easier and faster to get my undergraduate degree in physics and then get my masters in marketing, which, in combination, gave me a competitive

I LIKE CREATING NEW THINGS AND DOING WHAT HASN'T BEEN DONE BEFORE.

GIAN FULGONI

advantage as an entrepreneur in my chosen field.

Marketing is a critical skill?
I think on a continuum with arts on one end and science on the other that I do pretty well in both areas. I'm able to leverage very strong analytic skills with very good communication skills. In our business, we have to be able to analyze data, translate it into business tactics and strategies that make sense for marketing people (our customers), and communicate the results.

Early on, could you have seen the arc of your career?
No, I thought I'd end up as the brand manager for some kind of technical product.

How did IRI and comScore succeed so brilliantly?

Neither company created the technical dislocation (point-of-sale scanners in the case of IRI and the Internet in the case of comScore), but we leveraged the dislocations very effectively to create better application products in the information business. By dislocation I mean a game-changing new technology, and a big dislocation generally means there's a terrific opportunity for entrepreneurs.

Why?
Because people in established and profitable businesses don't like to change. They're making money in a certain way and can't embrace the need to change for the future as easily as the newcomer, who is able to move and innovate faster because he or she has no legacy baggage.

Why start comScore? You already hit a home run at IRI.
I enjoy building new businesses. I like creating new things and doing what hasn't been done before. But I do think the financial rewards go hand in hand with enjoyment. Both have to be there for me to be interested and motivated.

How did you know there'd be a market for comScore?
When we founded comScore, there were two companies, Nielsen and Media Metrix, already in the Internet measurement business but they were just counting "eyeballs" — how many people visited a site, for example. They had a combined market cap of over $2 billion, and combined revenues of maybe $30 million, but they weren't measuring what people were buying. I did a back-of-the-

envelope calculation to figure out how much money companies spent on ratings—TV, radio, print, etc. —versus how much they spent figuring out how consumers buy products. It turns out companies spend four times as much money figuring out consumers' buying behavior. In 1999, everything in online measurement was simply based on counting unique visitors to web sites and measuring their demographics, and we thought, well, that's going to change. Companies are going to also need to measure e-commerce and other types of online transactional activities.

How do you measure online buying without a UPC code to scan?
You have to scrape all the information off the web page during an online

People in established and profitable businesses don't like to change. They're making money in a certain way and can't embrace the need to change for the future as easily as the newcomer, who is able to move and innovate faster because he or she has no legacy, no baggage.

Gian Fulgoni

Gian Fulgoni

checkout and turn it into a numerical database, and that was not easy to do. We knew what we wanted to do, but we had no bloody idea what technology would allow us to do it.

Was raising money easy?
If we were two fresh entrepreneurs, they might have laughed us out the door. The fact that we had been very successful before at IRI got us the meetings. And we were able to focus more on the potential of the business rather than how we would do it. Of course, that was 1999 and back then it was almost as if any Internet business could get funded.

Is there a regional bias in venture funding?
We're in California, it's August 1999 and the Internet is going full bore. We

meet with one of the biggest venture funds and the VC partner tells us we have a really interesting idea. "Now where will you put the headquarters?" he says. We say, "Virginia," and he says, "That's a deal killer. You can't expect me to jump on a plane and fly four hours for a board meeting." I'm thinking, let me get this right. There's no office space at any reasonable rent in the Bay area. It's going to cost a fortune to hire software engineers because they will each want 5 percent of the company's equity to join. And you think we should base the company in California because you don't want to get on a plane?

Did you persuade him to invest?
I told him I had a solution—we'll base the company in Virginia but come out

to California for the board meetings. That was the end of that discussion. But, it proved to me that some VCs are more interested in making their own lives easier than in doing what's right for the business.

You're at about 1,150 customers. Was growth steady?
We ran into two unexpected problems: the tragedy of 9/11, and the bursting of the Internet bubble. Revenue growth slowed and our cash burn increased more than we had planned.

Was it hard to keep on raising money?
We raised $88 million in total and I think we could have done it for $30 million less if not for 9/11 and the bubble. It was a little frustrating every time we did a round because the

existing investors said, "We're going to invest, but we need a new outside investor to lead the round and set a value for the company." That burned up a lot of time going on the road to find the new investors.

If you were doing it all over again, what would you do differently?
The most important thing is to move quickly when something isn't working right. "Time is money" is true. When you're a start-up and burning cash, you're basically diluting yourself as you use the cash. Maybe we raised too much money in our second round. It almost seems that the more you raise, the more you spend.

Was there ever a point where you doubted the business would make it?

THE MOST IMPORTANT THING IS TO MOVE QUICKLY WHEN SOMETHING ISN'T WORKING RIGHT

GIAN FULGONI

No, but we worried about money and dilution. We knew we were being diluted pretty badly. At one point, we had to go to the VC investors and say, "We've been diluted down so much, you're going to have to give us a stock option package," which they did. If they wanted a return on their money, they had to have our management team motivated to continue building the business.

What do you say to the youngster starting a company now?
You've got to get some reliable confirmation that there's really a market for your idea. By the same token, this can get tricky, because I don't believe most breakthrough ideas originate from marketplace feedback. Henry Ford once said: "If I'd listened to my customers, I'd have built a very, very fast horse."

What's the secret sauce?
Surround yourself with the right people who have complimentary skill sets. For example, just because "Jack" was involved with the creation of the original idea, if he brings nothing to executing it well, then God forbid you end up with Jack in a pivotal management role. I read that 95 percent of great ideas fail on execution, so the management of the execution is vital. Above all else, I think assembling a team where each individual brings his or her unique talents is critical.

What's the most brilliant thing you've done with comScore?
I think we were very smart to buy Media Metrix, one of our competitors. In 2002, the Internet had imploded. Nielsen had cash. Media Metrix had burned through theirs. Nielsen offered to buy them for $70 million but the FTC blocked the transaction. We were able to snap up Media Metrix for $1.5 million.

Okay, that was a good move.
With all due modesty, I also think we developed some brilliant data collection and warehousing technologies and very powerful application products that help marketers better leverage the power of the Internet.

Do you text message?
Very infrequently. I either call or email. Most of my career is from the time before the Internet. But I have to confess that it drives me nuts when I see an e-mail that contains a spelling mistake or a PowerPoint deck with a typo.

Just a typo?
It just looks so schlocky. Do today's young executives attach much significance to it? I'm not sure they do. Does it matter? I think it does. For me it says that someone didn't pay a lot of attention to detail. That can be a killer in any business.

What was it like taking comScore public in 2007 versus IRI in 1983?
Remember "Doogie Howser," the television show that featured a 16-year-old teenager as a brilliant surgeon? It seems like Doogie Howsers are now running $20 billion funds. We'd be on the IPO road show

When you're a start-up and burning cash, you're basically diluting yourself as you use investors' money.

Gian Fulgoni

Ronald Galowich

sitting across the table from some very young-looking person who managed a really large fund, and I'd think, this kid can't really be running a fund this big, can he? I wonder whether computers, to some extent, haven't taken the place of human experience and allowed much younger people to manage very large funds today.

So now the 800-pound gorilla, Google, has entered your arena.
What Google has done is put together a tool that makes it easy for media planners to buy ads on Google's ad network. Does Google provide anywhere near all of the tools and functionality of comScore's broad portfolio of offerings for advertising anywhere on the Internet? No. Plus, there's a natural desire for ad agencies

and advertisers to avoid using audience measurement data supplied by the same company that's selling them the advertising. A case of the fox guarding the chicken coop, if you will.

Does technology make strategy go faster?
Today, there's pressure to make fast decisions and to recover quickly if it turns out to be the wrong decision. That's all well and good with tactical issues, but when it comes to strategy, I prefer to spend a little more time thinking things through. I don't think it's particularly easy to recover quickly from strategic mistakes.

First Health, Initiate
Systems Inc.
Illinois

You, Howard Tullman (see Howard A. Tullman, page 152), and Stephen Shank (see Steve Shank, page 118) are lawyers. I'm going to have to rethink law school as actually being a good training ground for company founders.
I'm a reformed lawyer.

But you practiced for a while.
I practiced law for 20 years, then ran real estate operations for the Pritzker family. I'm also a real estate developer on the residential and commercial side.

You started First Health with Dr. Robert Becker in Joliet and it became a large healthcare cost

management company with 6,000 employees. When did you first know it would survive?
We felt like we had turned a corner when I got the right president and CEO and a couple good customers.

Why was the president a sign?
I found a CEO with a sales and marketing background who understood the word "profit." I wanted somebody from a sales environment as opposed to an operations environment to be my president and CEO. You can always find operations people, but you can't always find top sales talent with a financial background.

How did you find him?
He was a business friend I had known. He reported profit and loss statements on a weekly basis, not monthly. I knew at that point we would be fine.

If I'm talking to two people about a CEO position and it appears both are strong personalities and could do the job, I'm going to take the one who I believe is a nice guy with strong values and ethics. I think in the long run, a nice guy is going to win out with the people he surrounds himself with.

Ron Galowich

How much money did you raise for First Health?
I raised $2 million. In the entire history of the company that was the total raise.

One initial investor put in $1 million. You paid back $750,000 upon completion of the IPO. The remaining $250,000 grew to $200 million three years after the IPO?
Correct. We were the biggest winner on the NASDAQ up until the Internet bubble.

I guess you prove the point about the Midwest being okay for start-ups.
We would go to $30 a share and split two for one and then go back to 30 and split two for one, and it just kept going.

What's the secret? How did you do it?
By having the right people with a strong work ethic in the right places, starting with the chairman, Bob Becker, and the CEO, Jim Smith.

Then what?
We expanded the group of people who had great capabilities. And they identified the right market and how to get to that market.

And everyone says hire smarter than yourself—
The team has to produce not just better products but more appropriate products. The trick is not to give the marketplace what you think it needs, but what it thinks it needs.

Did your competition simply miss the opportunity or was this still so new that you had open ground to run with?
Both. It was a new field, little understood, and the competition that we might have had was the big healthcare insurance companies, but they were too busy doing their own thing to look at what we were doing.

They missed it.
I wouldn't say they missed it. I would say they didn't give it the significance that we did. We took a gamble—and we gambled right—that it would become a major issue. Bob Becker, who was one of the leaders in a yet-to-be-discovered industry, thought that the cost containment that the government had figured out for Medicare, called Peer Review

Organizations, was something that would have to happen in the private sector as well. He said, "Let's go do it and make it better."

You were one of the leaders in pre-admission certification, which has become standard procedure for all hospital stays. First Health was public for 20 years, then you sold it. Why?
We saw the market changing. In '05, we sold the company for $1.8 billion to Coventry Health Care.

Your next start-up in '96 was Initiate Systems, which you co-founded with your son, Jeff.
Initiate became the leader in the healthcare industry in identifying duplicate medical records, then branched out into government and

I found a CEO with a sales and marketing background who understood the word 'profit.' I wanted somebody from a sales environment as opposed to an operations environment to be our president and CEO. You can always find operations people, but you can't always find top sales talent with a financial background.

Ron Galowich

Ronald Galowich

commercial. We linked disparate databases and were able to identify people who looked different as being the same, and people that looked the same as being different. You can imagine how many Jim Smiths there are in this country alone.

How did you fund Initiate?
I funded the first $4 million myself and was choking on it. We built a product but needed to find a beta site.

What did you do?
Our CTO, Scott Ellard, had been a troubleshooter for Informix. The CIO of a California hospital—Uni Health, which became Catholic Healthcare West—knew our CTO as a person who got the job done. They bet on him. We got the job over major software companies.

You got your beta site. Were you able to raise money?
That's when I went out and raised the first $10 million from my friends.

You wanted proof before risking anyone else's money.
I thought we were going to get market proof and that we would be able to build the kind of software that would work.

Any pros or cons about being in the Midwest?
We wanted to stay here because I wanted to keep control and normalcy. The longest-standing Illinois state senator, Richard Barr, happened to have been from Joliet, my hometown. He coined a great saying: "The best fertilizer for a man's land is his own footsteps."

What does that mean?
It doesn't matter whether it's land or software or healthcare companies, if you're not around to see what's going on, it's too late.

But you did branch out.
We have offices in Phoenix, Austin, Toronto, London, and Sydney because we found that it was essential, especially in the foreign jurisdictions, that we have people there, not because of the location but because they were locals.

Kind of like the expression, "all politics are local."
Our offices have worked out fairly well. We have people traveling for implementation and software support from various offices and travel is extremely expensive. We couldn't keep it all here.

Sometimes the institutional money forces the company to move.
One of our VCs wanted to see us move to Boston. We wanted to know what was going on and be able to move rapidly if we had to, and that meant the company needed to stay in Chicago. One of our requirements was that the company could not move out of Chicago without my and Jeff's approval.

Thoughts on hiring?
If the person who hired you is smart and nice, the people that person hires will be smart and nice. If the person who does the hiring is smart and a jerk, you're going to end up with a lot of smart jerks. You need to find somebody who not only is smart and capable, but who cares about people,

If the person who hired you is smart and nice, the people that person hires will be smart and nice. If the person who does the hiring is smart and a jerk, you're going to end up with a lot of smart jerks.

Ron Galowich

Try not to take money from people you don't know or know about, whether they're angels, private equity or VCs.

Ron Galowich

shareholders and investors, not just about himself.

You are the first company founder in this book to single out niceness.
If I'm talking to two people about a CEO position and it appears both are strong personalities and could do the job, I'm going to take the one who I believe is a nice guy with solid values and ethics. I think in the long run, a nice guy is going to win out with the people he surrounds himself with.

What would happen if you made the wrong pick?
I have been fortunate and have never made a wrong pick. What you find is people take too long to make a change once they discover they've hired the wrong person. No matter what the implications, you must bite the bullet

and get it done. Jeff and I found and hired the right CEO at Initiate in '02 when we hired Bill Conroy. Bill's values matched ours, and he came from the sales side with broad enterprise software experience. He did a great job building the company, and didn't drag his feet when it came to making a few changes in senior management.

Any crises?
Try not to take money from people you don't know or know about, whether they're angels, private equity or VCs. We took money from someone who became very difficult and although it did not adversely affect the outcome for the company and shareholders, it did cause headaches for management. On reflection, I wish we didn't have his money.

And once you take in investors you can't automatically show them the door.
It was a very unusual deal because, luckily, we kept control of the company, in large part because we had a very significant investment pool from angels who invested in every round.

It's such a balancing act between needing the money and wanting desirable terms. You raised money because you landed new contracts?
No, I wish it was because we landed a new contract. It was because we had to staff up in order to land the big contract, because the sales cycle wasn't a two-month cycle, it was a six-month-to-a-year cycle.

That'll keep you up at night.
It kept me up many nights.

You recently sold Initiate to IBM. Congratulations.
It was not only a good outcome for us and IBM, it was a good outcome for 300 shareholders, including many of our employees.

How do you have balance in your life? It's such a dedicated effort to really build the business.
Well, first of all, it helps that I have a wonderful, supportive wife and great, smart, hard-working kids. When I started out practicing law from my home office in Joliet, Illinois, it was day and night. My dad owned a small shoe store and paid the first month's rent on our office. I had a twin brother who died in an airplane accident many years ago and his kids are like my kids, so really I have five kids—three of my own and his two. His son, David, runs

You try to think ahead and be sure that whatever surprises come up, you are prepared to move ahead aggressively and positively. The last thing an entrepreneur wants when starting a business is to lose momentum.

Bill Gantz

52

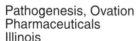

Bill Gantz

our real estate business and my son, Jeff, was number two in our software business. By working with them, every day is Father's Day.

Pathogenesis, Ovation
Pharmaceuticals
Illinois

What was it like to go from being the president of Baxter Corporation, a $40 billion company, to launching Pathogenesis, a start-up?
It was, well, talk about getting shell-shocked.

What caused you to do it?
I was watching a lot of people go into biotechnology and very successfully develop and create companies and I thought, you know what? I'm at a point in my life that either I do it now or I'm not really going to have a chance.

How did you do it?
I had an idea for the product that I

thought would work. I was introduced to some people in venture capital and some wealthy families that liked the idea. We put together what, at that time, was the second largest seed round ever raised in the biotech industry.

How much did you raise?
We raised $42 million to start the business. In 1992 that was a lot of money.

And that amount turned out to be important.
That turned out to be one of the keys to success because in pharmaceuticals as you go along, you need a lot of funding to develop products. That gave us the wherewithal to work on, what I thought, would be a great product—a cure for an infectious disease. We

focused on cystic fibrosis, which involves infections of the lung.

Any lessons learned that were critical to your success?
I learned that when you identify an opportunity, make sure you stick with it. People would come in with funding and say, "You know what? Your idea's okay, but why don't you try to do a little more of this and a little more of that." So one of the keys is to be sure you remain focused on a strategy and a program.

Focus is important—so many people have a scattershot approach. What else?
Make sure you recruit people who are experienced and have the same passion for doing what you're trying to do. And if you can, make sure you have solid funding.

I thought I better cover my bases, so I had a Plan B. I didn't think we would ever need it. I just thought it could be a good idea. It turned out that our Plan B saved the company.

Bill Gantz

What was the biggest crisis you faced?
The first product failed to work.

That's bad.
We had a product from Baxter that was an antibacterial, monoclonal antibody—state-of-the-art technology. After doing a clinical trial, we found out that we had the perfect drug, no side effects, but it didn't work.

How did you recover from that?
Fortunately, working with the Cystic Fibrosis Foundation, we had identified a drug that really worked well. As luck would have it, I was able to convince the owners of the drug to license it to me before I knew my other drug failed.

Was that luck or superior planning?
I thought I just better cover my bases, so I had a Plan B. I didn't think we would ever need it. I just thought it would be a good idea. It turned out that this drug really worked; it saved the company. We would've had a real problem funding a drug that had failed a year and a half into the company.

Did you have to convince others on the team, or your board or investors?
Absolutely. There was a lot of doubt. We licensed it for a small amount of money, but even so, the venture capital investors didn't want to spend additional capital. The backup program idea was one that I really had to sell hard and it turned out to be a lifesaver.

That led to the sale to Chiron Novartis for $720 million all cash.
It turned out to be a very good outcome for us, for everybody involved.

It paid off in other ways. Didn't that backup plan help launch a TB drug?
I was just reading today that one of our drugs for tuberculosis continues moving toward getting approval.

Most entrepreneurs have to rely on friends and family for early funding. What was your experience?
One of the advantages coming from a large company is that I had access to a lot of sources of capital that I never would have had otherwise. I did not have to go to friends and family. We ended up with some really interesting investors, including Bill Gates.

You may be the only champion founder selected from the Great Lakes states with Bill Gates as an investor.
He was very interested in biotechnology. We had this interesting mix of VC and wealthy families, plus some friends of mine that had been successful in their entrepreneurial activities.

Your blue chip list of investors must have helped immensely.
That's why we were able to raise such a large amount of money. When Bill Gates invests in you, people follow.

People followed as investors—and that also attracted management?
I was able to attract management because we were well funded and we had people with really good reputations. I was able to get a board together that was absolutely world-

We like to say we do a lot of 'littles.' We do a lot of little things a little bit better than everybody else.

—Jim Gray

Bill Gantz

class. I had the ex-CEO of Merck, the ex-CEO of Upjohn, and the ex-president of Eli Lilly on my board. Again, I never could have done that without our investors.

Was it hard to deal with that caliber of investor?
Thank goodness our investors were really willing to listen to the board. And listen to management.

How did your experience with Pathogenesis influence launching Ovation?
I was able to identify some sources of products and ideas that we were able to move ahead on very quickly. We got up and running much faster, and we learned how to recruit and get the right people on board. I believe we did our first acquisition 120 days after funding.

Your backup strategy also carried over to Ovation.
You try to be thinking ahead, and to be sure that whatever surprises come up, you are prepared so you can move ahead aggressively and positively. The last thing an entrepreneur wants when starting a business is to lose momentum.

Was your location a help or a hindrance?
We have great resources here in the Midwest. Roughly 20 to 25 percent of healthcare industry CEOs come from Abbott and Baxter. This is an enormous strength in the Midwest.

You and Jeff Aronin (see *Jeff Aronin, page 1*) just sold Ovation for $900 million. Congratulations. How did you come to work together?

Jeff founded the company. I joined him and we went out and raised the money. I had the concept of a specialty pharmaceutical company. I felt that at that point in time it was going to have some opportunity of building a very nice business. Jeff had exactly the same concept in mind and was a little bit further ahead in terms of getting something in place and so, best of all worlds, I joined with him, we went out, and we raised the money.

You had two incredible mentors at Baxter—Bill Graham, former CEO, and Vernon Loucks, chairman of the board. Was their mentoring helpful when you went off on your own?
Yes. Bill Graham really understood business strategy, but more than that, he could define how you look at and

find opportunities in the marketplace. He taught us how to aggressively move forward, and how to take an idea and turn it into a business opportunity. And then he gave us the opportunity to run businesses. I ran a number of businesses in the international sector so I actually had the experience of going out and doing it.

You are uniquely positioned to coach former corporate managers seeking to start their own companies.
A lot of companies are cutting back on their research and development, and some of them are really good programs. I think there are opportunities for people in large companies to take these programs, get them funded, and build successful businesses. Research is being spun

We always knew we were going to be successful. It's just that our idea of success isn't what actually happened.

Jim Gray

Jim Gray

out because companies—and not just those in the pharma industry—don't have the funding to continue it.

optionsXpress (OXPS)
Illinois

***Barron's, Kiplinger, SmartMoney, Forbes**—they all say you're the best online broker.*
We took the company public about five years ago. We started in '00 and today we've got over 300,000 customers. It's just been a lot of fun. We work with some tremendously bright and successful people, and they're really the drivers of our business.

At the time you launched, there were many online brokers, large and small. How did you think you could succeed?
We really built our business on the premise of wanting to level the playing field and adding better products and

capabilities to allow retail customers to trade like the pros. A lot of these new products were being treated more as an accommodation by the traditional online brokerage firms. We wanted to deliver it at a cost that was very competitive and compelling for our retail consumers.

What inspired you to start optionsXpress?
As one of my partners likes to put it, "options traders were being treated like lepers." He had this great idea to build a "leper colony"—a place that embraced traders.

Great metaphor. You were already running a trading company?
We started optionsXpress as an offshoot of a proprietary trading company. One of the things we

underestimated was the pent-up demand in the marketplace for people who wanted to use derivatives—primarily options and futures—as part of their investing portfolio.

Too bad about the timing. You went out for funding in 2000?
Financial markets cratered, investing cratered, so we ended up funding it ourselves. Instead of someone giving us a lot of money that we could spend maybe a little more aggressively or recklessly, we really made sure every dollar we spent made sense.

But you had an angel at some point, didn't you?
We funded it for the first few years on $2 million. We never found one specific angel. It was a lot of people

We didn't know what we couldn't do or weren't supposed to do, so we just did it. We built it in a way that made sense to us. And we broke a bunch of conventional rules.

Jim Gray

putting in $50,000 or $100,000, and so forth, and we funded the bulk of it.

As successful traders, didn't the delay in funding drive you nuts?
I think it really suited our temperament and our style very well. Immediately after the financial world and technology businesses cratered, many of our customers, though they weren't our customers yet, were very unhappy. People were losing money with their brokers. That actually turned into a competitive advantage for us.

People were losing money and that became a competitive advantage for you?
People were unsure about the financial marketplace. They were unhappy with how things were being done and they were looking for new alternatives. We

were there with a solution that actually provided them with better returns and better yields at lower cost with less volatility. We started as a very niche player and continued to grow and build upon that, continually adding tools and technologies.

What's the secret sauce?
Execution of the plan. The team we put together executed phenomenally. As the market changed, we were able to reevaluate and continue to execute and adapt to that market.

But there has to be more. It sounds like there was some belief or mission behind that.
We're built on a lot of very simple philosophies. We always ran businesses to make money. We thought about it from Day One. The

other core strength for us is we like to say we do a lot of "littles." We do a lot of little things a little bit better than everybody else. When you put a lot of these "littles" together it changes the overall business experience.

And did the "littles" really make a big difference?
It made a dramatic difference in the end-user experience, like how many keystrokes it took to get from Point A to Point B. We also invested heavily in our back-office because we felt that anything we had to do more than once we ought to automate. That gave us a platform that was more efficient than our competitors'. It allowed us to adapt to the market and have further iterations come out at a far more rapid pace than any of our competitors.

It sounds like constant reinvestment or reinvention.
We were very dynamic in what we rolled out and how we rolled it out to our customers. We didn't know what we couldn't do or weren't supposed to do, so we just did it. We built it in a way that made sense to us. And we broke a bunch of the conventional rules in the financial industry at the time. We continue to follow those same philosophies.

What kind of rules did you break?
We priced our product at $15. At the time I think Merrill Lynch and Schwab were charging $80, and we could have priced it at $50, but this is what made sense to us. And we knew we could make a very large profit and add a lot of value to our customers.

Get some kind of product out early so that you start getting feedback from customers. Don't put all your eggs in one basket because you're doomed if that launch fails. With feedback you can hone your products.

Roland Green

Chicago is not an obvious choice for a tech start-up.
I think we had an advantage in that Chicago is one of the financial centers of the world, certainly in terms of derivatives. There was a wide array of talent to draw from for ideas. There were lots of people who understood the exchanges and how to continue to build and add innovation, which gave us a leg up.

Did that translate into publicity? Were you a home town darling?
We have always been strong believers in the benefits of good PR and have devoted significant efforts to it even when we didn't have a lot of money. This has paid off in good media both in Chicago and nationally.

Any big challenges along the way?
We went from three to 300 people with none of us ever having managed a large group of individuals. We were a very young management team. None of us had been educated on how to manage a large company or how to build that foundation efficiently.

That's a lot of hiring. How did you learn on the fly?
We had a strong belief that A people hire A people, B people hire C people, and C people drive away A people. We were very focused on bringing in top-tier people. I think most organizations have one or two people who really ignite and drive the firm. We were very fortunate in that we were able to find more than just a couple.

What's it like to work with your father?
My father and I have become close friends. I merged my original business with a family company.

You also hired friends. How did that go?
We had mixed success. In some cases it worked great. The people we hired were more dedicated, more loyal. In other cases, if they felt a sense of entitlement, those people didn't work out very well. The key is to identify which are which as early as possible.

Is there a recipe for hitting a home run in business?
If you hit a home run, it's because you built a good business and were fortunate in the timing—you hit the wave just right. We always knew we were going to be successful. It's just that our idea of success isn't what actually happened.

So in the end both your timing and lack of venture funding worked in your favor.
Yeah, but when we started investors would say, "You don't have a first-mover advantage—there's Ameritrade and Schwab. The whole world's already there. You're not that unique." I have a lot of friends who ask, "Why didn't you show me the business plan? Of course I would've invested." Not many remember the phone calls and emails. But it's all fun.

One of the tricks is to have this combination: the ability to be focused, yet flexible and reactive to changing environments. These are opposing but important characteristics, since most start-ups end up selling a product that's different from what was originally intended.

Roland Green

We had a complicated intellectual property situation that added to the difficulty of getting funding. It put a lot of pressure on the company, but it may have been a good thing because it forced us to be relatively lean and stay focused on getting product out and generating revenue.

Roland Green

Roland Green

NimbleGen
Wisconsin

How did you come to help start NimbleGen and serve as chief technology officer and head of R&D?
The technology was based on my thesis project as a graduate student at the University of Wisconsin. As Nimblegen grew, I gained responsibilities. Eventually I headed up the engineering, manufacturing, quality assurance and chemistry divisions. We had a chemistry division in Germany and a manufacturing division in Iceland. At the time of the acquisition, I had 80 people under my control—about two-thirds of the company reported to me.

Who were the other founders?
Three University of Wisconsin professors—Francesco Cerrina, Michael Sussman, and Fred Blattner—and two venture capitalists, Bob and Tom Palay, who took very active roles in managing the company. The Palay brothers were the initial money behind the company but they also each served as CEO at different times.

Affymetrix had the original idea of light-directed DNA chemistry, but you took it further. NimbleGen had the idea of building instruments to allow labs to create microarrays. Instead it became a services company selling DNA testing and eventually expanded into product sales.
Professor Cerrina thought up the idea of using micro-mirrors. The existing microarrays were quite expensive and could not be changed once they were made. Right away we recognized that the use of digital light control was a great idea.

For what use?
Scientists working in the gene expression market were trying to understand which genes were being turned on or off in different organisms. The bigger markets now are studying the integrity of genomes for cancer research. They'll track the DNA from a tumor biopsy to see which parts of the genome have been deleted, amplified, or mutated in some way and then compare that to a normal one to try to get and idea of what is driving the cancer and also what possible therapeutics could fight that type of cancer.

How long did it take to commercialize a product?
Four or five years.

The sale to Roche in 2007 for $272.5 million occurred just as you were getting ready to go public. Was that a coincidence?
Gearing up for the IPO precipitated a bidding war. We filed our S1 and within a week we had four serious offers.

Why do you think that was?
A fair amount of effort goes into filing an S1 and preparing for an IPO, so it showed the company had itself together enough to go after it. It put us on the map and lit a fire under the companies that were interested in acquiring us. Once you file for the IPO there's a period of time you are still private but typically you are more

We filed our S1 and within a week we had four serious offers. It put us on the map and lit a fire under those companies that were interested in acquiring us. While filing for an IPO there's a period of time you are still private, but typically a company is more expensive to buy once it has gone public. This precipitated a bidding war, which was a perfect situation for us.

Roland Green

expensive after the IPO. A bidding war was a perfect situation for us.

No doubt. How was the business funded along the way?
Venture capital, a loan from the state of Wisconsin, and several grants, which made up approximately 10 percent of the funding. It took 20 to 30 million dollars to get the product out.

How was the process of raising money—easy or hard?
It was definitely touch and go. There were several times we were almost out of funding. It was a tough economy in '00-'02, and a tough time for biotech funding. The Palays were able to keep the company afloat. We always got the money in the end.

What about the IP issues?
We had a complicated intellectual property (IP) situation that added to the difficulty of getting funding. It put a lot of pressure on the company, but it may have been a good thing because it forced us to be relatively lean and stay focused on getting product out and generating revenue.

It is a bet, because if you pick the wrong product, you're done.
Many of our competitors did go under. When you go through a lean period and survive, but your competition doesn't, it's a lot better landscape when things improve.

A technology company with an IP issue. That's not good.
We didn't have the freedom to sell our product in the US at the time, but we

could perform services and sell the data from those services. So we set up a service operation. People would send in their DNA samples and we would do the tests and send back the data. It was a low margin business but it allowed us to improve our core technology and products. It also put us in a good negotiating position when we were able to acquire the licenses to the IP. By that time we had honed the products so they were the best on the market.

Why were there IP issues in the first place?
Affymetrix had patents covering any microarrays that used photo chemistry for synthesis. Once they saw our service business was viable, and they were getting nothing from it, we

were able to negotiate a license. Now we can sell product anywhere in the world. NimbleGen still runs a service business. It's more lucrative now and it gives us intimate contact with the customers, which is an invaluable source of feedback.

If you were doing NimbleGen all over again, what would you change?
In the early days we tended to have too many senior managers and not enough foot soldiers.

Why was that?
The company was born during the boom in the late '90s right before the bust. A lot of companies were getting formed and then flipped rapidly, before they had real revenue and real products. I think initially we thought we could do the same thing. We built

A lot of companies are too rigid. They don't see the changing market opportunities, so they miss with their product. Or it can be the opposite, where companies shift with every latest trend and never stay on topic long enough to develop a real product. The challenge is in striking that balance.

Roland Green

Starting with a service business wasn't easy. But if you can survive, you come out strong. In our case, it really helped that our R&D scientists often talked directly to our customers, because they learned exactly what customers wanted. We were able to improve the product in a very short cycle, and I think that was key.

Roland Green

Roland Green

up a pretty top-heavy management team because that team would be able to sell the company. When the bust happened that whole model evaporated, but the company was left with a fairly top-heavy structure. It was expensive. Eventually the board let go quite a few senior managers, so that we had more people actually working and developing products instead of sitting around in meetings.

Any advice for someone starting a company right now?
Get some kind of product out early so that you start getting feedback from customers. Don't put all your eggs in one basket because you're doomed if that launch fails. With feedback you can hone your products.

How did that apply to NimbleGen?
Starting with a service business wasn't easy. But if you can survive the tough route, you come out strong. In our case, it really helped that our R&D scientists often talked directly to our customers, because they learned exactly what customers wanted. We were able to improve the product in a very short cycle, and I think that was key.

What do you think the best qualities are for company founders?
One of the tricks is to have this combination: the ability to be focused, yet flexible and reactive to changing environments. These are opposing but important characteristics, since most start-ups end up selling a product that's different from what was originally intended.

True! But why is that?
As the company matures, R&D finds that the original plan was not on target. They have to adjust to get to the opportunity. But once you find the right opportunity, you have to be able to stay focused and not get distracted.

How does the average mortal deal with that?
You want to have a team of people to cover those bases.

Still difficult for the average company to pull off.
A lot of companies are too rigid. They don't see the changing market opportunities, so they miss with their product. Or it can be the opposite, where companies shift with every latest trend and never stay on topic long enough to develop a real product.

The challenge is in striking that balance.

You left after the company was acquired. What's next for you?
I had an agreement with Roche that I was free to start another company in a different space, so I founded a new company called Greenstone Technology, which makes solar film in windows.

It's a bit like what my mother taught me back in Alabama: "If you want to find a worm, you gotta look under many rocks". That is to say, in solving a medical idea to commericalize you have to be willing to look pretty extensively and to recognize your first choice may not always work.

DONALD C. HARRISON

Donald C. Harrison

AtriCure (ATRC)
Ohio

Don, you are the only cardiologist to make the cut.
I have always been interested in developing new concepts and new approaches—both for the diagnosis and treatment of heart disease. The four companies that I have either founded or co-founded all relate to my belief that I had something to contribute that would improve patient care.

Most doctors don't have the entrepreneurial bug, especially someone who had been chief of cardiology at Stanford for 20 years.
I think it was my training and my time at the National Institutes of Health. I

was with a very entrepreneurial group that was really on the cutting edge of cardiovascular disease—thinking through new concepts, looking for ways to develop new approaches to treatment.

What was your first company?
EP Technology developed a method for a form of heart rhythm problem that was common in younger patients and caused much consternation and occasional death. We developed a technique using a catheter that could abolish the site that was causing the abnormal rhythm and developed that into a successful company.

EP Technology had an IPO and a secondary and ultimately was sold to Boston Scientific. What was your second company?

EP Technology continues to be a successful company. I co-founded Venture Inc., using the same technology as that for treating a women's health issue called menorrhagia. The company was ultimately sold to American Surgical, a branch of Pfizer. The technology was never totally pursued.

Your third and fourth companies were founded in Cincinnati.
I had studied atrial fibrillation—irregular heartbeat—for about 40 years so I knew all the problems with it. We came up with a way to change the structure of the atrium of the heart, stop the atrial fibrillation, and keep it from recurring. That's AtriCure. The fourth company, UMD, also treated women with dysmenorrhea and was a drug delivery company.

What's the common element for you in these start-ups?
Taking advantage of what I knew about medicine, realizing there was an unmet need and a problem, and working with engineers and others to solve that problem.

Let's talk about AtriCure, your second successful IPO.
AtriCure was formed by a merger with Mike Hooven's company, Enable, which made medical instruments. I was on the board of Enable. Mike wanted to work in a bigger arena and one day he asked me, "What are the big unsolved problems in cardiology?"

Great question for an entrepreneur.
I said that really there are two. One of them is congestive heart failure and the other is atrial fibrillation. And we

A poorly written business plan is a mistake, and so is a poorly organized presentation. When you're making a presentation, if you can't convince the potential investor within 10 minutes that you've got something novel or a solution to a problem and you're dedicated to doing it, you're not going to succeed. Most venture investors are looking at hundreds of opportunities, so you've got to clearly have an edge.

Don Harrison

Donald C. Harrison

spent a couple days talking about how we could make a novel contribution here. Mike eventually came up with some ideas that were good enough to test out. After some of that testing it was clear that it would work. We filed some patent applications and four of us did some angel funding to get it started.

In most fields, just having a new product isn't enough. But AtriCure had something better and that was it?
We simply made a device that allowed people to do things they had not done before. And it was clear that it was a big field. It's still a growing field. I consider AtriCure still an infant.

A better mousetrap—
You have to understand why you need the mousetrap. Even though I was primarily an administrator, I was still practicing as a cardiologist. I kept up with what was going on and was aware of new research that showed you could change atrial fibrillation with a technology. Having a prepared mind and understanding the nature of the problem that you're trying to solve is the first key. And then developing the new technology that allows you to intervene is the second. It's a little bit like what my mother taught me back in Alabama: "If you wanna find the worm, you gotta look under many a rock." You have to be willing to look pretty extensively and know that your first choice may not always work.

Any crises along the way?
There's a lesson in the companies that didn't achieve IPO status. For example, we were approached by a large conglomerate that wanted to partner with us after one of our companies received several patents, so at that early stage we took them in. Later on, I heard they had an internal shakeup and they subsequently stopped funding. That made it very difficult to get funding from anyone else because they wondered why a partner would pull out. My view now would be to find some other funding method for an early stage company. Although the IP portfolio was sold to a new venture, that company was destroyed by partnering too early.

Some entrepreneurs don't have the highest opinion of venture funds and think of strategic investors and big corporations as their savior. That's not your experience.
Not always, but I understand the desire to partner.

Any rule of thumb about finding the right people at the right time?
In my case, to get venture funding we had to have a credible CEO. A credible CEO is someone who knows the industry, and has, perhaps, already succeeded in taking a company from an early stage all the way through to an IPO. Find somebody who is energetic, who's got experience, and who's had some previous success.

There's a lesson in the companies that didn't achieve IPO status. For example, we were approached by a large conglomerate that wanted to partner with us after one of our companies received several patents, so at that early stage we took them in. Later on, I heard they had an internal shakeup and they subsequently stopped funding. That made it very difficult to get funding from anyone else because they wondered why a partner would pull out. My view now would be to find some other funding method for an early stage company. Although the IP portfolio was sold to a new venture, that company was destroyed by partnering too early.

Don Harrison

Rich Heise

What about the entrepreneur just starting out?
First: Be certain that there's a problem that you're solving that's meaningful. Second: Carefully do your background research so that you can get the intellectual property you need for the company you're going to found. Third: If you need people to help you, make sure you get compatible partners. Lastly: clearly lay out a business plan that is credible and can be used to raise funds.

You also help start companies more proactively.
I run the Ohio office of a venture fund, Charter Life Sciences. My task is to look for opportunities in the Midwest.

What are the biggest mistakes that company founders make?
A poorly written business plan is a mistake, and so is a poorly organized presentation. When you're making a presentation, if you can't convince the potential investor within 10 minutes that you've got something novel or a solution to a problem and you're dedicated to doing it, you're not going to succeed. Most venture investors are looking at hundreds of opportunities, so you've got to clearly have an edge.

Magnitude Networks,
InnerWorkings (INWK),
Echo Global Logistics (ECHO),
MediaBank, Forseva
Illinois

What do you advise entrepreneurs starting out at zero?
You have to be extremely persistent and optimistic. Data, friends and family may suggest you're on the wrong track. You need a lot of energy. You need to have something that's pushing you.

Something pushing—
People are motivated in business by one of three things: money, power or acknowledgement.

And for you?
I try to figure out which of the three is most important to the person I'm working with.

For you the drive was money.
It was. That was the score card for me.

What about fame and power? You have created companies, all from zero, that total billions of dollars in market value and employ thousands.
I'm not interested in exercising power. I'm a very private person. If I'm dealing with people that really want recognition, or really need to exercise power, I can trade those away, because they don't have any value to me.

People are motivated in business by one of three things: money, power, or acknowledgement.

Rich Heise

I understood how to use financing to enforce discipline on what the management team needed to accomplish and in what order. New businesses need to have a strategic operating plan and advance from benchmark to benchmark, and to focus on the needs of clients rather than the capital markets.

Rich Heise

Rich Heise

It is somewhat of a fatal flaw in some entrepreneurs, the need for acknowledgement. You must see that all the time.
All the time. And the need to exercise control. Not many people who are able to start businesses are able to let go when they probably should.

You and I have been friends for 24 years and I've only seen you wearing a tie once. I understand at your first finance job at Northern Trust you wore a suit and tie daily.
Northern is a great company, but I refer to working there as life in the slow lane. Northern has a very successful, defined culture, and if it's not a culture that you're comfortable in, it will repel you. Which is good, that's what cultures are supposed to do.

But a great education.
It turned out to be the best take-away for me. I got my first exposure to accounting and finance principles. These things came easily to me. I'm grateful for what I learned there, and I'm still a client.

But you had entrepreneurial urges even at the bank.
I organized a barter operation from inside Northern Trust. They had excess capacity to provide cash management services, which is a commodity. The bank spent a lot of money on airline tickets, hotel rooms, and rental cars, so I wanted to swap cash management services, which had an incremental unit cost of virtually zero, in exchange for blocks of hotel rooms, rental cars, and airline tickets. The guy I was reporting to hated it. So naturally I

went to someone much higher up, who ran with it. I was fired not long after that. Good lesson.

Then you went into real estate with your dad in the late '80s.
The office market in Chicago was going through a depression. I thought I could help my father and his partner restructure the mortgage debt, based on what I had learned about how banks make decisions.

Everything is by committee.
The partnerships were still current on their mortgages, but leases were due to roll over and huge concessions would follow, so income wasn't going to be able to service the debt much longer.

What happened?
My goal was to renegotiate the debt and allow the partners to defer their tax liabilities. We rewrote the business model for those assets and then convinced the lenders we were the right team to execute the plan.

Trial by fire.
We were constantly fighting with the lenders, tenants, and lawyers. Capital was non-existent. It was a long five or six years. If we ever lost these battles, they'd just take the keys and throw us out. It was miserable.

Somehow you got interested in the Internet and started Magnitude Network.
I thought there was an opportunity to combine radio and the Internet, so we bought a radio station in Champaign,

A typical screw-up for entrepreneurs is to underestimate the time and capital needed to build new technology. Or to try to perfect the whole technology suite before bringing it to market. By the time the developers get everything working reasonably well, the market has shifted. Or maybe it wasn't really there to begin with. By the time they lift their head up to look, they've missed the opportunity.

Rich Heise

Illinois, built a website, and simulcast the radio station over the Internet.

How did you fund Magnitude?
My savings, plus about $1.5 million from individual investors.

You sold it 18 months later to CMGI Ventures. CMGI and ICG were the two most favored stocks on Wall Street as Internet aggregators, each with market caps in the billions. There's a lesson in this because you simply made a cold call to Dave Weatherall, CMGI's famous founder.
It boils down to some person on the other side saying, "I get it." CMGI had no exposure to broadcast media, and we were the best alternative at the time to Broadcast.com, run by Mark Cuban.

So what was Magnitude for you: money, power or fame?
Money. I told CMGI, "I'm here as a shareholder. If you want to bring someone else in as chairman or CEO, I won't stand in your way."

How did they respond to that?
They replaced me. I think my willingness to step aside was a breath of fresh air for Weatherall. I'm sure he had a lot of entrepreneurs he was dealing with who were saying, "just give me the money and let me teach the world a lesson."

Magnitude sold for $34 million, about 1,000 times revenue.
It was a great outcome, but that was an unusual moment in time. I thought, naively, that to provide Internet solutions to radio stations, I had to own a radio station and figure out how an Internet service could actually enhance the business of radio. In reality, there was a tidal wave of capital looking for high growth tech stories, and we had one. I'm glad we chose to sell when we did.

I guess you figured it out. You then did Starbelly, which went from start-up to $240 million valuation in 11 months. Then InnerWorkings, which went public and could do over $500mm in sales in 2010. Then Echo Global, which had a successful IPO in 2009. The list goes on with investments in MediaBank and Groupon. What am I missing?
Brad Keywell, another founder of Echo Global, is a brilliant, passionate entreprenuer, and Eric Lefkofsky's the best operator I've ever seen (*see Eric Lefkofsky, page 75*). I understood how to capitalize a high growth start-up, and how to use the financing process to enforce discipline on a strategic operating plan, but those two deserve the credit for what's happened. Since Groupon, I've gotten involved with Liquidus Marketing and Forseva, two more Chicago-based technology companies showing a lot of promise.

You developed a unique strategy for raising money.
I fund the A round and then a series B round, where we bake in some strict control preferences. The series C round is where friends and family, the first outsiders, come in. We won't take outside money until revenue is coming in and we know the outside money is safe.

Everybody underestimates the sales cycle. The sales cycle is always much longer and harder and more expensive than you think it will be, because if you have a product that people actually are willing to pay for, it means you'll have to dislodge an existing vendor relationship. That's hard to do.

Rich Heise

Until a business is self-funding, it's just a really expensive hobby. Your first goal as an entrepreneur is always, no matter what, to get your business to break even.

Rich Heise

Rich Heise

How would that affect the team coming into the start-up?
I never want to overcapitalize businesses because if you throw too much money in front of really smart, ambitious people, they'll try to do 10 things at once and they will screw them all up. But if you give them just enough money to do two things, and they get them done, then you bring in money to do the next two things. And if they get those done, you give them money to do the next two things. Also, by funding in increments, you can preserve more ownership for management and founders.

Then this feeds back in going for more money.
Institutional investors don't want to see a huge gap in share price from the previous round, so by staging the investments, you can stair-step the valuation as the company achieves its goals.

And the power of focus.
No group of people can do more than a couple of things well at a time. It just never happens. So make management focus on a couple things, get them done. Good execution is the key.

Your businesses amaze me because you take traditional industries and stand them on their head. Starbelly was technology applied to promotional products. InnerWorkings: technology applied to print brokering. Echo: technology applied to transportation and logistics.
Starbelly was the right answer to the wrong industry. Promotional

products is a $5 billion industry with 4,000 suppliers. Commercial printing has 40,000 printers with $170 billion in sales. The first print broker we partnered with had 42 percent gross margins, without buying power or technology. The margins in print are hard to believe. It's a very inefficient market.

InnerWorkings took five years to go from zero to $150 million sales. Echo Global's growth is even more dramatic. How did you do it?
If commercial print is a $170 billion market, transportation is probably $800 billion. And it's much easier to win the freight client than it is to win the print client because print relationships are stickier.

But how did Echo Global grow that fast?
There are 300,000 trucking firms in the US, with no pricing transparency, so buyers of freight need massive data on carriers and lanes to understand what best prices are. We solved those problems with technology. At the same time, one of the founders was learning how to migrate elements of the trucking process to India with technology and low-cost labor.

Trucking help in the US—from India. What about MediaBank? It's on track for $30 billion in advertising billings running through the network.
Yes. It's on an IPO track, but I suspect a strategic buyer will emerge.

I never want to overcapitalize businesses because if you throw too much money in front of really smart, ambitious people, they'll try to do 10 things at once and they will screw them all up. But if you give them just enough money to do two things, and they get them done, then you bring in money to do the next two things. And if they get those done, you give them money to do the next two things. Also, by funding in increments, you can preserve more ownership for management and founders.

Rich Heise

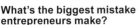

Scott Jones

What's the biggest mistake entrepreneurs make?
They underestimate the time and capital needed to build new technology. One typical mistake is trying to perfect the whole technology suite before bringing it to market. By the time they get it all working reasonably well, the market has shifted on them. Or maybe it wasn't really there to begin with. By the time they lift their head up to look, they've missed.

That's technology.
Also: everybody underestimates the sales cycle. The sales cycle is always much, much longer and harder and more expensive than you think it will be, because if you have a product that people actually are willing to pay for, it means you'll have to dislodge an existing vendor relationship. And that's hard to do.

Even when the technology's better?
Even when you can measure and guarantee lower costs. Customers sometimes say no because somebody in the organization controls the vendor relationship and they don't want to give it up. They'll fight it, and fight it, and fight it.

How do you deal with that?
I ask management to define sales goals, then I'll fund to the first benchmark. If they hit it, we'll do the next tranche of funding, and so on. Until a business is self-funding, it's an expensive hobby. Your first goal as an entrepreneur is always, no matter what, to get your business to break even.

If you were doing it all over again, would you have done anything differently?
I hired my best friend as president of one of the early companies and that turned into a very difficult experience for both of us. As successful as it was, it just destroyed our friendship. That said, if that particular deal hadn't had as good an outcome as it did, I wouldn't be sitting where I am today, so I'm grateful for what we were able to achieve.

Boston Technology, Gracenote, ChaCha, Precise Path Robotics
Indiana

You spent your undergraduate years at Indiana University, then went to MIT as a research scientist at the Artificial Intelligence Lab. What a great learning environment.
It was. I spent a couple of years exploring a lot of cutting-edge technology, not just AI, but vision, robotics, Internet, computer graphics, laser printing, speech recognition.

Let's talk about voicemail.
I met my future business partner, who was at Harvard, and we decided we should start a company together. He had been studying the divestiture of AT&T and we believed that there

We were building a business to be a dominant force in the industry. The numerous technology patents we accumulated were used defensively to say to everybody else: 'You can't do it this special way that we figured out how to do it.' That gave us a big leg up in the market. And with the multiples of a public stock, that created the value in the company.

Scott Jones

Scott Jones

would be a lot of opportunity from that, so we created a company called Boston Technology. We discovered a new technology called voicemail that nobody had ever heard of, but it was starting to permeate business. I had some ideas about how you might be able to get rid of the busy signal for phones around the globe. So we got to work building a very different kind of scalable architecture than the business voicemail systems that had started after mechanical answering machines. I filed patents and started to work on the prototype while my partner got to work on a business plan.

Your technology became the voicemail platform we all know and use today.
We built a product around my inventions and patents and we built

a sales team that was able to go out and work with the "Baby Bells." We were the first to sign up Bell South, Southwestern Bell, and Bell Atlantic (the biggest of the seven Baby Bells), and sell them on this concept of enhanced services.

Luckily for you, Judge Greene—the federal judge who was responsible for the divestiture—told the Bell companies they could not be in the businesses of fax, email, and voicemail early on.
One day, about a year after starting the company, we woke up and on the front page of the *Wall Street Journal*, Judge Greene said now is the time. The Bell companies can enter those businesses. They can't make it, but they can sell it. That was our ticket.

There were competing technologies.
Octel, probably the dominant voicemail company out of Silicon Valley, became Lucent's voicemail technology. There was another company that emerged internationally called Comverse, and we spent some amount of time in the early '90s suing them for infringing on our patents. After a couple years in competition, we were each at about $200 million in revenue. We decided to stop fighting and merge. The company exists today as Comverse, and it is still leveraging the technology I invented.

Billions of dollars of voicemail to billions of subscribers around the globe, and it's your creation!
Right. I had ideas about how you would build something that would handle voicemail for the entire world and get rid of busy signals. Voicemail

that would even work in space. I didn't just have area codes and country codes, but galaxy codes and all that. So I was thinking big.

Galaxy codes. But how did you win against all that competition?
Our technology was significantly better and more scalable. When we went to Bell Atlantic we were competing against everyone, but we had a technology that was not just a voicemail system with a great user experience, it scaled 20 times bigger than anything that had ever been built.

Some founders believe patents give up vital information.
We weren't using the patents offensively, we were using them defensively. We were building a business that was intended to be

My mantra at ChaCha is "fail fast." So try things. What doesn't work, throw it away, and what does work, run with it.

— Scott Jones

public and to grow and to be a dominant force in the industry. The numerous technology patents we accumulated were used defensively to say to everybody else: "You can't do it this special way that we figured out how to do it." That gave us a big leg up in the market. And with the multiples of a public stock, that created the value in the company.

How did you fund the company?
We had friends and family funding up until we created a really good working prototype and a business plan. Then we were able to merge with a public company that was looking for a great idea.

Public shells became acceptable, but when Merrill Lynch showed up— that was your credibility?
It was one of the most profitable services that the telcos had, because they couldn't really make much money on their standard regulated wire line and wireless services. With these enhanced services they were able to charge $5 per mailbox per month. This was "found money" and it turned out to be extremely profitable for them. It really took off.

Merrill Lynch helped us go out with a $17 million offering, and that's really what allowed us to expand globally. We had a thousand percent growth from our second year to our third year, going from about $2 million to $20 million in revenue.

Your customer was the telephone company, not the consumer. How did the telephone companies do with those new products?
It was one of the most profitable services that the telcos had, because they couldn't really make much money on their standard regulated wire line and wireless services. With these enhanced services they were able to charge $5 per mailbox per month. This was "found money" and it turned out to be extremely profitable for them. It really took off.

The sale to Comverse was for $850 million. When did you leave?
I left a couple of years before the sale. My whole career has been start-ups.

Speaking of risk, you learned how to fly airplanes and helicopters. How did that fit into your start-up world?
I accumulated about a dozen aircraft and started a company called King Air Charters. We flew celebrities on jets coast to coast—to places like Nantucket and Martha's Vineyard. As much as we leveraged the name, we capitalized on a great phone number, 800-AIR CHARTERS, so we got quite a few calls.

What a way to avoid traffic.
I'd go to New York City and grab a hot dog and come back.

That's like the story about the Marx Brothers. They were sitting around in Hollywood one day when Groucho said they should knock over their agent. They went over to his office in Hollywood and he wasn't there. They learned he was in New York. This was before air travel, so they got on a train, arrived in New York two days later. They found the agent on a golf course. They walked up to him, Harpo knelt down behind him, Groucho pushed him over, all without saying a word. They left, got back on the train, went back to Hollywood.
That's good.

Back to business. You exited voicemail and sold the air charter business. Then you started Escient, high-end home audio and video

We decided the right market to focus on and came up with a product that solved a lot of customer problems and labor issues. Robots don't need sunlight to see so they can mow in the dark while being whisper-quiet, so courses can open up earlier, which increases revenue.

Scott Jones

I'm in the business of start-ups.

— Scott Jones

Scott Jones

companies, which led to Gracenote.
Escient quickly acquired about a dozen companies, and I distilled them down into five operating companies. Escient became a leader in audio and video, particularly video storage, for high-end homes. The crown jewel was technology that recognized songs or movies on CDs or DVDs as they were put into a player. It could pull up the cover art off the Internet and get the tracking—

How did you think that up?
I was partnering with someone who was working with these big CD jukeboxes that you could put all the songs from your CDs in. A customer would send 500 CDs, and someone from the company would pull each one out and type all of the song names into a database and load it into a slot.

I thought there's probably a way, based on the length of each song—a fingerprint that could be identified—to put it in once, and have it recognized forever more. And so we built that.

There wasn't anything similar already online?
We discovered two guys doing something similar, a free service called CDDB. I called them up and said, "Hey, this is really cool. We've done something similar, but you guys have put it out there to the world and your database is growing faster. Can we work together?" First I asked them if I could acquire them.

Ah, music to the entrepreneur's ears. What did they say?
Sure, for $100 million. And they hadn't even incorporated yet. So instead we

became their first customer and paid them a small licensing fee.

How did you eventually acquire them?
We were their first paying customer. About a year later a large company made them an offer. They called me up and asked what they should do. I laid out their options and also made an offer that allowed them to keep a lot of equity and be involved in the development of the technology. They said yes. We merged the companies, then set it up as a separate company that could license the technology to lots of different companies, from Microsoft to Sony to Real Networks, to Yahoo, to Apple. A couple years later we started going after mobile phone companies and car companies that had GPS systems.

You became the dominant player with the largest music database in the world.
It was music recognition and identification—holding your phone up to the car radio or in a restaurant and having it identify the song. It also organized music collections. iTunes uses Gracenote technology as a core service. I sold the company a year ago to Sony for $260 million.

Congratulations. Can we change gears? I'm looking out your window at a simulated Mojave Desert as we speak, even though we're actually in the Midwest.
DARPA (Defense Advanced Research Projects Agency) had a competition to run a robotic car 150 miles through the Mojave Desert. There's about 50 acres here where we put together our

We would've had nice, two-digit percent growth every year, but we chose to take the big risk, which ultimately gave us a thousand percent growth and created hundreds of millions of revenue and billions in valuation.

Scott Jones

version of the desert with hills and valleys. I helped lead a team—made up of local business people, and faculty and students from Purdue, IU, and Rose-Hulman—and we built this robotic car. We were over 100 volunteers competing against Stanford and Carnegie Mellon.

And there was a moat surrounding the test track?
This is not a remote-controlled car—it's 6,000 pounds moving at up to 90 mph with sensors, 40 laptops in the back all connected together, and cameras so it can figure out where it is. We had to dig a ditch about 10 feet deep and 10 feet wide all the way around the property so that the robot didn't get loose in the neighborhood. But ultimately we moved out to the

Mojave Desert for a month with our robot to accelerate our progress.

You moved the whole show—computers, welding equipment, generators, everything—to the desert. How far back did you all stand when you hit the "on" switch?
The night before the race, I asked if the engineers felt confident enough to stand in the road and let the robot weave its way through them. And, yes, we had a safety driver sitting in the front seat.

How'd that go over?
The engineers survived. We performed in the race pretty well.

Being the start-up guy you are, you had to be thinking about a commercial application for the robot, right?

DARPA told us we'd done things that nobody else had thought of. Ultimately we decided to focus on the golf course industry. We built a robot that mows greens.

Roomba for golf—
Except Roomba does random patterns and our company, Precise Path Robotics, does those nice pretty lines that you see on a golf green or baseball field. It's precise to the centimeter, and nobody could do that before. What most people don't fathom is that mowing golf greens is a billion-dollar-a-year market, good economy or bad economy, doesn't matter. If you don't maintain the greens you're out of business.

You are spending most of your time on ChaCha, which is a mobile search service that uses voice

recognition and human searchers in the background. Does that take on Google?
I think the thing that Google has missed is that they want to do everything with computers and servers. We pull in a human when necessary, which turns out to be about 50 percent of the time, at varying levels of human assistance. There are different kinds of human guides in the system who might be involved for a split second or for several minutes.

ChaCha has just been named the fastest growing web site in the Quantcast Top 100. Any advice for someone starting a company right now?
My mantra at ChaCha is "fail fast." So, try things. What doesn't work, throw it away, and what does work, run with it.

VC investors have always said I have giant ideas, but nobody would be able to execute them, which is what I love to hear. When I did voicemail, and then Gracenote, everybody said, 'You'll never get that done. You can't do that. That's not possible.' That's what fuels me to go bet big on an idea that can have significant impact on the world.

Scott Jones

Scott Jones

Can entrepreneurs have balance in their lives between work and play, or is sacrifice a given?

I work very hard not to think in terms of sacrifices, but in terms of what the possibilities are to have everything work out. I know that a lot of people try to strike a balance. I represent the antithesis of that—I don't believe in balance. I believe in a combined, holistic approach to life where, at the family dinner table, for example, we can discuss the number one ChaCha business problem. Or vice versa. If it's the middle of the afternoon at ChaCha and there's a key thing going on at home or my kids' school, I have built a team there that can carry on without me, and I can go to the baseball game. It has to be holistic. Sometimes that

means I'm working at midnight. But that's what I want to do. It's not a sacrifice.

Is there a secret sauce, how a business becomes a home run?

Tune up quickly. Noticing what's going right and what's going wrong, and doing something about it quickly, will put you at the front of the class.

Any crises?

All of these companies had crises. It's usually a matter of not figuring out the revenue equation fast enough, cash has run out, and investors are getting weary. It is an annealing process that makes the company stronger. It usually comes with cutbacks and layoffs and really tough decisions.

Can you be specific?

With the voicemail company I had to make a decision to basically shutter two profitable segments of our business and bet on the thing that wasn't proven yet, but was the really big idea. It was the central office-based solution. In retrospect it seems like an easy decision, but at the time that segment was losing money and the other two were making money.

You ended up shutting down two profitable business units to make a bigger bet. That's a tough one.

That's an eat-your-young type of decision. We would've had nice, two-digit percent growth every year, but we chose to take the big risk, which ultimately gave us a thousand percent growth and created hundreds

of millions of revenue and billions in valuation.

What inspires you now to keep starting companies? You're at a dozen and counting.

VC investors have always said I have giant ideas, but nobody would be able to execute them, which is what I love to hear. That's what people have always told me. When I did voicemail and then Gracenote, everybody said, "You'll never get that done. You can't do that. That's not possible." That's what fuels me to go bet big on an idea that can have significant impact on the world.

We licensed Spyglass to nearly 100 companies, but the only one anybody remembers was Microsoft. It became Internet Explorer. It put Spyglass on a really fun growth trend and allowed us to become the very first Internet software company to go public—in 1995—a month before Netscape.

Tim Krauskopf

Tim Krauskopf

Spyglass
Illinois

How did you come to be an Internet pioneer?
I went to the University of Illinois in 1985 and worked at the National Center for Supercomputing Applications (NCSA). I worked on Internet networking software and then shifted over to imaging technologies. The VC thought that was going to be a huge market.

And was it huge?
The estimates for market size turned out to be wrong but we started a company called Spyglass right in the middle of it. We had the first set of desktop computer applications that could handle millions of data points,

do graphs and images, and things like that. We got venture funding for that, which was pre-Internet and pre-web.

What about your claim to fame—the NCSA's development of Mosaic, the first popular Internet browser?
NCSA was giving it away and it was becoming very successful. They asked me to help them make it commercial—sell it to the outside world and make it something big.

A brilliant license on your part—
Not at first. I said, "You know, we're working on scientific imaging applications and networking software is too hard. I don't think we can do it."

You must have changed your mind?
Luckily we changed our minds. One of our VC board members decided

that this web stuff and Mosaic was terrific. We ended up licensing from the university and becoming their commercial partner to bring Mosaic to market.

When does Microsoft enter the story?
We licensed it to nearly 100 companies, but the only one anybody remembers was Microsoft. The Spyglass version of Mosaic became Internet Explorer.

That's a defining moment for the Internet.
Then we continued to support that software base for Microsoft and did an additional licensing deal for the Macintosh platform a year later. It put Spyglass on a really fun growth trend and allowed us to go public.

Tell us about the IPO, which raised $30 million at a $90 million valuation.
We were the first Internet software company to go public—in 1995—a month before Netscape. By '96 the market cap hit $900 million and by '98 it was down to $30 million.

You helped grow what has become an industry standard worldwide. Internet Explorer is used by a billion people. How did you get your product to that level?
Luck. But the kind of luck that favors the prepared. We had a great engineering team already in place. We had VC backing, as well as management and salespeople that were better suited for the new product than our previous product line. Then we made some pretty good

You have a commitment to your good people to get rid of the people who aren't pulling their own weight. As you build your team, you're going to make a few mistakes. Sometimes you need some idiosyncratic personalities to be a part of the company because they add a lot of energy. So you can take a chance on this one or that one, but if they're not pulling their own weight, if they're bringing other people down, or if they're distracting people in ways that don't work, you've got to get rid of them. It's not that they're bad people. It's just that you discover it's a bad fit.

Tim Krauskopf

Tim Krauskopf

"bet-the-company" decisions and the luck followed.

Congratulations. Spyglass was sold to OpenTV in 2000 for $2.5 billion, but you didn't want to stick around?
I went to business school at Kellogg (Northwestern University). After that I went back into other start-ups. One was Parlano, a secure instant messaging technology company.

How did Parlano do?
The investment company that owned most of it went into bankruptcy after the Internet bubble burst. I was gone by then, and it was purchased by another fund. They sold to Microsoft in 2007.

Apparently all paths lead to Redmond. How did you then become a truck driver?

On a lark, I decided to learn to drive a semi, so I got my commercial license. That got me interested in transportation and I started my own trucking company. Then I sold it to a larger trucking company and became their CFO. They got sold out later and now I'm doing another start-up in transportation technologies called FreightZone.

I'm still wrapping my head around the fact that you went from Internet Explorer to trucking.
The way I go about creating a great solution is exactly the same, very experiential. For browsers, I was solving problems for someone like myself or the scientists I was working with—information workers. In transportation, I drove semis and

ran my own trucking company. You go do the job in order to find out the real story: How does this company make money? How do we position it in the market? What are our cost drivers and efficiency drivers? Then we create some of the software that solves those problems.

You used a great word—experiential.
I always get more energy and can focus more on the right problems when I've actually tried to do something myself. A lot of technology people have approached transportation and they've either failed outright or really struggled while they get to know the business.

Why do they fail?
They look at a portion of the business and they say, "that's an auction

problem" or "that's a distribution list problem." It's not quite so simple.

You need an integrated approach?
It's a series of interlocking relationships where price and capacity are both supply and demand-driven. We're trying to create tools that directly address a lot of that subtlety that you're only going to get from having tried to do something yourself.

Being in Illinois for Spyglass was necessary, but beyond NCSA, was it a help or a hindrance?
Sometimes that question comes from a very cynical point of view: assuming Illinois provides only disadvantages. But it has advantages, too. For example, in the Midwest, technical talent was easy to get to be loyal. It was easy to build a good, stable team.

After developing Mosaic, which became Internet Explorer, I got into transportation. I drove semis and ran my own trucking company. I always get more energy and can focus more on the right problems when I've actually tried to do something myself. You go do the job in order to find out the real story.

Tim Krauskopf

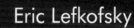

Eric Lefkofsky

Being leading edge was no problem at all.

Did your VC investors object to the Midwest?
We were funded by a group out of Boston and a group out of New York. They didn't have any trouble finding an airplane. They're on airplanes all the time. Being near a major airport played a part.

We hear that entrepreneurs seek employees who will be passionate on their behalf. Is that what you look for?
They're never going to be as ingrained as you are, but you want to see the little spark of interest or some sort of bond that grows, so that they aren't completely clueless about what they and you are trying to do.

Any advice for someone starting a company right now?
You have a commitment to your good people to get rid of the people who aren't pulling their own weight. As you build your team, you're going to make a few mistakes. Sometimes you need some idiosyncratic personalities to be a part of the company because they add a lot of energy. So you can take a chance on this one or that one, but if they're not pulling their own weight, if they're bringing other people down, or if they're distracting people in ways that don't work, you've got to get rid of them. It's not that they're bad people. It's just that you discover it's a bad fit.

InnerWorkings (INWK), Echo Global Logistics (ECHO), MediaBank, Groupon
Illinois

You created InnerWorkings from scratch and took it to $150 million in revenue in five years. Then you did it again with Echo, zero to $250 million in three years. Give it up, my friend, what's your secret?
The common theme at Starbelly, Innerworkings, Echo, MediaBank, and Groupon is that we developed some expertise applying technology to service-oriented problems.

Let's start with Starbelly (nice reference to Dr. Seuss!). Initial funding to exit took all of nine

months and you reached a $240 million valuation. How did that happen?
We started in March of '99 and sold it in January of '00. We rode the height of the dot com insanity.

But the acquirer, Halo, didn't do well.
The company that acquired us was a failed rollup. We spent about a year over there. It began to implode, so I left in April of '01.

Then you started InnerWorkings in 2001 with Rich Heise (see *Rich Heise, page 63*). I have to admit, at the time I thought, what's the big deal with print brokering?
Again we're trying to apply technology to the service-oriented problem of buying print. InnerWorkings has about 800 employees now—growing about

We've lived through bankruptcies, lawsuits, fighting with states— endless insanity. I think if you're in business long enough and you move at a fast pace, you get to a certain scale and business just gets crazy. It's not a perfect science.

Eric Lefkofsky

Eric Lefkofsky

30 percent a year—and roughly $450 million in revenue. We took it public in '07.

How do you keep pace with that kind of growth?
We are probably one of the fastest growing employers in Chicago, so it's hard to keep pace. We try and practice controlled chaos.

You and your partners run four technology companies, with about 2,000 employees in total, and hire 50 people a month. All this while the world goes through a massive recession. Help me get my arms around that.
We are a technology anomaly. We're sucking so many resources out of the system so fast that it's hard to keep pace, and there are only so

many engineers you can hire who happen to live in Chicago. Most of the engineering population is concentrated on the coasts or overseas so we have to tackle that problem.

Would it be easier on the coasts?
Different. If you need capital, I think being on the coasts would be an advantage. You can also probably pull a lot more technology talent by being on the coasts but you're competing with lots of other people.

How hard or easy was raising money for you?
We have a different profile in that we are our own mini private equity firm. When we launch companies, we do our series A, B, and C on the same day.

You do three rounds on the same day?
On the same day. And we typically will do a D or E round from only one firm, NEA. We have a long-standing relationship with Peter Barris, who is the managing general partner of NEA, and he sits on most of our boards.

Then came MediaBank in June of '06.
MediaBank applies technology to the media space. It helps people buy radio, television, and Internet ads more effectively. We built the system to help people handle the migration of analog media to digital.

And now it handles $40 billion in media spending. Is that luck or talent?
Caught a wave, probably more out of pure luck. We started technology company number five about a year

ago called Groupon with its founder, Andrew Mason. Groupon harnesses the power of the Internet to allow groups of people to achieve discounts every day through collective buying. It's currently one of the fastest growing sites in the US with about 1.5 million daily subscribers.

You run all this?
No, but I'm the only common theme in all of them.

What's your role?
I found them or think of the idea and then get them off the ground. Typically I serve as the CEO or at least the guy running the business. My partner, Brad Keywell, and I also swap CEO roles at times. Eventually we bring in a CEO and round up a management team and then hand the company off.

The only problem I'm ever trying to solve is revenue. How do I get more customers? Every other problem can be easily fixed.

Eric Lefkofsky

You're a lawyer who's built five technology companies.
I'm not a technologist, but I am by default. We start off looking for somebody who is going to build the technology, but typically we are looking for just brilliant engineering talent.

Is it better to hire experienced people or those fresh out of school?
InnerWorkings is predominately people who've had experience in the print industry and who understand printing. Echo is all kids, ages 22, 23, 24 or 25. We typically hire 40 kids a month. You should see it, it's comical. You walk in this room, it's 100,000 square feet, and you see five to six hundred 25-year-olds. Literally, it's frenetic.

All of this sounds like something out of a book. And you wrote a book called *Accelerated Disruption*?
I wrote it for my students at Kellogg (Northwestern). One of the challenges that we have in general is that it is very hard to teach some of these entrepreneurial skills.

Can you teach that kind of entrepreneurial ability?
I spend a lot of time with students who are trying to figure out how to be entrepreneurial. Teaching entrepreneurship is a little bit like trying to chase a ghost. You can't distill down the attributes to a lack of patience, for example, or a Type A personality, because it's just not that general. There's a certain risk-taking characteristic, as well as an ability to think on the fly, to problem-solve,

to work your way out of complex issues, to kind of bend the rules, to sell, and to persuade people. All of these are attributes of a successful entrepreneur; they're just difficult to teach.

It's not the same thing as academic intelligence.
You can take a kid who's fantastically intelligent out of Northwestern, and you probably can turn him into a brilliant analyst at BCG or McKinzie, but I'm not sure you can turn him into Bill Gates.

Too true. What is that quality?
There's an attribute that Bill Gates and Steven Jobs have that just can't be repeated even when there's unlimited amounts of money. Microsoft and Google have unlimited amounts of

money, so if they could recreate it, they would over and over again. There's a reason why when Steven Jobs leaves, Apple suffers.

The thing that's most striking is that you've been able to repeat this over and over. How did you do that?
We've been able to take the experience of things we did that did not go well and avoid them at every subsequent engagement. We've also found a way to take everything that did go well and repeat it in every subsequent engagement. We've become very methodical.

You're in a room right now being interviewed for this book with some of the highest achieving entrepreneurs in the Midwest, and everyone is talking about wanting a

> # A lot of folks are afraid to hire good people because they think they'll make them look stupid. That's obviously terribly wrong. You can hire people who are better than yourself, and then if they hire people better than themselves, pretty soon you'll have a world-class company.

Rock Mackie

Eric Lefkofsky

stronger entrepreneurial community. How do you do that?
The challenge is that people who've achieved a high degree of success typically hate networking. The word networking causes instant anxiety. They don't want to meet anybody. The best part of reaching a certain level of success is that you don't have to meet anybody; you can kind of form your own cocoon.

Well, it's true—we didn't use the word networking to gather this group of people, who've all achieved $100 million to a couple billion in company value.
I think it's about finding a forum that's not networking, which can address common issues or structural deficiencies or what can be done. It's more about giving back a sense of community or maybe it's got an educational purpose. These successful founders want to figure out what more they can do while they're on this planet.

What's your biggest challenge?
The only problem I'm ever trying to solve is revenue. How do I get more customers? Every other problem can be easily fixed.

Any time when you went through crisis?
There have been so many crises. We've lived through multiple bankruptcies, dozens of lawsuits, fighting with states—endless insanity. So, I think if you're in business long enough and you move at the pace that we do, which is quite frenetic, you get to a certain scale and business just gets crazy. It's not a perfect science. You're gonna wake up one day and have to let go a bunch of people, you're gonna have things that go wrong, you're gonna be in contract disputes that can't get resolved—all those nightmares.

That's a definition of masochism.
Yeah. It's the business world we live in today. I think if you want to be in it, and you want to be in it consistently, you sign up for some level of insanity.

Thomas Rockwell "Rock" Mackie

TomoTherapy (TOMO)
Wisconsin

How did you come to think up the idea for TomoTherapy, a radiation company treating cancerous tumors?
We were looking for a solution to a problem, how to avoid normal tissues while irradiating tumors with a uniform dose. Stuart Swerdloff, a nuclear medicine graduate student, helped me one summer to investigate how we could create these non-uniform beams of radiation.

Got it. Your grad student helped.
We came up with a number of ideas to produce non-uniform beam modulation and distribution with both high and low intensity. The second major idea,

Make sure you empower your employees. You do that by giving them credit, letting them make decisions, and allowing them to make a few mistake.

Rock Mackie

adding a CT scanner, came from another graduate student of mine, Tim Holmes, who thought up the name "tomotherapy." And then the third big idea was something called Spiral CT. When those three ideas came together, I realized this could actually work, so we started filing patents.

Three big ideas that eventually led to an IPO and a billion-dollar valuation. But there's a leap at some point, because not every PhD can create a company, execute a highly engineered product, and then complete an IPO.
Well, it's a progression. It doesn't happen overnight. We were just university people.

How did you get started?
We tried to find a partner to execute and build a prototype, and ended up getting General Electric to take on the challenge. For four years this was a GE research project.

GE's a pretty impressive partner coming out of the gate.
Yeah, this was a marriage made in heaven. The CT division for GE was just down the street in a neighboring town in Wisconsin.

And the Wisconsin Alumni Research Foundation (WARF) licensed the patents to GE?
That was the plan, but then General Electric decided to get out of the radiotherapy business, I believe because of an accidental death involving a patient. And so we were

just excess baggage at that point. GE sold their business to another company and I think they tried to sell the contract with us, but it was non-transferable.

What did you do?
I was horrified. We tried to convince them that we should be transferred to another division.

You were not able to convince them.
It looked like the whole game was over. We had to lay everybody off,

Oy vey. But you already had some experience and cash from launching Geometrics, a radiotherapy treatment planning company.
We had sold Geometrics to Adak. Paul Reckwerdt and I decided to spend some of our money to start

TomoTherapy on our own. We asked WARF for the same deal they were going to give General Electric.

Nice idea.
A good deal for us. We essentially got the same terms as GE, which obviously bargained a wonderful deal. Then we proceeded to try to find venture capital.

It's impressive that you spun Geometrics out from the university, and that Philips now owns it and employs 70 people in Madison. Not bad for a first company. On to TomoTherapy: you are the only founder I know who had to lay off his entire staff before starting the company. How did you eventually raise venture capital?

The dangerous thing is that you will micromanage employees to death. You have to know what are important and not-so-important decisions. Let your employees make smaller decisions even when you disagree. It's too easy to continuously correct and give your opinion.

Rock Mackie

It helps to have cold winters and nothing much to do to get people to stay late or come in early!

Rock Mackie

Thomas Rockwell "Rock" Mackie

We were in the dot com bubble so it was really hard to find capital, but we found it in '99. Then we got some office space and eight of my researchers from the university left and joined the company.

It's ironic that in the midst of the bubble, with all that money being invested in vaporware, you had a substantial product—
We were told things like, "This is so old school. Companies don't worry about making a profit anymore, they worry about equity valuation." And they said, "The US is not going to be manufacturing 'things' anymore—only software and services."

Why not just find another partner or buyer like GE?
We almost sold the company to one of the largest global industrial companies. We wanted to see if we could quickly flip it and make a few bucks, because our reputation was on the line. We had put most of our "reputation capital" into the idea of TomoTherapy, and had been talking about the concept for years at this point.

Luckily you didn't sell low and the funding came in. How were the terms?
I was happy with the terms. I think they were very fair. And we made a bet on the pre-money valuation. The VC said it's worth $5 million and Paul and I said it's worth $10 million. We bet the valuation would go up ten-fold in six years.

How did you do?
Paul and I won half the bet. It turned out our effective pre-money valuation was about $7.5 million. I haven't seen any other university start-ups get a $7 million valuation.

What mistakes do company founders make?
A lot of folks are afraid to hire good people because they think they'll make them look stupid. That's obviously terribly wrong. You can hire people who are better than yourself, and then if they hire people better than themselves, pretty soon you'll have a world-class company.

So many founders say that but would never actually do it. You acknowledge the three big ideas that

created TomoTherapy all involved your students.
Exactly. Make sure you empower your employees.

How?
You do that by giving them credit, letting them make some decisions, and allowing them to make a few mistakes.

It's hard to sit on your hands though.
I know, but the dangerous thing is that you will micromanage employees to death. You have to know what are important and not-so-important decisions. Let your employees make smaller decisions even when you disagree. It's too easy to continuously correct and give your opinion.

If I get a kid from a dairy farm who's studying nuclear medicine at the university, I think, this is the guy for me. I know he'll work hard—he isn't afraid to get up at dawn and work until the cows go to bed. And I know he can probably fix anything that breaks, because he's had to do it on the farm.

Rock Mackie

With a scientific and an academic background, how did you come to have management intuition?
As an academic, you have to manage people sometimes when the stakes are phenomenally low. Some of the most ridiculously hard decisions you have to make are when the stakes are the lowest.

What do you mean by "low stakes"?
Lots of times people get upset about little things, like, "she's got a bigger desk than I do" or "his chair's not as comfortable as my chair."

Who knew a university could be good management training. Any advice for someone starting a company right now?
Make sure you know how you're motivated. There's nothing wrong with wanting to become rich or wanting to be the boss. You may want to be able to control your own destiny. But you need to ask yourself why you want to start a company. Lots of people get in the trap of getting involved in a business and not knowing why they're doing it.

What do you mean?
For example, if you don't care about money and the business is all about making money, then you'll be very unhappy in that business. You need to match what you want to do with the kind of business you start and then be able to communicate the motivation.

What was your motivation?
I was headed for infamy if our project failed. I staked my whole career on the idea of TomoTherapy. I didn't want that fate.

Eventually you took in $32 million from investors before the IPO in 2007. Did you think when you started you'd ever employ 600 people and hit close to a billion-dollar valuation?
Hell, no. Are you kidding? No way.

What are the best qualities in an entrepreneur?
Stick-to-it-ive-ness. When you're faced with a problem, find every possible way around it and don't give up. When really good entrepreneurs find something is impossible, they'll change their whole business model and retool it for an entirely different product or service.

The Midwest—a plus or minus for you?
It helps to have cold winters and nothing much to do to get people to stay late or come in early. In the Midwest, it's just like Garrison Keillor said, "everyone's above average."

But it's true.
If I get a kid from a dairy farm who's studying nuclear medicine at the university, I think, this is the guy for me. I know he'll work hard—he isn't afraid to get up at dawn and work until the cows go to bed. And I know he can probably fix anything that breaks, because he's had to do it on the farm.

Most entrepreneurs are in too much of a hurry. Everyone wants to have a huge company and make a million dollars overnight. The truth is, growing a business is a process, like planting a seedling. It takes awhile to develop, you have to water it and nurture it. Sometimes you just need to spend time to get to know your customers better, figure out what they really want, and fine-tune your products to make sure they meet clients' needs.

Joe Mansueto

Joe Mansueto

Morningstar (MORN), Mansueto Ventures
Illinois

You have a classic background for being in the investment world.
Yes, in some ways. I went to the University of Chicago business school, where you'd think I developed my passion for investing. I did take a class on investing, but it really didn't click for me. The U of C's business school is all about efficient markets and the message is "you can't beat the market." So I didn't get excited about investing at that point.

But you did have entrepreneurial genes?
I have that tendency. During college I sold soda from my dorm room. I also sold Christmas trees.

So from Christmas trees to investing?
I didn't get excited about investing until I read about Warren Buffett in the late '70s, early '80s. At the time he was a pretty obscure figure. But once I read his investment philosophy based on "economic moats," something clicked. He demonstrated a way to invest that was ethical, fun, and made sense. I wanted to combine an entrepreneurial venture with a passion for investing, and that led me to Morningstar.

Mutual funds were pretty obscure back in 1984. How did you decide to focus on that?
I worked as a stock analyst at Harris Associates in Chicago. I loved the job. They had a mutual fund called the Acorn Fund. From that I got some exposure to the mutual fund business. Funds were not mainstream at all in the early '80s and investors had very little information to study when selecting a fund. As a stock analyst, I had tons of data, including stock charts, and fundamental and qualitative research going back decades. Fund investors had only one line of total return data. So my thought was to bring that same level of fundamental analysis that stock investors had to fund investors.

How did the rise of the Internet affect Morningstar?
I started in 1984. With the introduction of the PC in the early '80s, electronic delivery of information was part of my plan. We did everything in database form from the beginning. When the Internet became popular in the mid-'90s, we quickly adapted our databases and made them accessible on the Internet.

It's kind of stunning to think that you started this in an apartment in Chicago, and now Morningstar is global, with 2,000 employees, $82 million in earnings, and $479 million in revenue. So what's the secret sauce, my friend?
We've always been a very product-driven firm and tried to create great products. In many ways it was investors creating products for investors. We were our target audience so we created products we wanted to use as investors.

If you can control your destiny, then you've got the luxury of time to really figure things out and create great products.

Joe Mansueto

Joe

And the secret sauce is?
We saw an unmet need in the marketplace. Fund assets were growing and investors were investing blindly. So we tried to offer them navigational support. It was just an intense focus on doing the right thing for the investors. I think our secret sauce is our mission of trying to help investors—to be their advocate and watch out for their interests. We're not just a firm selling data or software.

That would be the definition of trust.
We run the firm with an investor-centric attitude. We believe if the investor wins, Morningstar wins. That created an unusual degree of trust in our brand from investors. That's important in a financial services business where the big question is,

who can I trust? My broker is trying to sell me something. Morningstar has been an independent third party, a Consumer Reports-like firm, that's developed trust with investors. Our mission and reputation have been the key things that differentiate us and make us successful.

You are one of the Hoosier state's most famous sons. Was the Midwest better or worse for launching Morningstar?
There is a terrific population to hire from here, and there are many great schools. There's also Midwestern values—a solid work ethic, integrity, and friendliness—that make it desirable for growing businesses.

How did you fund Morningstar at the start?
It was a bootstrap start-up. We had no venture capitalists, no bank debt. We grew steadily over a long period of time. The first year we did $100,000 in sales. Then it was $120,000, then $200,000, $400,000, $1 million, $2 million, $4 million, $11 million, $20 million. So we had a very nice, steady compounding.

Any bumps along the way?
I think we were always pretty frugal and prudent in running the business. But of course there were bumps. We tried to expand internationally a little too quickly. In the mid '90s, we opened up an office in London. At the same time, certain things happened in the US that dampened our cash flow, so we had to pull back from London. I

think I got a little ahead of myself. For the only time in our history, we had to lay off some people and pull in the reigns a bit. We had to cut out some products that I thought had potential but weren't making money.

But Morningstar is global?
We eventually came back. International is now about 25 percent of our revenue.

Entrepreneurs seeking funding sometimes have the attitude, "just give me the money" and they don't focus enough on the terms. Have you found that to be the case?
I've seen it happen all too frequently. The typical scenario is founders get diluted because they don't value the equity enough in the early stages. They bring in venture capitalists and

I think a lot of founders either give up too quickly or sell prematurely. You just have to hang in there and be patient.

Joe Mansueto

Joe Mansueto

give up more and more stock until they're left with a very small sliver. You really have to view equity as a precious commodity and stay in control.

A number of champion founders interviewed for this book were very conservative about distributing equity. You are still the majority shareholder in Morningstar. How were you able to hire people without giving away equity?
It's a matter of degree. I think it's a good thing to spread some equity around the team, have your key managers invested. I just didn't bring in outside investors.

That same philosophy applied to bringing in your first investor—after

you'd already been in business 14 years.
Yes, we did bring in an outside investor as a defensive move in 1998. But by then we were sizable and had a good market capitalization.

Since the economy slowed in 2007, Morningstar has acquired 15 companies. Is this a new strategy?
If we can acquire a business faster and cheaper than we can build one, we'll make the purchase.

Joe, you now have a customer base of 7 million individuals; 250,000 financial advisers; and 4,200 institutions. Where do you go from here?
We'd like to be able to track any investable asset.

You have been chairman and CEO for 25 years. Are you still "operational"?
Yes, I'm still operational. I enjoy it. I got into this business because I love investing. So I still like reviewing our products and helping to make them better.

If you could do it over again, is there anything you would do differently?
I don't think there's much I would change. I like the way things turned out.

That's what we call an understatement.
The only thing I can think of is that being more aggressive in the early years could've let us grow more quickly. I was pretty conservative about how I ran the business. It

took us awhile to get up to a million dollars in sales. I did all the computer programming in the early years which was probably not the best use of my time. But again, maybe that's that bootstrap mentality of trying to conserve cash that drives you to profitability more quickly.

What advice do you have for aspiring entrepreneurs?
Be patient. I think most entrepreneurs are in too much of a hurry. Everyone wants to have a huge company and make a million dollars overnight. The truth is, growing a business is a process, like planting a seedling. It takes awhile to develop, you have to water it and nurture it. Sometimes you just need to spend time to get to

I'm not the most visionary person in the world, but I'm very persistent. I'll keep going at something until I get it right.

Joe

Joe Mansueto

Don Maurer

know your customers better, figure out what they really want, and fine-tune your products to make sure they meet clients' needs.

What's the biggest mistake entrepreneurs make?
I think a lot of founders either give up too quickly or sell prematurely. You just have to hang in there and make sure you control your own destiny. I was really glad I didn't have outside investors. I had the luxury of time to figure things out. If you keep coming at something, eventually you'll get it right.

There's too much desire for instant gratification?
To build something great, the payoff is long-term.

Are you lucky or good?
A little of both. We were fortunate to have a bull market from August of 1982 to today. Funds went from niche to mainstream. When I started, the fund industry was about $350 billion. Today it's $12 trillion. Funds have grown 30 times. All that benefited us. At the same time, I think we did many things right. Not just me, but our whole management team.

Empi, Inc.
Minnesota

How did you get involved in medical device design?
I was an R&D director at Medtronic for 11 years.

Did you have a mentor?
My mentor was Earl Bakken, founder and CEO of Medtronic. Earl is the focus and the inspiration of what's called Medical Alley, a non-profit, progressive healthcare association in Minnesota. The medical device industry was a result of Earl's genius. He literally started Medtronic in his garage and created the first transistor-operated, wearable pacemaker. I would guess dozens of companies have spun off as a result of Medtronic.

What was your typical day like?
This was before the FDA's medical device act, so the industry was very loosely regulated. As special projects engineer I would go out and talk to physicians who had an idea they wanted to try. I would come back to the plant, design, build and test it, and bring it back to them. The physician would try it out and see if it worked.

Yes, that's what you could call very loosely regulated.
The pacemaker, under today's regulations, might have been delayed 15 years. It is hard to find funding under those circumstances.

Good point.
I came in not knowing a great deal about medicine, but Medtronic was probably the best training ground that

You have to view equity as a precious commodity.

Joe Mansueto

Don Maurer

a person could have. Management pretty much left me alone. I worked with the top cardiovascular surgeons and cardiologists in the country and they had some unusual requests. One of my designs was a heart fibrillator, which held the heart still during open heart surgery making it safer for the patient. I had to come up with things that no one had ever really thought of trying. I figured out how to do it—and do it well.

You left to pursue your master's degree and then came back to a big company with thousands of employees. What was that like?
It was stifling for me. When you get large, you get bureaucratic. You can't have all these crazy entrepreneurs running around doing their thing.

I stayed five more years and then decided to do something different. I took my resignation in to Earl Bakken, which was the hardest thing to do. Earl is a very quiet and kind man and had done so much for me. I left Medtronic to work at a rehabilitation center.

So you left a high-paying job for one paying a third as much. It wasn't about the money, was it?
No. I think that true entrepreneurship isn't money-driven.

What kind of work did you do at the rehabilitation center?
I started an engineering department at Courage Center, a comprehensive rehabilitation facility for the disabled. The people there were medically stable but they needed to learn how to become more independent. I started

to make devices for activities of daily living—ADL is what it was called.

Not life-sustaining, more about improving the quality of life?
Right. The patients were highly disabled—usually from a spinal cord injury. My goal was to maximize whatever residual movement they had left to allow them to feed themselves and pursue things that interested them. For example, I had a very bright young man who had a diving accident. I came up with a keyboard cover for a computer and a mouth stick. He was able to program with the mouth stick because he could move his neck. That sounds like a simple idea but there was nothing commercially available like that at that time. Another young man wanted to be a deer hunter,

so although it frightened me a bit, I adapted his wheelchair to support his high-powered rifle and he went deer hunting.

The deer hunter had a problem that gave you another idea that became a commercial product.
Transfer boards allow quadriplegics to slide from their wheelchair to places like, say, a shower. The problem is they can cause pressure sores that are very hard to heal. One patient developed skin abrasions so his doctors wouldn't let him use the boards anymore. I came up with the idea to wrap the board with Teflon tape, which was the only thing commercially available at the time. It worked and he was ecstatic as it let him transfer to the shower by himself. I contacted a company in

True entrepreneurship is not money-driven.

Don Maurer

Chattanooga, Tennessee, that makes devices like that, and I didn't patent it. They were able to coat transfer boards with Teflon and that is now a commercial product.

How did your work lead to pain control devices?
As one of the founders of Medtronic's neurological division, I developed electrotherapy for control of chronic pain and worked with patients who had spinal cord and brain implants. Dr. C. Norman Shealy, a leader in the holistic medicine field, was a neurosurgeon who did pain control implants. He and I were part of a study group of neurosurgeons evaluating electrotherapy devices, and they had a problem. They would put spinal cord implants in and turn them on, and after

a short time, some patients couldn't stand the sensation and wanted it taken out.

What was the solution?
They wanted to test patients' tolerance levels to electrical stimulation before the stimulator was implanted. They had an external test device but it was very difficult to control and use, so I made a battery-operated external device that was highly controllable and comfortable for the patient.

How'd that work out?
The study group sent their patients home with these devices. After a month, Dr. Shealy called me and said, "I think we've got something. The neurosurgeons are giving these devices to their patients and some of them never come back. They don't

want the implant—they just want to use the device because it relieves their pain." So the testing device turned out to be a treatment device.

It's serendipity, like Goodyear accidentally coming upon the process to vulcanize rubber. So is that what launched Empi?
My salary at the Courage Center needed to be supplemented somehow. I set up a small office and started importing German transcutaneous electrical nerve stimulators. I raised $50,000 in private funding and put all my savings into it. I hired a salesman and a bookkeeper. So Empi was born—the first year we had $30,000 in sales and $50,000 in expenses.

How did that go over with your investors?
They said, "You need to come in and run this thing or we're going to shut the doors."

Not an unreasonable position.
I regretted having to leave the Courage Center. I came in as president of Empi because I'd started it. Unfortunately, the German exporter decided to sell their business to a large drug company, which had come up with a drug called thalidomide. I met with the drug company and they said they really wanted to buy Empi for a million dollars.

What did you say?
No thanks.

By the time the factory was up and running, and we had international distribution and significant sales, I hate to admit it, but I was getting less interested in the business.
I did not like being purely an administrator. I still had passion for patient care, so after 17 years I hired a president and CEO and I became chairman.

Don Maurer

Don Maurer

You had a salary of $19,300 from the Center and your start-up was losing money.
You know why I said no? Several of my clients at the Courage Center were disabled people born without arms and legs.

What next?
I said to myself, "I have a company, now I need a product." I set out to design something I knew best, a pain control product. While I was at the Courage Center, the *Star Tribune* ran a front page story about my work and it attracted an investment banker. When I left Courage Center I contacted him and he said he could do a private placement for us. We put together a wooden model of my concept, painted it, and glued on some knobs. It was totally non-functional. I went out and

gave a talk to some investors and we raised $500,000.

You made an empty box that didn't work and you raised a half million bucks.
Yeah.

That is a nice start for a company you took public. Do you still have the box?
I don't know what happened to the box. That funding gave us enough to start. We leased a 10,000-square-foot facility in Minnesota. In a few years we ran out of manufacturing space. The state of South Dakota offered us a 20,000- square-foot manufacturing facility in Clear Lake for one dollar if we guaranteed 15 jobs for seven years. Clear Lake's Empi currently has more than 80,000 square feet with more than 200 employees.

And you went on to raise another $15 million in later years.
The investment banking firm Dain Bosworth took me on a road show for that. I went to 18 cities in eight days and gave four to five presentations a day.

Back to the launch—how did you go about building the first product?
I needed an engineer to take it to the next step. One of the things I'm glad I did was to put together an assessment of what I thought I could and couldn't do well. I knew I was going to need a good accountant and a good mechanical engineer, because I had no idea how to make molds, cases, and enclosures for electronics. I was an electronics engineer and, by training, a medical engineer.

So you had some key hires to make.
I came back from my travels in the field supporting the sales people and asked if we had gotten any response on my ad. At that time things were hot and it was hard to find an engineer. It turned out that the only applicant who responded was a Whirlpool engineer and we met. I asked him why he'd want to leave his job designing washing machines and he said that some co-workers approached him in the parking lot and said, "You're working too fast and too hard, and if you don't slow down we're going to beat you up." I told him he wouldn't have that problem here.

How did you think up the name TENS for Empi's pain control device?
Transcutaneous electrical nerve stimulation. That acronym came

Entrepreneurs can be arrogant bastards and sometimes difficult to work with. The biggest mistake I saw in company founders who were technically trained is they discounted the importance of the sales force: getting very high quality sales people and supporting them. Gadgets don't sell themselves.

Don Maurer

from a friend, Dr. Charles Burton, a neurosurgeon out of Philadelphia.

And what about the name Empi? Lemme guess: "Ex-Medtronic People Inc."?
Everybody asks me that. It was just a name I liked. As it turned out, people remembered the name because they assumed it stood for something.

When you entered the field with your TENS product you had dozens of competitors. Did that bother you?
It didn't bother me. It helped that the devices out there were competing only on a cosmetic level. I had years of studying how the nervous system worked with both implantables and externals and I had a lot of knowledge about pain relief. To relieve pain you have to produce a very strong counter irritation and recruit the nerve system that subserves the area of pain. The counter irritation causes a release of endogenous opiates to relieve the pain. The market was being soured because these competitive products only provided temporary pain relief due to an improper design. So I decided our priority was to produce an effective pain control device. We weren't going to be the smallest or the lightest. We were simply going to design and build what was needed to relieve pain. We figured patients weren't wearing it as a piece of jewelry.

How did the market react?
The therapists loved it. They called it "the little tank." One guy even ran over it with his car and it still worked.

So "build a better mousetrap and the world will beat a path to your door," is still true.
Well, I think my biggest entrepreneurial contribution to the field is that I wrote up a series of sales materials I called Technotes. I believe in giving your sales people all the support you can. You can have the greatest product in the world but if it doesn't sell, it doesn't mean much.

You added intellectual property around the product. That's good.
I traveled in the field, met the customers, and gave seminars to the physical therapists, explaining how to use the device. They loved Technotes, and so did my competitors. They were out there using Technotes to sell their products, too, which was fine.

Your strategy worked. By the time you sold the company in 1999 to the Carlyle Group for $26.50 per share—$161.4 million in cash—there was only one other competitor.
At that point only about 40 percent of our $90 million revenue was from TENS product. We had a number of other products and patents. One of them was a drug delivery device where you set the dosage on a little external box connected to drug-saturated electrodes on the skin. The electricity would push a diffuse dosage of lidocaine or steroids through the skin, producing the same effect as needle-injected steroid shots without deteriorating the joint membrane.

Any advice for entrepreneurs?
Have a real passion for what you are doing. Don't be driven just by

Getting the right people in the business early was key for us.

William Merchantz

financial reasons. Success is paved by many little setbacks and failures. I'd started a company before Empi where I was making electronic test equipment in my home and selling it through free catalogs advertised in Popular Electronics. I got a lot of orders for catalogs but didn't sell very many products. The company failed miserably.

What is the biggest mistake entrepreneurs make?
The most obvious one is being underfunded. Beyond that, in some ways we entrepreneurs can be arrogant bastards and sometimes difficult to work with. The biggest mistake I saw in company founders who were technically trained is they discounted the importance of the sales

force: getting very high quality sales people and supporting them. Gadgets don't sell themselves.

What are you working on now?
I am helping a brilliant engineer, Nick Van Brunt, to commercialize a wearable, lightweight medical oxygen concentrator.

William Merchantz

WhittmanHart, Lakeview Technology
Illinois

You are a true Chicagoan—a product of the Chicago Public School system and the University of Illinois at Chicago. What did you major in?
I majored in basketball.

That's a good start. What happened next?
After graduation I started Whittman Hart. It was a services business that helped companies implement business software.

WhittmanHart went public, so that was your first home run.
It did well. I sold it to my partner in 1990 and spun off a little piece of

software into Lakeview Technology. That software collected real-time transactions for high availability or disaster recovery purposes.

Another home run.
I ran that for 17 years—I can't believe how fast it went—and then sold it to a private equity fund in June 2007.

What inspired you to start a company?
I was running the financial systems at Skidmore, Owings and Merrill, the famous architectural firm in Chicago that designed the Sears Tower and the Hancock center. Since these are great showplaces, attracting talent was relatively easy. But retaining talent was difficult. I had taken Skidmore through the process of taking on a new financial package—implementing

When the product works, it gives you a lot of confidence to invest in and grow the business.

William Merchantz

it, customizing it, and modifying it to fit their business. My idea was that I could do this for more than one company, while being able to retain good people.

So what did you do?
Four of us set out in February 1984, and we put a few hundred dollars in the bank. We didn't have a board. We didn't need venture. All we needed were our hardworking people, our good ideas, our experience, and a little bit of money in the bank. And clients. Clients were number one.

Which means you had to do a great job taking care of them?
Getting the right people in the business early was key for us. We would go through 10 resumes to find the one really good hire.

How fast did WhittmanHart grow?
We started out in '84. In '85, we doubled revenue, and it just kept on doubling every year thereafter.

Your idea proved to be right on the money.
The dream of being able to help more than just one company improve its business operations and profitability, through the use of these new financial packages in the marketplace, was what WhittmanHart was all about.

What was the secret sauce—what enabled you guys to succeed?
At Lakeview, we identified an opportunity to take a little piece of software that we had built at Tellabs. We negotiated up front to own the intellectual property. We knew that no one else was filling this hole in the

market for high availability systems or disaster recovery systems for protecting data in the event of an outage. We left the services business behind and began to focus on a few target customers who had a real need to protect their data 24 hours a day, 7 days a week.

No one else saw it?
We were filling a hole that IBM had at the time in their product offering.

When did you know it was going to be successful? What was the turning point?
I knew early on that it would be successful because the product worked. In software, you don't have to go through, say, clinical trials, like drug development, to determine whether or not a product works. You write the

software, get the bugs fixed, and put it out into a test environment and then a real live environment. If it works, then you've got something.

Which, in a way, points to the biggest crisis you faced.
We took our software and put it in at the New York City Housing Authority. And in this situation it didn't work. And it not only didn't work, it destroyed some of their data.

That's not good.
It was the perfect storm. The engineers were either off or traveling at customer sites on this particular weekend, so there was no one in the office but a support guy and me. We had to go 24 hours a day for about three days to dig into the code to find out what the problems were. We

If I could do it all over again, I would have a formal board of directors.

William Merchantz

William Merchantz

eventually solved the problem but lost the customer.

That's painful but you survived it.
And we solved that particular issue for all future customers.

Was the Midwest a plus or minus for your company?
It just so happened that IBM landed its laboratory for this particular hardware and software solution in Rochester, Minnesota. After we got our product up and running, we attracted engineers away from IBM and opened up our lab in Rochester, where to this day they still develop the product. Access to business application talent has continued to grow and is readily available throughout the Midwest.

Any rules of thumb for hiring?
We really tried to look at people's behaviors and value systems—dig a little bit deeper than just their technical skill. We wanted people who would have a passion for solving problems for our customers. We also wanted to create somewhat of a community within the business. We had very loyal people working for the business, and that continuity with the customers was very helpful.

Was it luck or talent?
Well, everyone has some luck. We happened to have the niece of the general manager at IBM working for us and he thought that our software was a good fit. Having IBM as an early partner gave us access to international customers. Our second or third customer was a soft drink business

in the UK. When the product works, it gives you a lot of confidence to invest in and grow the business.

Who helped you early on—friends? family? Professional resources around you?
If you have experience in a particular area—tickets, shipping, manufacturing, whatever it may be—it's relatively easy to take an idea and put together a software product in your home office. However, when we got the business up and running, there wasn't the healthy source of business lawyers, intellectual property people, accountants, and trade associations that are available today to connect founders with more experienced tech people. Access to those people in an advisory role is absolutely critical.

What would you have done differently?
I would have a formal board of directors. I had an informal advisory board at Lakeview.

Not many entrepreneurs admit to wanting a board of directors.
We were too conservative financially. We could have used leverage to accelerate the growth of the business because it was profitable from the very beginning. We built a cash hoard and I now know through experience that we could have leveraged that cash flow into significant growth, had I had a board advising me to do that.

If you were talking to a young start-up company getting going right now, what would be the top three lessons

> We were too conservative financially. We could have used leverage to accelerate the growth of the business because it was profitable from the very beginning. We built a cash hoard and I now know through experience that we could have leveraged that cash flow into significant growth.

William Merchantz

Dane Miller

you'd give? Obviously one would be more use of leverage.
Number one: Create a good board that will bring a lot of experience and advice to the table. Number two: Attract very talented people and take a chance on younger people. We hired a lot of professionals and I think we could've brought more kids in from the universities that abound here. Number three: Don't be quite as conservative as we were with the balance sheet.

Any advice on acquiring customers?
Motorola is a good example of one of our early customers that teamed up with us to help us understand their problems. This drove right into making our products better for companies all over the world. Teaming up with larger companies that need your problem-solving is an ideal way to grow. There

are large companies that still have a lot of problems that need to be solved in software and technology.

You have a unique point of view, Bill, not from your product outwards, but from the corporation's worldview.
Yes. And let's not forget that Sears is here and needs problems solved. I think there are probably tons of opportunities there. We did a lot of business with Allstate and McDonald's. Whether it's in financial services, fast food, or retail, there are quite a number of industry-leading, large companies that need help. You can get great ideas if you know what their needs are, and then you take those ideas and do a start-up.

Being the most native Chicagoan nominated for this book, any thoughts on the Windy City?
Chicago is a city that works. It's clean. It has culture. It has both an urban center as well as very attractive suburban areas. It's a terrific place to grow a business.

Biomet
Indiana

You left the security of an established company, Zimmer, to start Biomet.
I was not happy with the politics of the organization. First I left for a division of Bayer in San Diego, then I moved back to Warsaw, Indiana, to start Biomet.

You also could have had the security of a teaching position.
I had many opportunities to return to academia, but there was a turning point. I was asked to take over Zimmer's custom products department, which produced implants specifically for individual surgeons based on their patients' needs. That provided me an opportunity to

One of the problems with highly educated, technical people is that they get caught up in analysis and can't make a decision. I've always been a believer that the last part of a good decision is based on intuition not fact.

Dane Miller

We made virtually our entire team shareholders. There was a sense of ownership, a kind of self-enforcement process, because virtually everybody all the way to the janitor had stock options. Owners think differently than employees.

Dane Miller

Dane Miller

experience full P&L responsibility and, despite my technical background, I found it to be extremely stimulating. I really enjoyed it.

When you started Biomet, did you have any customers or investors lined up?
No. We knew we had a certain amount of funding, but the big piece of funding was a $500,000 SBA guaranteed loan that didn't fall into place until a month after I moved back to Warsaw from San Diego. If that hadn't fallen into place, Biomet wouldn't be here today.

You cut the risk a bit with simpler products in the beginning.
We started off with soft goods and bracing products—a low barrier-to-market entry. It was easy to talk a doctor into trying out your arm sling or rib belt. If he liked the product and service, maybe someday he would think about putting in some bone plates or hips and knees as well.

Biomet sales went from $17,000 in the first year to $500,000 in the second; to $1 million in the third; to $2 million; then $3.5 million; then $7.5 million in the sixth year. Those are exciting leaps.
I would agree, but keep in mind that until we reached about $3.5 million, we were still losing money.

When did you know you were on the right track?
In our initial debenture offering with warrants, we sold $1.25 million in corporate bonds and that made us think that the investment community had given us some validation that we were going in the right direction. The warrants were exercisable after 18 months, so that was the first time we were technically a public company with common shares outstanding. Then we did our IPO in '83. Somewhere in between we began to realize it wasn't a matter of if, it was a matter of how far and how fast.

Your PhD in bioengineering doesn't predict you'd become the CEO you've turned out to be.
That's correct.

Or that you would develop such a strong skill set in operating and growing a business.
I hope the message that lots of entrepreneurs can take away from this is that there is no defined means of becoming an entrepreneur, and becoming a successful entrepreneur. I found over the years that each week, probably each day, was a learning experience, and you didn't have to be in a Harvard or Wharton MBA program to experience those learning processes. I didn't know what a debenture was 30 years ago. I had to learn along the way.

What separates a smart academic from a smart business leader?
One of the problems with highly educated, technical people is that they get caught up in analysis and can't make a decision. I've always been a believer that the last part of a good decision is based on intuition not fact.

There is no defined means of becoming a successful entrepreneur. I found that each week, probably each day, was a learning experience, and you didn't have to be in a Harvard MBA program to experience those learning processes. I didn't know what a debenture was 30 years ago. I had to learn along the way.

Dane Miller

Everybody should go through a humiliating experience early on.

Dane Miller

From four founders you eventually grew to 5,500 employees plus a sales force of 2,000. Any tips on hiring?
At all levels we tried to hire "roll up your sleeves and get the job done" kind of people. I think it's worked out pretty well. We have very low turnover.

Biomet eventually grew to sales of $17,000 every three-and-a-half minutes. How did you do it?
It's a whole combination of things I think luck tends to follow good decision-making and hard work. The technologies that we brought to the market—and I'm proud to say that many of them are the gold standard today in the orthopedic industry—were a product of sound, technical thinking. We avoided the temptation

to let marketing affect good technical thinking, and we made the right decisions.

I know you don't like this question, but what was the secret sauce?
This reminds me of an interview with a Wall Street guru who had a reputation for picking the next home run in public companies. He wanted to know, in 10 words or less, what it was at Biomet that was going to make us successful. And I said there aren't 10 words that can explain that. It's a whole lot of things. It's blocking and tackling. Doing all the right things from a business standpoint—treating people properly and fairly, getting out of their way, and letting them use their creative energies to do the best job they can. "Well," he

said, "I have no interest in investing in Biomet. I don't know how you guys think you're gonna make it."

That was right after your IPO in August '83, with a market cap of—
$20 million.

And the market cap hit $11.4 billion when Biomet went private. He missed the mark.
A little bit.

I take your point about oversimplification.
One important thing we did early on was make virtually our entire team shareholders. There was a sense of ownership, a kind of self-enforcement process, because virtually everybody

all the way to the janitor had a stock option. Owners think differently than employees.

It's a great incentive, although it sometimes has a downside.
If the share price took a dip, it created a little bit of depression around the company. That was temporary.

Let's get to the good stuff. Did you really have a piece of titanium implanted in your arm for nine years?
Yes. Right here.

Let the record state I'm looking at a scar on your arm. You wanted to prove to yourself that titanium was the safest metal for implants. Did anyone else in the industry do that?
Not that I know of, but I did have a good excuse. We had a series

The more important the decision, the higher it tends to go in an organization. There need to be checks and balances, but when a decision gets pushed to the top, the likelihood of that decision being made incorrectly is greater. We try to keep decision-making as low as possible, where the real knowledge base exists.

Dane Miller

Dane Miller

of tornadoes in 1974 that cut off electricity to the county for seven days. Our home and our office had no power. I had downtime and nothing to do, so I called a friend in Fort Wayne, an orthopedic surgeon, and said, "Hey, if I come over, would you put a piece of titanium in my arm?"

The power's out. I think I'll insert some titanium in my arm. Your friend said yes?
He was skeptical—

Apparently not a violation of the Hippocratic Oath.
No. The biggest difficulty I had was returning home. My wife saw this bandage on my arm and wondered what I'd done. The titanium was about one centimeter long and probably a quarter of a centimeter in diameter.

At the time stainless steel was used for implants. This is also amazing because when you started to champion titanium, and did the business with your arm, you were still an employee at Zimmer. Did you point this out on sales calls?
No. Early on very few people knew. My daughters thought it was kind of cool.

Can I see that scar one more time please?
Actually, the scar is not because of the titanium. The scar is because of the use of a product called Derma Zip, a closure device that we helped develop and intended to commercialize, but it simply didn't work.

So that was the second self-experiment. Did any of your partners join you?
No.

That's the reason why you've lasted and they didn't.
I guess.

There's a story in your biography by Patrick Kavanaugh, *The Maverick CEO*, about deciding to sponsor Lynn St. James, a race car driver, on your first meeting with her. Do you think one element to being a successful entrepreneur is being a good decision-maker?
I think organizations can become risk-averse when it comes to decision-making. The more important the decision, the higher it tends to go in an organization. There needs to be checks and balances, but when a decision gets pushed to the top, the likelihood of that decision being made incorrectly is greater. We try to keep decision-making as low as possible, where the

real knowledge base exists. Decisions are important, but they need to be made at the right level.

You didn't try to control everything.
When it came to IT decisions, for example, I had great difficulty keeping up with the IT world. When we were adding a half million dollars worth of hardware, I signed "Pedro" on a couple of capital appropriations requests and that was to indicate that Pedro, the illegal alien from Mexico, probably knows as much about this decision as I do.

USA Today ranked the 25 most successful companies on their 25th anniversary, and you are number seven, at 30,531 percent. You're ahead of Microsoft. You're ahead of Berkshire Hathaway—you're ahead

Don't look for shortcuts. Until you've got a few singles, don't look for a home run. Sometimes when you cut corners, you avoid the learning experience you might have had, if you stayed on the path and did the whole thing.

Dane Miller

The biggest mistake company founders make is misuse of capital.

Dane Miller

of Warren Buffett! Doesn't that amaze you, that you did that?
It does. Yeah.

Berkshire Hathaway was ranked 20, a lousy 19,424 percent increase. How does an entrepreneur achieve this kind of success?
Don't look for shortcuts. Until you've got a few singles, don't look for the home run. Sometimes when you cut corners, you avoid the learning experience that you might have had if you stayed on the path and did the whole thing.

Eventually you had a first home run.
The first home run was taking full advantage of the biocompatibility and mechanical characteristics of titanium, which no one else in the industry was doing. They laughed at us for a long time. Now virtually every company has copied our Taperloc hip, which has been in use since the early '80s and has amazing long-term clinical results.

What's the biggest mistake company founders make?
Misuse of capital. I frequently hear people say, "well, we just ran out of capital" or "we weren't properly capitalized" or "we were under-capitalized," or whatever.

What's the reality here?
On occasion, I think that start-up companies are unsuccessful because of excess capital. I've served on the boards of several venture capital-backed companies that acted like companies, when in fact they were R&D projects. You don't need a VP of sales or a VP of marketing when you've only got a product in development. You don't need a personnel director if you've only got 10 employees.

Did you really plan for this to happen?
Yeah, this is what we wanted to happen. We wanted to take the company public and share the results of success, including ownership, with a broad component of our team. We wanted to treat people right and avoid developing the political infrastructure that often affects larger companies. And so this is exactly what we had planned. That's been my typical response, but recently I've begun to think that's a pretty simplistic answer. It's a little like playing golf. You walk up to the tee on a 375-yard hole, swing perfectly at the ball, watch it roll down the fairway and up on the green, and fall into the hole. Your partner says, "Did you really intend to do that?" That's what we intend to do every time we hit the ball, but how often does it happen?

An investor helped out with $500,000. What did that turn into?
The $500,000 turned into approximately two-and-a-half billion dollars.

That is a 5000 times return and five times the return VC reportedly got on eBay (a lowly 1000 times). You take the grand prize for company launch success in the region. Was Indiana a plus or minus?
The Midwest is a very large plus. There is a great work ethic and, as

Other firms would tout all of these skills, but the problem was that they were only two inches deep. We made sure that we had very deep experience in multi-disciplinary teams. When we needed a technologist or a process engineer, the guy came in with 15 or more years of experience. Our clients loved it.

Chris Moffitt

CFOs are in a great position to be the pessimists.

Chris Moffitt

Chris Moffitt

Technology Solutions Company, Diamond Management and Technology Consulting, Rubicon Technology (RBCN) Illinois

you probably found out, it's almost impossible to get here, which isn't all bad.

You're three home runs in one guy. First, Technology Solutions Company (TSC), where you were a co-founder and took that company public. Then Diamond, another IPO. Then Rubicon, another IPO. What's number four?
I don't know yet.

No pressure. What inspired you to start TSC, your first company?
I had just made partner at Arthur Young. But the impetus was to free myself from the institutions. I wanted

to be a millionaire and that wasn't going to happen there. I also wanted to control what I did the next day. I knew the six guys I was doing it with and they're all really smart guys.

Those home runs were not all sweetness and light. At TSC, for example, there was conflict among the founders?
Yes, and I left, and then came back, and then left again. So Mel Bergstein and I sat down and wrote the business plan for Diamond Management and Technology Consulting.

Lots of people write business plans for companies providing IT services. How did you get funded? How was it different and better?
We talked to a lot of venture funds and Safeguard Scientifics fell in love with

Mel and me. We started a company that had extremely strict protocol and regimen around recruiting and training and providing client service. It was really well done. Lots of it came from what Mel learned from Accenture. Lots of it came from what I learned at EDS. And that's the root of the success at Diamond. We had a talent machine in place. Our recruiting process was very specific, about how to weed out the talent. For the first year you were with Diamond, you were in a training mode for three months. That's the secret to how Diamond succeeded.

Initially TSC disputed that model.
After we started Diamond we got sued by TSC, because a number of people followed us within two months. But we had all the paperwork straight and the lawsuits were thrown out.

You think I'm a classic entrepreneur? I find it to be relatively unpredictable behavior, but okay. I've never stayed in one place more than five years.

Chris Moffitt

Most services companies just grow helter-skelter.
That's right. You get the bodies in there, we'll take care of it. The more senior people will just pick up the slack when the other ones fall out. The problem is you end up with 25 percent turnover. Our turnover never went above 11 percent, even through the Internet bubble and including involuntary layoffs. You always let go five percent. There was an up or out protocol. You got promoted or you got let go. One of the two.

GE and Accenture popularized that.
It's the only way you can do it because you've got to make room. You're not going to be 100 percent on your recruiting calls. You're gonna be 50 percent at best.

The Internet bubble gave rise to all kinds of IT services companies that would furiously pitch one-off projects and application development.
We didn't sell that way. We wanted to have a relationship with the client for 10 or 15 years. And we knew the work was gonna go up and down. Other firms would tout all of these skills, but the problem was that they were only two inches deep. We made sure that we had very deep experience in multi-disciplinary teams. When we needed a technologist or process engineer, the guy came in with 15 or more years of experience. Our clients loved it.

Was there a crisis at Diamond?
The Internet bubble bursting was a problem, but it wasn't nearly as bad for us as for everyone else. I don't think we ever got more than about 20 percent of our revenue from Internet-related work. Our problem was that we bought Cluster, a telecom company. The bubble that burst hit telecoms and the Internet. Our revenues disappeared in Europe.

You have lived with public markets hanging over your head, repeatedly. Diamond, for example, went from $12 per share to $106 to—
Two dollars.

Down to $2. Did you hang in there?
I was an insider. I was on the board. All I could do was watch it disappear. It recovered to about 15.

Why did you leave Diamond?
I was selling—bringing in revenue of $20 million a year—and Mel was selling $20 million a year. And we were teaching a whole bunch of guys how to sell $20-$30 million a year. It was going fine, and I was bored. I wanted to do something else. Rubicon was extremely exciting, I enjoyed the hell out of that. And if I could find another one it would be great. But finding Rubicon was serendipity, so I gotta figure it out.

Rubicon fabricates sapphire wafers needed to make LEDs. That's a far cry from IT. What was the serendipity?
My co-founder was my father-in-law. Once I got engaged to his daughter, he asked me to help seed this little thing he wanted to do.

What inspired you to jump in?
It was the replacement of the light

If you have to raise money you have to get over the fact that you are not going to control everything. You'd like to, you want to, but you're not. Do not expect to manage your business on the basis of always having 51 percent of control.

Chris Moffitt

If customers visited, we conducted the meeting in their language, in Japanese or Chinese, even though we were sitting in Chicago. And our staff members were not just translators, they were professionals who understood technology and spoke both languages.

Chris Moffitt

Chris Moffitt

bulb. I was in love with the concept of being part of the advent of solid state lighting. It was a clear path, and the big play was, we're going to import 70-year-old Russian technology. And run past everybody because they're all invested in completely different technologies that weren't scalable to make the wafers for the LED industry. I had the pitch down fast. And it was easy to raise money.

Easy?
I seeded the first five million bucks myself. We didn't bring in our first venture investors 'til two years later. That was for $10 million. It's a very capital intensive business. When I left in 2005, we'd raised over $60 million.

You were raising big money when nothing else was getting funded.
We were raising money hand over fist because we weren't in the services business. All of these venture funds—their portfolios were getting whacked. And they were investing in us because we were going to save their portfolios.

Along with the Russian technology came a number of scientists?
We brought 25 Russian scientists and 15 Japanese scientists to Chicago. There were a number of impoverished Russian and Japanese guys who are millionaires now. A lot of them had to learn how to drive. They didn't own cars. Not to mention the language thing. We ran meetings in English, Japanese, Russian, and Ukrainian.

Your strategy paid off.
Today, Rubicon is probably 60 percent of the sapphire substrate market for LEDs. We're talking about white LEDs behind all the LCD screens, phones, and tape recorders.

What about patents?
We were developing stuff that should've been patented. The problem with patents is that you have to publish them. The problem with the industry was most of it was in Japan and China where they're perfectly happy stealing it.

How did you protect yourself?
We put deep teeth into our employees, our scientists, and our engineers, and then paid them lots of money for those teeth. We did not patent anything.

That must have freaked out the VC.
They were freaked out every day, but they finally got it. They said, "Let's take the plant and go to China. Let's go to Mexico, because we can lower the labor costs." No, no, no, because you start going out there, and then they'll rip it off.

When was it that you knew Rubicon was going to be okay, it would survive and thrive?
Five years in.

Tell us about the $50 million glass ceiling.
Entrepreneurs underestimate the difficulty in growing a business beyond $50 million sales. They underestimate the complexity and energy it takes to scale. All of a sudden you've got to spend millions of dollars—an amount

The problem with patents is that you have to publish them. The problem with our industry was most of it was in Japan and China where they're perfectly happy stealing it. We put deep teeth into our employees, our scientists, and our engineers, and then paid them lots of money for those teeth. We did not patent anything.

Chris Moffitt

To succeed you have to have failed before. There's this adage about leadership, that you can't lead until you've failed. You have to know what failure is all about because you're gonna fail a lot while you're starting the company. You're gonna make mistakes right and left, and it's kind of like the salesman who is said 'no' to 99 times and once he hears 'yes.' But that took care of the year. He would never have gotten to that 100th answer if he'd given up on the 30th 'no.'"

Chris Moffitt

Michael Pape

of money that you can't spend—to get to a hundred.

Any advice for someone starting a company right now?
The biggest problem with starting a business and taking it from zero to $100 million in sales is that it can only be done with an enormous amount of optimism. Obviously, you need energy and some smart ideas, but you have to be optimistic, too, or you can't get through the day. There are so many "why you can't do its" thrown at you. You've got to have a measure of pessimism, caution, and discipline, but optimists aren't terribly disciplined. These traits—you don't get all of them out of one person.

So you hire pessimists?
Mel and I are terribly optimistic. We had a CFO who was our gatekeeper, and that was really important. Because we'd say, "Let's hire 500 people in the next six months," and he'd say, "No." And then we'd fight. In a couple of weeks, we'd decide to hire 150, but we'd say, "If we sell this, this and this, we're gonna go to 250." We would refine it.

You are a classic entrepreneur.
If this is classic...I find it to be relatively unpredictable behavior, but okay. I've never stayed in one place more than five years.

**Esperion Therapeutics
Michigan**

What does it take to be an entrepreneur?
You have to leave something behind, step out and give it a big try. I don't think that differs from person to person.

Lipitor is the most successful drug ever developed. You were at Parke Davis on the development team working on the next generation of heart disease drugs. What was the team's goal?
Lipitor lowers LDL, which is your bad cholesterol. We were looking at ways we could raise HDL, which is your good cholesterol, to reduce heart disease— regress it. This hadn't been

done before. Lipitor only prevents it from getting worse.

You didn't stay with that?
We did. We just took a different approach but not within the walls of "Big Pharma." We got a call asking whether we'd be interested in leaving a big company and starting a biotech company based on some technology that came out of the Pharmacia and Upjohn merger in the mid-'90s. That technology was to infuse HDL particles which could reduce the plaque burden level in arteries.

On the strength of that you left?
It was an innovative and radical approach. We ended up getting that license through the help of David Scheer, an expert in pharmaceutical spin-outs. David thought that if he

Our inspiration was the replacement of the light bulb. I was in love with the concept of being part of the advent of solid state lighting. It was a clear path, a big play, running past everybody else because they all had invested in different technologies that weren't scalable. I had the pitch down fast. And it was easy to raise money.

Chris Moffitt

Michael Pape

could get the Lipitor team it would be a top-tier biotech company.

I guess he was right!
We started with $15 million from VCs on the East Coast as well as one in Europe, and we're based in Ann Arbor. We ended up consolidating the intellectual property around the world on this one particular avenue of trying to regress heart disease.

You were able to raise more than a hundred million dollars in the course of a few years and have an IPO two years after starting the company. At the point of the IPO was a product out?
No, but we had four clinical drug candidates. Before the IPO we were trying to test in animals the hypothesis that if we infused these particles we

could reverse heart disease. We did. After the IPO and five years after starting, we showed they did the same thing in humans. It was pretty fun to see the news on the front page of *USA Today.*

Once those positive results were in, Pfizer bought you.
Pfizer bought us in 2004 for $1.3 billion.

Was there a crisis at any point?
We woke up one day with 100 people. We had over-hired. We just went too fast. The market had turned and the cost of the trials went up. We had to lay people off rapidly. That was a tough time.

When the four founders left Parke Davis to start Esperion, what did you know about starting a company?
We didn't know the first thing about starting a biotech company. We got a lot of help from VCs along the way.

And then after selling you decided to join the ranks of the venture capital community.
After the Pfizer exit I raised a fund and entered the VC world with one of my business school colleagues. It's still very entrepreneurial on the VC side. Co-founding a venture fund is like starting any other company. It just happens to be a service company, rather than a drug company.

How so?
For example, our venture fund spun a company out of Procter & Gamble

after they closed their R&D facility in Cincinnati. We pulled out two programs, wrote the business plan, seed funded it, and recruited the management team.

Do you still see yourself in the mode of a start-up?
Exactly. Fundraising is a skill set that I think we're always developing. It's never over and the network is never complete. It's important to be aggressive and meet as many investors as you can, and to understand what portfolios people have and what their specialty is.

Sometimes great entrepreneurs become quite reclusive. But it sounds like you're still out there?
It's difficult to be an entrepreneur as a complete recluse. You want to

To be an entrepreneur you have to leave something behind, step out, and give it a big try.

Michael Pape

FUNDRAISING IS A SKILL SET THAT I THINK WE'RE ALWAYS DEVELOPING

MICHAEL PAPE

meet people, but the most powerful networks are the ones you're kind of in battle with to get in.

You're not only still out there but you're a scientist.
The idea of building a network wasn't first and foremost on my mind. I'm kind of an academic at heart, but I really got the business bug. If you're into it because you just like people and like creating something new, you might choose to be in business rather than sit on the beach.

Are you mentoring any entrepreneurs?
Not right now since I've co-founded another biotech company. But, yes, I served as a "mentor in residence" at the University of Michigan after the Pfizer exit.

When you helped out at the University of Michigan, how did you encourage start-ups among scientists?
I met with the faculty and listened to their research stories to see if they'd discovered something that could be commercialized or licensed. There's a real drop-off in knowledge for top-notch researchers when it comes to business. I explained how the biotech business worked.

Great science is entrepreneurial, isn't it?
Although they might not see it this way, many scientists are entrepreneurs in the laboratory. Thinking outside the box and pushing the paradigm of science are very entrepreneurial in nature.

You and Tim Krauskopf (see Tim Krauskopf, page 73) share a common trait—you both scored home runs and then went to business school.
I decided it would be fun to get an MBA and meet some people that have done some neat things. I went to the University of Chicago and met my current business partner, but it was more to try to figure out what to do next. It opened up a whole new vein of relationships that I hadn't had before.

Was there someone who mentored you or shaped how you are in business?
On the science side, it was my thesis advisor. He asked us to think about what the next question in the field would be. I learned that good companies are innovative and attack the next frontier. On the business side

of things, I think it was the VCs that came in and took that raw material that we had as technical and scientific people, and formed us into more of an executive team.

Venture investors don't always get such high praise from company founders.
They showed us how to raise money, how the story needs to be told, how that world works. There are some technology entrepreneurs that are going to catch on to the business side and I think that one-two punch can lead to great success.

If your parents give you the education, you've got to do something with it. If you fail, what's the worst thing? You move in with them for a little bit and then get going again. It's a lot harder when you get a little older. If you don't have kids, you've got nothing to lose. You gotta go for it.

Thomas Parkinson

My BROTHER AND I AREN'T IN IT FOR THE SHORT RUN. WE WANT OUR KIDS TO BE DRIVING THE COMPANY TRUCK SOME DAY.

Thomas Parkinson

Thomas Parkinson

Peapod
Illinois

You started young. Ten years old, selling eggs, only to end up launching and growing Peapod, the first online supermarket ordering and delivery service.
I had a chicken coop. So at the age of 10, I was an entrepreneur. When I got to college, my brother (Peapod co-founder Andrew Parkinson) and I had this thing called the beer keg carrier. Then I created a T-shirt at my university that everybody bought. That turned into a T-shirt company. After a stint at Procter & Gamble I started a software company in New York selling relational database systems for executive recruiters and employment agencies.

How did that get you to launching Peapod?
My brother and I wanted to start a company, so I sold that software company in New York. I took a backpacking trip around the world, and then moved to Chicago and started Peapod. I think it's just in your blood. If your parents give you the education, you've got to do something with it.

That's the spirit!
If you fail, what's the worst thing? You move in with your parents for a little bit and then get going again. It's a lot harder to do this when you get a little older. If you don't have kids, you've got nothing to lose. You gotta go for it.

You and Andrew thought this up well in advance of the World Wide Web.
Andrew's into market research, and back in the '90s he thought service was going to be important. He was at P&G, then Kraft, thinking about grocery shopping. We wanted to figure out how to save time for people, by building an online service that had all these online stores, but we decided grocery would be the first one. I had worked with executive recruiters who wanted to work at home over modems instead of going into New York. I hooked them up with early modems and learned all about online bulletin boards. Instead of taking a telephone order, we wanted to see if we could take the order on an online bulletin board and then sell advertising at the bottom.

From that idea you succeeded in taking Peapod public.
I think it's interesting that the minute we went public we were no longer able to improve our business. Because any big strategic decision was just like, "Oh, we have to hit our numbers." Everything was a short-term, quarterly kind of thing. So I would never, ever go public again. I would just sell my company.

So how did an IPO come about?
We worked really well with William Blair, the investment bank. They were so patient with us. We always seemed to get people who believed in us. What's funny is their wives were users of Peapod, so even though they didn't really get it, their wives would say, "This is a good thing to invest in."

When we hired MBAs, they felt entitled. They didn't want to do the hard work. We hired an MBA for a senior financial role when really all we needed was an accountant, a comptroller. He didn't want to do the dirty work. We said, 'See you later.' Our culture is based on the philosophy that you're not too good for anything. Be willing to do anything.

Thomas Parkinson

Usually something happens that tests the underlying concept and mettle of the business and its founders. Peapod had one of those moments, didn't it?
We had a very large moment. This was in 2000. We were about to raise $200 million from some very large funds. On the day we were closing our hired CEO didn't come in to work. He called in sick and was unable to continue working. All the financing collapsed, and we only had two weeks of cash left in the company, with 1,500 employees. That was the darkest moment of my life. I was 40 years old and I didn't have a penny to me. If this went—I was done, I was cooked, with a family and everything.

What did you do?
Andrew and I went into his office. We looked at each other and he said, "I'll worry about the money. You make sure the company doesn't fall apart." So my job was to reassure everybody by saying, "Things are great. We'll make it through this." And, because we had a culture built to last, they stuck it out.

And that's the point when Ahold invested?
My brother went to one of our biggest customers, Stop-and-Shop, which was owned by Ahold on the East Coast. They didn't want their whole home shopping business to collapse so they invested—they basically bought Peapod.

And that was a better experience than being public.
From that moment we were a private company. We started growing our sales 25 percent a year because all we did was focus on the business.

Were you always patient or only by necessity?
My brother and I aren't in it for the short run. We want our kids to be driving the company trucks.

How did you find talented employees and managers?
We were always looking for talented employees. If someone good came to us we often tried to find a place for them at Peapod.

I understand that same benevolence applies to consultants.
We test out consultants and if they're good, we bring them in. We may even hire them if we can. We also have a lot of corporate employees who are part-time—three days a week—and they produce as much as any five-day-a-week person. It's amazing. And I would never hire anybody with a grade point average of B or higher.

Seriously?
When we hired MBAs, they felt entitled. They didn't want to do the hard work. We hired an MBA for a senior financial role when really all we needed was an accountant, a comptroller. He didn't want to do the dirty work. We said, "See you later."

We were always looking for talented employees. If someone good came to us we often tried to find a place for them at Peapod.

Thomas Parkinson

I SAY THREE THINGS TO FOUNDERS. FIRST, YOU NEED TO PUT YOUR WHOLE HEART AND SOUL INTO IT. SECOND, NO ONE IS GOING TO SOLVE YOUR PROBLEMS EXCEPT YOU. AND THIRD, IT'S GOING TO TAKE A LOT LONGER THAN YOU EXPECT. YOU NEED TO COUNT ON AT LEAST 10 YEARS.

Thomas Parkinson

Vince Pettinelli

Our culture is based on the philosophy that you're not too good for anything. Be willing to do anything.

That's like Guy Kawasaki's joke about Cisco purchasing tech companies in the Internet bubble: he said Cisco valued staff at the company to be acquired at $3 million per engineer but took off $250,000 for each MBA.
With technology companies you need to find tech guys who are part of your management team. You're never going to be able to hire a tech guy—you have to make him an owner because technology is a strategic part of your business. You better make sure that the person who is involved in the strategic part of your business lives and dies for the company.

Any advice for someone starting a company right now?
A famous entrepreneur told Andrew and me when we started, "Everybody wants to screw you." We thought that was rather skeptical. I always say three things to founders. First, you need to put your whole heart and soul into it. Second, no one is going to solve your problems except you. And third, it's going to take a lot longer than you expect. You need to count on at least 10 years.

PeopleServe
Ohio

Vince, how did you start what became one of the largest providers serving people with mental retardation and developmental disabilities?
I am a psychotherapist by training, and I was the commissioner for mental retardation for the state of Pennsylvania. I was then recruited by the governor and legislature of Ohio and discovered it was extremely political. I was talking about developing private sector opportunities for people with disabilities in Ohio. I was doing this for the state, and then I thought maybe it's time to do this for myself. We started with a group home in Columbus for 10 people.

So from 10 residents, you grew to serving 7,800?
Well, we were really good at what we did. And we had a no-reject policy. We would serve anyone so long as we had reimbursement to pay for services. So we quickly grew by taking people with difficult challenges that other providers were not interested in taking. We were one of the first proprietary companies to do that.

There aren't many psychotherapists on any list of champion company founders. Was that an advantage or disadvantage?
Both. My colleagues were very skeptical. They suffer from a "sack cloth and ashes" mentality: you shouldn't profit, and doing good is enough.

I found myself with my wife gnashing her teeth: 'You're going to do *what*?' Our son was just born, I was 35, and if I was going to do it anytime, I was going to do it then. I started with my own personal credit card with a limit of $10,000, which I would borrow and pay back, and borrow and pay back.

Vince Pettinelli

You started PeopleServe in 1979, thought about an IPO in 1999, then sold to ResCare for about $200 million. Why did you sell?
We were doing $380 million a year in revenue and needed to get to $500 million before we would be ready for an IPO. We needed to do acquisitions, and ResCare came to us with an offer we couldn't refuse. We were the largest company of our kind when we sold.

Was there a key hire?
Not in the beginning. I met individuals in the business community who were fascinated by what we did, and I was able to glean information from them on how to set up the business. As we grew, I was able to afford more. My accountant, who had just passed the CPA exam, eventually became president of the company and I became chairman. I told this young accountant, "Your job is to teach someone who can't read financials--how to. And that includes me." We needed to know how to stay within budgets and operate judiciously. That was a very, very good move for me.

What's the toughest problem you ever had?
Litigation. This is a very litigious business. We dealt with people who were fragile. People would pounce on us like no one's business. The minute a consumer was hurt we got sued.

Was Ohio an advantage?
The advantage was being in Columbus. It's a big small town. I had access through business contacts to some wonderfully gifted individuals, who really cared about what we did. And bankers who cared. The environment in Ohio was perfect for me. I think it would have been much harder in New York, LA, Miami, or Houston. I think the Midwest is a good incubator for entrepreneurs.

Why?
It's more familial. There's a lot less hierarchy. There is less of the "old boy network" to break through. By the time you get noticed in New York, you've already made it and don't need a lot of help. And I'm originally from New York! I think Midwesterners are willing to share their ideas and help. That's how we grew to be in 21 states and have 9,000 employees.

To go from solo to 9,000 employees—was there a turning point?
My personal credit card was with Huntington National Bank in Columbus. We had our first line of credit with them, so I got to know the president of the region. We had an opportunity to get a huge contract for $5 million. I was playing golf with the bank president and he says, "You know, Vinny, I think you're doing great. We're going to deny your request for a $1 million line because I think you're growing too fast."

Ouch. That couldn't have helped your golf game.
That's like getting shot in the head. I went back to my office and called the bank's chairman. Luckily, his assistant

You guys are giving your lives to venture capitalists.

Vince Pettinelli

I think most entrepreneurs try to do it all, instead of delegating, and they fail.

Vince Pettinelli

Vince Pettinelli

had stepped away from her desk. The chairman answered the phone and I said, "You don't know me. I'm a client."

Good! Chutzpah. What'd he say?
He said, "Come on down." I went to lunch on the 34th floor of the Huntington Bank building, carting files. That was something for a guy from Brooklyn. We sat down for lunch. He asked me nothing about the business—for an hour. At the end I asked him about the loan, and he said, "I'd be very disappointed if you didn't get it." And that made it. When we sold the business we had a $40 million line with the bank.

Was the business completely financed on bank debt?
I sold 25 percent of the company to do a major acquisition in Texas. I learned that giving up a little to the right person or company can net great rewards. Prior to that all our financing was through commercial lenders.

You think entrepreneurs give up too much equity?
Most entrepreneurs—you guys are giving your lives to venture capitalists.

What's the alternative?
You need to develop great relationships with your bankers. Here's how: you don't schmooze them. You ask them to give you a try. People are afraid of commercial lenders. People think they are there just to say no. You want to get the highest level people at the bank to love you. And as people come and go at the bank, the word goes down, that you are going to be there. Without financing you can't do anything.

How did you keep your best employees? You were in a tough business.
We did employee surveys before any competitors thought of it. What's right about what we do and what's wrong. It's very tough to hear negative feedback, but it was worth it, because whether you're selling ice cream or serving people, your employees are the most important asset in building and maintaining a successful business. More than anything else, that shaped what we were doing.

What else besides surveys?
We also had a tuition reimbursement program that would pay two-thirds of an employee's tuition as long as they maintained a C average in anything they wanted to study. I was blessed with having a wonderful education. We found that people in school increased their self image. Even if they left our company, they had a degree, and we'd get letters back thanking us.

Where do you think entrepreneurs get it right—or wrong?
I think most entrepreneurs try to do it all, instead of delegating, and they fail. They wind up selling too soon because they are start-up people and do not realize the full value of their efforts.

What was the high point for you with PeopleServe?
Walking into my homes, which I visited at least once a year. I spent a lot of time in the field. I would see our customers develop skills they

If I had to hire me, I never would have, because I never had the prerequisite business skills.

Vince Pettinelli

109

Joseph A. Piscopo

Pansophic
Illinois

didn't think possible. To see people with severely limiting handicaps go to work was very satisfying. And to watch those, who were so withdrawn they wouldn't talk to anyone, begin to make telephone calls to family really reinforced what we were doing. I'd take my coat and tie off and help. One day I was helping to lift a patient and an employee said, "We better hurry up, the president's coming."

Let's start with the day in 1985 when someone erased all of the data in your company with an electromagnet.
I got a call one night around New Years' Eve from my data center manager and he said someone just walked through the computer room with a magnet and erased everything on every disk drive in the place.

How could that have happened? You were a public company with safeguards in place.
We're talking about a rather significant electromagnet, not something little—something industrial strength. All our programs were erased overnight.

How did you recover?
As it happens, we sold a software product that promised security for a customer's software library, so we had backup for all our programs. It took us about two weeks to rebuild everything.

You usually wouldn't carry a powerful magnet with you in a data center.
We hired an outside investigator to come in and talk to our people. It turns out that an employee, who was behind on a development project, sought to hide the fact that he had screwed up. We believe he destroyed an entire library of all the programs. The best we could do was fire him. We couldn't put him in jail and we couldn't sue him. We couldn't even prevent him from getting a job somewhere else.

That's what you call a defining moment.
For a couple of weeks, it was panic-ville.

Back to the good stuff. You started Pansophic Systems at the age of 24 at a time and place without much support for technology start-ups.
I was enrolled in graduate school at Southern California and, rather than go to grad school, I started Pansophic in Chicago. We developed and marketed mainframe-size system software.

Why did you start the company?
I was a technical guy working for Montgomery Wards and I learned a lot about computers and software and kind of knew where the flaws were.

Hiring poorly prepared people, weak people, or bad people— and each has a different kind of background—is probably the cause of 75 percent of company failures.

Joe Piscopo

Joseph A. Piscopo

And your software solved those problems, such that every year you had increasing sales leading to an IPO in 1981, NYSE listing in 1985, and sale of the company to Computer Associates in 1991.
We grew by leaps and bounds every year.

You started without venture funding and grew the company to 1,100 employees. How long did it take to turn the corner—for you to know you'd survive?
About a year.

Did everyone on the team see that?
We started with $150,000. We had a banker on our board and we had our money in his bank. He got out after the first year because he kept seeing our money go down. We were down

$10,000 after about a year, but we had just finished developing our first product, which we knew was a winner. From that point on, it was duck soup.

No bumps along the way?
For a number of years, we hired application programmers rather than computer science types and what we got were good employees in one sense: they did what they were told. However, they weren't creative. They were unable to keep developing new products and keep the new product basket full and that became one of Pansophic's negative points.

After Pansophic, you became a professional investor. How did that work out?
I was a director of a long-distance telephone company and a Chinese

fast-food restaurant chain. Those went belly up.

But there was a winner in there.
I made an investment in a very small company called Software Artistry in Indianapolis. The company had a product that managed the help desk function and telephone calls—tracking, problem-solving, record-keeping—for large-scale companies. I was an investor for three years and then I was elected to the board of directors. I then became chairman and the company went public. In 1998, after three years public, Software Artistry was acquired by IBM Tivoli Division for $200 million in cash. We had sales of $50 million. It was a rather handsome return on investment.

The Midwest gets slammed for not having much tech innovation. Did location help or hurt you?
We had to sell a $3,000 product to every big company in the world and it had to be installed by a technical person. Being able to travel to either coast in equal time and go direct to every city in North America was a tremendous advantage.

You set up a large number of offices in the US and around the world. Did that strategy pay off?
One of our biggest advantages was that our operations went international when we were four years old. We set up eight subsidiaries in Europe plus Brazil and Australia. Each one of those subsidiaries became very profitable.

If I was starting a new company tomorrow, my first order of business would be to take an up-to-date seminar on how to hire people.

Joe Piscopo

Spreading out quickly sounds like the critical advantage, and this was pre-Internet.
Software is a worldwide market and we found that our competitors were probably five to 10 years behind us. After just two years, international revenues became 36.5 percent of our total revenues and those businesses were running at a 75 percent annual growth rate. Even 10-plus years later, at the time Pansophic was acquired by Computer Associates, international still had a higher growth market opportunity than domestic.

Was managing worldwide difficult?
We had subsidiary managers, like the local president of Pansophic Germany. I couldn't fire him. In my 18 years as CEO, I went through 25 vice presidents and six CFOs.

That's painful.
I did a lot of on-the-job learning. I ended up with a venture capitalist on my board because he bought shares from one of my vice presidents whom I'd fired. We didn't get any money out of the venture fund. He bought other shares. That got rid of a thorn in my side, but I'd rather have the thorn of venture capital than the other thorn. I won't name him.

What else was on-the-job learning?
Each country had to have a separate organization. The laws in each country were different, and the currency controls and cash transfers were tightly controlled in some of those areas. The hiring processes were different. We had green card and immigration laws to deal with since all the international employees had to

come to the US for weeks at a time for training. It was a great deal of up-front cost, but it was worth it. Many of my counterparts in the US software industry never grasped the benefits.

What would you have done differently?
If I could have cut turnover in half, I probably would have tripled the amount of money the company made in all those years. It's extremely expensive to hire people and then hire again. I want to emphasize that. It's really costly. I learned this lesson about halfway through my career. It took that long.

How expensive?
If you hire a dud for a certain position, everybody that person hires is a dud. You have to fire them all, and that's

really expensive. Plus you have the opportunity cost of whatever you didn't accomplish during that time.

It sounds like hiring right (or wrong) was the biggest factor in your success.
Hiring wrong undermines the culture of the company all the way around. It doesn't mean you should turn tail and run, but I wish I had learned this lesson earlier. If I was starting a new company tomorrow, my first order of business would be to take an up-to-date seminar on how to hire people.

Do you think this is true for all founders?
I'll bet that hiring poorly prepared people, weak people, or bad people—and each has a different kind of background— is the cause of at least

If you hire a dud for a certain position, everybody that person hires is a dud. You have to fire them all, and that's really expensive. Plus you have the opportunity cost of whatever you didn't accomplish during that time.

Joe Piscopo

I DID A LOT OF ON-THE-JOB LEARNING.

JOE PISCOPO

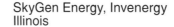

Michael Polsky

75 percent of company failures. That's my opinion anyway.

We've heard how hard it is to have a balanced life while growing a company. Was your life in balance?
It's tough. It's a trade-off between your family and your business. I have two sons and when they were growing up, I'd go to work before they got up in the morning and I'd come home after they were in bed. There is something lost in the trade-off. I would say I would do it over again, but you can't ignore the impact. My sons are now 37 and 35, and I have grandsons and I enjoy them greatly. But what happened to those years when my kids were 9, 5 and 2? It's a cost, a real one. You can't pretend that it isn't.

I'm astounded that you earned for your original investors 850 times their investment.
I really believe if you don't have the return, you ought not be in the business. It's wonderful to make many of your family members and good friends and shareholders millionaires.

After you left the company, your successor didn't last. When you tried to get back in, your board refused. Can we talk about that?
I tried to go back to the company four years after leaving and my own board, which I had put in place, dropped me. I was only 46. I was stunned. I wish I hadn't left.

SkyGen Energy, Invenergy
Illinois

How did you get into the energy business?
I was trained as an engineer. In the late '70s, when the laws changed to allow private ownership of electric generation facilities, many people who did not have technical expertise tried to build and own power plants. I thought, if these guys can do this with little training or knowledge and I understand the business, then I should be able to do it well.

How were you going to fund the business?
I looked for an investor because I didn't have any money. I had to find someone who would at least pay my salary. So

that was my first business—I found an investor who basically paid my salary and gave me a space. I started that way.

You had the technical expertise and an entrepreneurial desire.
I think I did not know what "entrepreneurial" meant at the time. I just saw the opportunity and felt I could do it. I never connected it to the glamour of having your own business. The thing was I really did not like big companies. I did not like their culture. I did not like that management was so far removed. I worked for an engineering company, but none of the management had a clue about engineering, so it was difficult for me to be there.

If you want to grow, you always stay ahead of your means

MICHAEL POLSKY

My objective is unlike some people's. I don't want to give the money guys the keys. When I'm raising money, I want to make sure that it comes with a cost that makes sense.

Michael Polsky

You're on your third company. If I remember right, the first one was okay...
I was a founder but I owned a minority piece—a substantial minority piece. The man who owned the majority suddenly realized I had built more than what he thought he had and things went haywire and I ended up leaving. I started the second company, SkyGen, on my own. It was very successful and I eventually sold it. Invenergy is my third company, also started from scratch.

Some people might have gone to sit on the beach, but you got into wind power. How did you know wind power was going to go where it's going?
Actually Invenergy began in 2001 in thermal power, not wind. But things

started to change. The cost of natural gas went up, there were increased concerns for national security after 9/11, and people were becoming more environmentally aware. I believed renewable energy would address these issues. Business-wise, it just made sense. And it has gone well.

Why build generating facilities from scratch—why not just acquire something?
I've never been good at acquiring projects. I've always been lucky that there were enough green-field opportunities so I didn't need to acquire another company's projects. Acquisition always sounds good, but to absorb another business is difficult. It always takes a lot of management time.

Why lead from Chicago and not Houston?
I like to run businesses technically, not financially. When you look at New York, for example, it's primarily financial movers and shakers getting in businesses by pooling money together and hiring somebody to work for them. If you go on the West Coast, it's more about finding the better mousetrap. I think that the Midwest and Chicago, in particular, fits very well with how I do business. I was always in the "execution business."

What does that mean—execution business?
I continually ask myself, how can I execute better than anyone else? It's not like I own technology that nobody else has. It's all about better

execution—finding a better way to accomplish business.

What's the biggest crisis you've faced?
I think I'm constantly in crisis.

Not really. Really?
We're in a very capital-intensive business. Our projects require hundreds of millions of dollars. In order to succeed, we have to make huge bets and commit to purchasing expensive equipment upfront. The power business is very institutional and it's unusual for an individual to own this type of business. So with a constant shortage of capital, I tell people: "My job, 95 percent of the time, is to look for money, big money." We are always looking for money and it is always difficult to get it. That is the crisis.

I did not know what 'entrepreneurial' was when I started. I just saw the opportunity and felt I could do it.

Michael Polsky

The thing was I really did not like big companies. I did not like their culture. I did not like that management was so far removed.

Michael Polsky

114

Michael Polsky

But when we think of large power companies there's an implied sense of stability.
Invenergy is one of the largest wind companies in the US, so people from the outside think there are no worries about the business. If you want to grow, you always need to stay ahead of your means. Our business is not grown on stable cash flow.

So you have to make big bets.
Right now we've ordered billions of dollars worth of equipment. These are firm contracts, so we've got to perform by installing this equipment someplace. If we don't, we're done.

How do you deal with that?
We raise more money, and we get a reprieve.

And then?
Then you've got another shortage. I call it "walking on the edge of the blade."

Even after all of your success. And your success has been very public, yet it's still hard to raise money?
It is and it isn't. My objective is unlike other people's: I don't want to give the money guys the keys. When I'm raising money, I want to make sure it comes with a cost that makes sense.

You mean some founders don't care enough about their equity?
Many entrepreneurs don't think forward. They just want to have money today at any cost. Later they regret that.

How so, if they get their money?
Because by the time the business goes public or is worth a lot of money, the typical founder owns a small piece. I still own most of my business, which is very unusual.

Your calculation is always between need for money versus dilution?
That's why you don't just say, "Give me the money on any terms, I don't care." I want to make sure the terms are such that it's not overly dilutive for us and, if we can raise debt, we should raise debt. If it's not done the right way, the financial people say, "I'll give you the money, but I want the keys."

And yet there are so many bright people who start businesses and immediately want venture investors.
That's a business they start to sell. This is just my opinion and may not

be true, but I think what happens is sometimes a person has a great idea, and then venture capitalists add to that the idea of how to flip it in a year or two, and they end up needing each other. One guy comes with an idea. Another guy knows how to exit.

Knowing what you know now, is there anything that you'd do differently?
There's been a lot of learning. I should've planned better as to what motivates people. I think you should be careful about giving employees equity in a company too soon. You want to reward your best employees and, sometimes, good employees come along later when the company is successful. I want employees to recognize the connection between

Most entrepreneurs don't think forward. They just want to have money today at any cost. Later they regret that they lost control.

Michael Polsky

Joel Ronning

Digital River (DRIV)
Minnesota

working hard and the company's success, and reward them accordingly.

Any advice for young entrepreneurs?
I sometimes feel strange when young people ask, what should I do? In my case, I build businesses around my skills. You go out there and try. It doesn't have to happen on Day One. You'll see what you're good at and what you can use as your base for building a business. I always felt I'd be better off doing something I really knew well. Even in the energy business, you can always find new ways of doing things. I don't agree with those people who feel that the only way to start a business is to come up with a totally new idea. I'm not even sure how that could happen.

What inspired you to start Digital River, a company that defined and continues to lead the industry in online software downloading?
I've always been very entrepreneurial. Digital River is kind of the logical culmination of a whole series of companies that I'd started or been involved with for the past 25 years. One thing we do a lot of here is direct marketing. I had a direct marketing catalog technology company before I started Digital River. Prior to that I was a partner in a software development company and a product manager. I have nine e-commerce related patents.

How did you know that software sales and distribution would move to the Internet?
It just made sense to me. The materials, the packaging, and all the stuff that was required to send a CD—or at that time a floppy disk—to someone's home, have them install it on their computer, and then throw it all away was very wasteful.

You started distributing free encrypted software in '94, then focused on the Internet in '97. Do you remember AOL—
Flooding the markets with those disks?

Yeah.
That was one of those things that got me thinking about alternatives that made more sense.

Did you have partners or did you launch solo?
Fujitsu was my partner.

Nice partner.
I had done well in a prior company called TechSquared. We were doing direct marketing of PC peripheral products and were one of Fujitsu's largest US customers. I had taken that company from zero to $50 million in about four years. I started fooling around with encryption, came up with a concept, applied for patents, then showed it to Fujitsu.

What did you want from them?
They said, this is a great idea and we'll throw in $600,000. They told me it was the best American investment they'd ever made. They made about $60 million off the $600,000.

You could see that if you didn't manage your cash flow, you'd go out of business. I watched a lot of companies disappear in the space of nine months because they didn't turn their burn off. When the downturn came, we turned our burn way down and went on an 18-month march to profitability. We had to recognize the situation quickly, then act fast, and that got us through.

Joel Ronning

Joel Ronning

They scored as a result of your IPO, and you're now at $400 million in sales. What prompted your inventive streak?
I don't have a degree in technology. I just have a huge interest in technology, and I had a bunch of friends who were programmers as well as hardware designers so we would collaborate on projects.

You left the University of Minnesota early to start your first company.
We used a computer to locate high-end, luxury cars, primarily Mercedes Benz. I put together a database, which ended up being the primary source for locating all Mercedes Benz cars throughout North America. I'd send out a weekly mailer and then broker the cars. I was selling probably 10

Mercedes Benz per month while going to college. In a good month, I'd make $14,000, which was serious money back in '82.

Not bad for a college kid. You had vision others lacked, which you took to your technology start-ups. Tech companies tend to only eat their own cooking, meaning protecting their own IP. Especially for a guy with a number of patents under his belt, why did you end up buying so many companies and competitors?
They had clients and contracts, so we bought them and migrated them to a superior technology.

After going public in the midst of the Internet bubble, you purchased a total of 29 companies, 13 of them during the recession from 2000 to

2003. **From a high of $60 per share the stock hit $2. Did either the frothy madness of the up market or the depression of the down market get to you?**
I think it just got to me a lot less than others. It's hard not to get emotional on either side of that. It absolutely impacts you.

How do you coach a management team through that?
In '99 the stock price was $60. We were losing $30 million on total revenue of $12 million and we hit a billion-dollar market cap. My executive team was congratulating themselves, and I told them to remember the moment because they weren't going to see it again for a long, long time.

What about when the stock hit $2?
I told my team it meant that everybody else is at a nickel and not to despair. That's when we really got aggressive about buying companies.

Many companies had no liquidity. How did you avoid having the company crash along with everyone else?
You could see that if you didn't manage your cash flow, you'd go out of business. I watched a lot of companies disappear in the space of nine months because they didn't turn their burn off. When the downturn came, we turned our burn way down and went on an 18-month march to profitability. We had to recognize the situation quickly, then act fast, and that got us through.

You may recognize a problem quickly but act slowly, or vice versa, but the best scenario is to figure out a situation quickly and then act fast. The worst scenario is not recognizing and not doing. Then you're dead.

Joel Ronning

In '99 the stock price was $60. We were losing $30 million on total revenue of $12 million and we hit a billion-dollar market cap. My executive team was congratulating themselves, and I told them to remember the moment because they weren't going to see it again for a long, long time.

Joel Ronning

Why did so many companies miss that?
You may recognize a problem quickly but act slowly, or vice versa, but the best scenario is to figure out a situation quickly and then act fast. The worst scenario is not recognizing and not doing. Then you're dead.

It sounds obvious, and yet the Internet bubble lasted from 1997 to 2000 with unimaginable access to capital, leading to crazy spending by entrepreneurs.
Many of those entrepreneurs were in their early 20s. If they had been running a company for four years, they had experienced 20 percent of their lives in a period of complete access to cash. I was in my late 30s and early 40s. I had a substantially different series of life experiences.

So the fact that you went through a recession in '82—
Mattered.

Was there a point in the business where you thought, we're going to make it. We figured it out.
About halfway through 2002, we added some large contracts, bought some small competitors, and prospects said, "You guys have really grown. Now you're a major player."

Was being early and defining the industry the key to winning?
It was the first key. We saw a seismic shift in how this whole industry was going to be run and we believed very deeply in it. We were early in seeing the opportunity and aggressive in execution.

It would have been a whole lot easier to do this in California.
I was very concerned about going to an environment where employees would jump from one company to the next based on what option package was offered. We knew we were going to be a significant player in the technology industry in Minneapolis and it would allow us to have access to top talent, and I think that's how it worked out.

How did you get the right people at the right time?
Because we were hiring so many people so quickly it was sometimes difficult to discern who was going to work out. When you are moving so fast, it's almost impossible not to make some wrong hires. We had to be very careful about who we kept.

How did you evaluate those you kept?
We focused on developing our best and brightest, so we put a lot of energy into helping them rise through the ranks. We made sure they were challenged, happy, and getting the right feedback. That process took four years to develop because you have to keep figuring out who is going to rise to the top. But it paid off.

How do you get to $1 billion revenue?
We're in a hurry to get there and to do it at the same level of profitability. We want to be the de facto global leader of Internet e-commerce. Things change all the time. It gives you an opportunity to be constantly fresh and challenged.

If I was starting a company, I'd start another Internet company. I love direct marketing. I love the ability to use crowd sourcing—using the wisdom of the crowd to determine what products should be—and I find the Internet to be an unbelievably powerful tool for building one-to-one relationships on a mass basis. This has tremendous possibilities over the next 50 years.

Joel Ronning

Joel Ronning

Steve Shank

You are selling software in 180 countries and your employees speak 32 languages. Do you see anything on the horizon that totally changes your game?
No. I mean, as long as you're not flat-footed. There's a whole series of opportunities that could be huge threats if you're flat-footed. Our focus is on the cloud and what impact the cloud has on the direction of e-commerce. If you ignore or don't embrace the opportunities, it is easy to get rolled over.

Doesn't the cloud replace your services?
Someone has to buy the software and pay for it. If you're using it on a cloud, it naturally turns into a subscription or pay-as-you-go model. You have

to make sure taxes are paid and notify customers when they need to purchase or when their credit card goes stale. All those processes are really complicated, and then you have to wrap billions of global transactions into something that looks like a single check and send it to the client. That's difficult to do. Around here we say, "Complexity is our friend." We simplify very complex processes.

What would you do differently?
I'd probably give away less on the front end and fund a little less aggressively. I wanted to make sure that things didn't go wrong. I think I probably made the right decision at the time, but if I knew then what I know now, with half as much funding, we would've seen the same level of success.

Any advice for somebody starting a company right now?
I think it's a great environment to start something.

Like what?
If I was starting a company, I'd start another Internet company. I love direct marketing. I love the ability to use crowd sourcing—using the wisdom of the crowd to determine what products should be—and I find the Internet to be an unbelievably powerful tool for building one-to-one relationships on a mass basis. This has tremendous possibilities over the next 50 years.

Capella Education (CPLA)
Minnesota

There aren't a lot of lawyers who succeed brilliantly as entrepreneurs.
I started out practicing law, and then at a fairly young age became CEO of Tonka Corporation, and then later started Capella.

So how do you have management DNA in you?
I am primarily oriented toward working with people and seeing ideas from start through completion. Those two things are probably not primary or positive attributes of a lawyer. A lawyer's job tends to be advisory and involves working with factual analysis and argument.

At some point I became a visionary, but for the first seven years, everyone in traditional higher education was campaigning to put us out of business.

Steve Shank

I never lost hope. We were beginning to build a growing cadre of wonderful learners. And we understood that being successful was about building a culture at Capella. We would only hire people who were passionate about our mission of enabling the success of our adult learners. I had the wonderful experience of working with true believers and you couldn't lose hope in that environment.

Steve Shank

Were your parents entrepreneurs?
They were extremely risk averse and non-entrepreneurial. My father was an executive with the Ethyl Corporation, which made the dreaded lead for leaded gas, and my mother had been a schoolteacher.

What caused you to launch Capella, which has gone from start-up to one of the largest for-profit educators in the world?
After Tonka was sold in 1991, I realized that the toy business was an entrepreneurial business and that I had a strong entrepreneurial streak in me. I grabbed on to the concept of applying technology to higher education. There was a need for higher education degrees for working adults.

Was it an idea you had been mulling around for a while or more like an epiphany?
An epiphany. I saw seeds of the idea lying around. If what I understood was happening with technology was combined with a business attitude of respectfully treating the adult student as customer and incorporating the values of higher education, it could be a pretty novel and high-value offering.

You had the idea and then what?
My first step was to attempt to purchase a couple of small emerging businesses that were related to the concept. That was how I spent 1992. That did not work out. Then I just decided to start an accredited university from scratch.

From scratch.
I was fortunate to have Cherry Tree Ventures as my partner. They really saw and understood my concept. And I was fortunate to hire Harold Able, who had spent his entire career in higher education leadership. He had the domain knowledge that was going to be necessary for us to succeed and he became our first university president.

Was Cherry Tree just cheering you on, or were they ready to write a check?
The understanding from the beginning was a fifty-fifty financial partnership. That's unusual, but because I had prior experience as an executive and there were prior relationships between this venture fund and me, they made the commitment.

Could you have launched Capella without your corporate experience at Tonka?
Unlikely. Tonka led me to an enthusiastic financial partner, and my corporate experience allowed me to see the opportunity with technology that was emerging: the need for remote adult learning in our society.

How did you start?
Higher education is intensely regulated, so the first thing we had to do was get approval from our state higher education authority as a university authorized to grant degrees. We were told by the state board that we would likely be approved, but first we had to create an entire university curriculum, faculty, and administrative structure, and return for approval before admitting a single

In 1992 the Internet was a really ugly thing. Once we achieved state authorization as a degree-granting university, we spent the next four years on a quest to achieve academic accreditation, and develop an online teaching method that would be effective and accepted. We achieved academic accreditation in '97 and a year later we were approved for the federal student loan program. We were still unable to raise any outside funding, other than with Cherry Tree. By 1999, the Internet had become a land rush and we became a darling.

Steve Shank

Steve Shank

student. A second, parallel path was to develop a level of confidence with the accrediting agency, then called the North Central Association, to achieve academic accreditation, which is a stamp of acceptance in higher education. Finally, we had to figure out how to use technology to teach.

That technology was not a given in 1992.
In 1992 the Internet was a really ugly thing. Once we achieved state authorization as a degree-granting university, we spent the next four years on a quest to achieve academic accreditation and develop an online teaching method that would be effective and accepted. We achieved academic accreditation in '97 and a year later we were approved for the federal student loan program. We

were still unable to raise any outside funding, other than with Cherry Tree. By 1999, the Internet had become a land rush and we became a darling.

You became an overnight sensation in just seven years.
Yes.

This reminds me of a story author Jay McInerney tells. His first book, *Bright Lights, Big City*, became a bestseller when he was 28. Until that point he was viewed as an old hack, but all of a sudden he became a child prodigy.
I can absolutely relate to that. At some point I became a visionary, but in the first seven years everyone in traditional higher education was campaigning to put us out of business, and would label me either a dope or a fraud.

Ever get discouraged?
I never lost hope. We were beginning to build a growing cadre of wonderful learners. And we understood that being successful was about building a culture at Capella. We would only hire people who were passionate about our mission of enabling the success of our adult learners. I had the wonderful experience of working with true believers and you couldn't lose hope in that environment.

It seems so obvious now.
This is something that people still don't understand. For the adult learner that we teach, online education is actually a more engaging, more effective forum than the traditional classroom-based education.

How is it more engaging?
Let's make a distinction between adult learning and learning in the traditional higher education years, which I'll define as 18-21 years of age. At 18 to 21, students have developmental needs based on socialization—learning how to relate to other people and living in a community—as well as the need to learn the discipline of study. There is also more acceptance of a one-way flow of knowledge from faculty member to student. The student is like a blank page willing to be written on.

Whereas Capella does not admit any students under the age of 25.
Our philosophy is that when people move into their adult years, their life and career experiences dictate different learning needs. This is well

The biggest MISTAKE FOUNDERS MAKE IS that they FALL IN LOVE with their IDEA. There HAS to be A CAPACITY to TAKE Feedback FROM other people AND FROM the MARKET, because the IDEA that you START with IS UNLIKELY to be the EXACT IDEA YOU'RE going to WIN with.

Steve Shank

documented in all learning research. People learn not by having other people tell them what to do, but by interacting and engaging with other people, and by experiencing and applying knowledge. So our whole approach is around collaborative and experiential learning, where students take what's going on in the classroom and apply it to their particular work situation and bring their knowledge and experience into the course room.

And you were able to make the technology for that to happen?
Our course rooms, for which we won a global award in education, are designed to create an interaction between an experienced set of adult professionals and faculty members. In a traditional classroom, the interaction goes on between a faculty member and maybe three highly active students. In our classroom, everyone participates. It's a required aspect of our education.

You built the entire university. How many students showed up?
We started offering classes in the fall of 1993. We were a university with five students.

Capella now has 34,000 students from all 50 states and 53 countries. Why did you wait until 2006 for your IPO—why didn't you go public in the Internet bubble?
We raised $40 million right at the peak and collapse of the Internet bubble. The lead investor honored their commitment and held to the valuation of the deal. Our plan had been to immediately go public, but the cloud around Internet companies made that not a good idea. We had plenty of cash so we just kept on going privately until 2006.

If you had not raised the $40 million, would you have been in trouble?
My experience is that successful entrepreneurs are not wild risk-takers. They take the intelligent risk. My perspective has always been that we had an obligation to our students to keep our university healthy. So we never over-extended ourselves.

That's smart, but University of Phoenix—
The cost of that decision was that the University of Phoenix was able to run much faster toward a much larger scale. We positioned ourselves as the high quality graduate online university, whereas University of Phoenix is more the mass online offering.

Those are both defensible positions.
There were well-known venture capitalists throwing money at us and one firm that wanted to invest $100 million. I said no to that offer, understanding that that firm would have pushed us down a growth trajectory that would've been too fast for us to maintain a quality proposition.

What if you couldn't get accredited?
Although we were the first exclusively online university to become accredited, we always had the belief that this could be managed as a rational process because we were doing the right thing.

Self-reflection is very important. People succeed by understanding what they love and what they're good at.

Steve Shank

Emphasis on innovation has to be matched with an emphasis on market thinking, because innovations get copied and markets get commoditized. You really have to be thinking about market positioning and differentiation.

Steve Shank

Steve Shank

At some point does online education become a commodity?
We position ourselves around this quality relationship with and commitment to the learner we are serving, and we hire employees who are totally committed to that quality experience with the learner. Since Capella offers a unique online experience, we are able to differentiate it from many of the more mass providers that we compete against and from traditional universities offering online learning experiences.

Was the location a plus or minus?
The North Central Association, which was based in Chicago, was the most advanced thinker in recognizing the need for new educational models, so being within its regulatory sphere was very helpful. Also, Minnesota has a reputation for high quality education generally, so that was good. There was also a very deep pool of people we could hire who understood using computers to teach.

Online education is something the US leads in. Where do you see it going?
Fully online, degree-granting education constitutes 15 percent of all higher education degrees granted in the United States. My expectation is in the next five years, you will see that go to 30 percent.

How does Facebook, LinkedIn, and social networking in general, fit in to online education?
We've been so heavily regulated during what I call the first phase of our lives. It felt like "you guys can do anything you want in education as long as you do it the way it's been done for the past 1,000 years." I think we are now in a new phase, where the tremendous power of social networking is going to take learning to a whole new dimension. My basic attitude is, "we're just getting started and you ain't seen nothin' yet."

I can imagine—
But our business is not technology, it's technology-enabled learning. Our focus ought not to be to get out ahead of our customers in how we apply technology. The emphasis has to be on people, people, people. We think of ourselves as a people business serving people.

Any advice for an entrepreneur just starting out?
Self-reflection is very important. People succeed by understanding what they love and what they're good at. If you're going to start a new business, you have to understand it's a very challenging process. This is not a walk in the park. You have to bring passion, commitment, and love of the idea to the table. What's really going to separate the winners from the losers is someone who can build a management team over time and navigate the challenges of financing. The leader of the business has to be out in front building that customer base and selling, selling, selling to get the business to a point of viability.

Our business is not technology, it's technology-enabled learning. Our focus ought not to be to get out ahead of our customers in how we apply technology. The emphasis has to be on people, people, people.

Steve Shank

Phil Sheridan

What's the biggest mistake founders make?
They fall in love with their idea. There has to be a capacity to take feedback from other people and from the market, because the idea that you start with is unlikely to be the exact idea you're going to win with.

What about the need to be stubborn, to persist no matter what?
If I had really listened to the weight of opinion, I'd have packed my bags a long time ago. Everyone told me I was crazy. But as we began to prove viability, I understood this was powerful and believed it would be successful financially and as an educational program.

Thank you for your contribution. Did you envision how successful Capella would become?
The total scope of this thing has exceeded what I expected. I never understood how big it was going to be.

Extended Care Information Network
Illinois

How did you start ECIN?
While I was a fellow at Loyola University in critical care, I got a call from my co-founder John Croghan (*see John Croghan, page 26*), who was a fellow at Johns Hopkins in geriatrics. He asked me if I was having difficulty getting patients out of the hospital. I said, "I can't get patients out of the intensive care unit because all the beds on the floor are filled with patients. So the answer is 'yes,' and it's making my day a lot longer."

What did that lead to?
When John finished his fellowship we started to put an idea together to

help match patients leaving hospitals with extended care facilities, nursing homes, and rehab centers.

A good idea, and I know from talking with Jeff Surges (*see Jeff Surges, page 141*) that it eventually resulted in a $100 million sale to Allscripts, but how did it really start?
We sent out an unsolicited, 10-page questionnaire to 300 extended care facilities in the Chicagoland area. We asked if they would be interested in being part of a database that might be used by hospitals to place patients in facilities like theirs. Fifty percent of them came back indicating they'd love to be part of this.

A promising start.
Then we went to friends and family and said we needed a little seed

We were very naïve when we started. We had no idea what source code was or what ownership of source code was.

Phil Sheridan

When hiring a business leader for a start-up, you need to find someone who's passionate and obviously capable, who is involved in every facet of the experience because it's not a business at that point.

Phil Sheridan

Phil Sheridan

money. Fortunately, we found Bob Ebersol, who had not been in healthcare but had been an executive at a small company and was looking to do something after he sold his company.

Doctors aren't usually experienced at running start-ups, so he helped launch. What next?
John and I were very naïve. We didn't know that you could make a database program around this idea. And we had no idea what source code was or what ownership of source code was.

You got lucky at that point.
We were fortunate to have Bob Ebersol on board. When it came time to get the source code, he convinced our programmer that this was ours and to not take advantage of these well-intentioned, young physicians. Then we were off to the races.

How did you hire people?
We tried to create a culture where everyone was invested in the success of the company and believed in our mission and the people they were working with. Some of the people we hired in the early days of ECIN came to us by serendipity, but they were willing to take a risk.

We think of founders as risk takers, but it's the same for employees?
The first and still only director of IT at our company was also an entrepreneur. We didn't have a whole lot of cash for software development but he saw it as a great opportunity. He folded his whole group into ECIN

and it became the backbone of our success.

So there you were, no business experience, hiring a management team. What were you looking for?
We needed to find people who were passionate.

Passionate and—
Capable. You need someone who is willing to be involved in every facet of the experience because it isn't a business at that point.

You go against the idea of a specific skill set.
You need someone who's willing to be a jack-of-all-trades, not someone who comes in with an "I'm the boss" attitude and farms out all the work to others.

You and John Croghan have started a couple more businesses since ECIN. Same for those?
We have quite a contrast—one company with a young leader who's very entrepreneurial and striving to make the company a success and another venture where we have someone at the helm who is a little older and a little more steeped in corporate culture.

What's been your biggest challenge?
Convincing people to invest.

If you have great customer service, you can be in any business. Scott Sheridan

I don't think in terms of when we turned the corner. I'm always thinking, you never know what's going to happen.

Scott Sheridan

Scott Sheridan

thinkorswim
Illinois

What inspired you to start an online brokerage?
My partner and I traded on the floor of the CBOE. By 1999, it was the height of the Internet bubble and we saw what was going on. We thought we could do something better as a website. The actual concept we came up with was not an online brokerage company. It was actually something else, but I can't reveal it. It's still in our back pocket and it's been carved out of our deal and we're allowed to do it.

Your secret is safe. Many traders left the CBOE floor back in the '90s because they realized that with

computerized trading there'd be nothing left for them.
And that's what happened, which has been great from a retail standpoint. I'm a retail trader now.

Fifteen years ago, you would call your broker and place an order. They called the wire room and put the order in, and then the runner would go out on the trading floor. It would take hours. How long does it take now?
Now it takes less than two-tenths of a second for a marketable order to leave your computer, go to our service to validate you have the money, go to the floor to get filled and come back to you. It's unbelievable.

How did you raise money to start things up?
We presented to a bank that was then purchased by National City Bank, the largest bank in Australia. They put together a global group of Internet companies and funded us. Then somehow they sold off the bank but forgot to include us in the deal. We became a huge regulatory risk for them. We were dangling out there. They had already given us $5 million, half of the total $10 million promised.

Not bad for a first time start-up.
It was amazing because we had nothing.

So how did you raise money?
With literally a concept, we went in and sold them 40 percent of the business for $10 million. That just shows how crazy the markets were.

What did you do when they refused to invest the other half?
We gave them a choice of either putting up the money or walking away. Eventually we took them down to under the five percent reporting requirement from NYSE. Our attorney said, "They'll never do it." We said, "Go. Fight with them." And they did it.

That was a time when funding felt unlimited for some entrepreneurs.
We took the exact opposite approach from most founders who started businesses in the late '90s. We funded it ourselves to begin with. Once we raised money, we watched every nickel. My partner and I didn't take a salary for the first few years. We said, "Whatever we have, that's it."

We took the exact opposite approach from most founders who started businesses in the late '90s. We funded it ourselves to begin with. Once we raised money, we watched every nickel. My partner and I didn't take a salary for the first few years. We said, 'Whatever we have, that's it.'

Scott Sheridan

Scott Sheridan

How did you survive?
I kept our CBOE trading operation going just to pay us. I traded and my partner Tom Sosnoff ran thinkorswim. It took us two years to write our software but we were cash flow positive after a few months in business.

When did you know you had a winner?
I don't think in terms of when we turned the corner. I'm always thinking, you never know what's going to happen.

Was there any other funding?
We talked to a couple venture funds that came to us, which was good because when you need it you can never get it.

True.
This was right after optionsXpress (*see Jim Gray, page 55*) got their funding. We figured it can't hurt to have an extra $20 million in the bank, so we said, "Let's just throw out a really stupid number and tell them it's not up for negotiation." They came in, we met, and they took our number. We were sitting there looking at each other like, what did we just do?

How did that turn out for everyone?
It was hugely successful for them.

I take it Chicago was an advantage for starting a financial technology business.
From a talent standpoint, yes, but we're really in the customer service business and we facilitate trading.

What does that mean?
I'm a big believer that if you have great customer service, you can be in any business. Our software development is all done in Russia, but it's not because it's a lot cheaper. That has nothing to do with it.

Your point is that you have to focus on being great at the most vital component of the business?
Yes, and as far as talent goes, I have an unlimited supply of people for customer service from the trading side. I receive resumes on a daily basis from people who are looking to get off the floor and put their unique skill set to work here.

Why Russia for software development?
It's actually a crazy story how it wound up going over there, but we have the best developers in the world working on our stuff and they just happen to be in Russia. If you ask them, they'll say their perfect world scenario is to have an American job, live in Russia, and drive a German car.

You successfully completed an IPO and eventually sold the company to Ameritrade. You are still growing fast and hiring more people. How do you go about that?
We don't take a traditional approach to most of the things we do and that's also true of hiring. I don't look at resumes, I just talk to the person. It's more about culture, it's more about a fit. I'll take somebody with desire over

We don't take a traditional approach to most of the things we do and that's also true of hiring. I don't look at resumes, I just talk to the person. It's more about culture, it's more about a fit. I'll take somebody with desire over somebody who has a good pedigree. I'd rather have somebody who's young and hungry and who has heart and character.

Scott Sheridan

somebody who has a good pedigree. I'd rather have somebody who's young and hungry and who has heart and character.

Gimme an example of that in action.
I hired the niece of somebody who works for us. She was fresh out of college with a degree in early childhood development. I needed somebody as a back-up support person to watch our systems, not for programming or anything, but just for watching, making sure the orders were going to the right place. I said to her, "I have no expectations because you're kind of a guinea pig. I want to see if I can actually train somebody who has no background in the trading world whatsoever. I know there's pressure on you because you're not going to

want to disappoint your uncle. I'm sure you're gonna do great." She just looked at me, put her head down and said, "Why'd you have to say that to me?" She passed her Series 7 securities test the first time through and she's learned everything she's needed to learn.

Any dark days for you, Scott?
Two. The first was a customer error that cost us 40 percent of our income for the year.

Oh, not good.
That was bad. It was in arbitration three-and-a-half years.

How did you handle it?
It was a very tough time because we knew what an expensive mistake it was. It was a situation where seven unbelievable things had all happened

at the exact same time. It couldn't happen again—that's how outrageous it was. The odds might be one in a million but apparently it was 100 percent for us on that day.

I'm afraid to ask about the other day?
We went totally dark one day. Our whole system imploded and we had nothing. Fortunately, we didn't have a lot of customers.

And those were mistakes you had to own.
It was our own stuff.

How do you also have a life?
I think I learned a lot from my dad about what I didn't want. He's a very successful real estate developer and has had a million businesses. I've told

him that he should write a book just because he's made it and lost it more times than most people can imagine.

What did you conclude?
I didn't want to work 16 hours a day. When I was a kid I'd ask my dad if we could go out and play catch, and we'd play catch in between phone calls. I hated it. So part of what I liked about trading was the markets closed at 3:15 and I was home by 3:30. Then I started this business and that changed dramatically. My hours, I'm 6 to 6. I used to work at nights and I've cut that out.

How was it, working with a board of directors?
We had one venture fund investor who was a board member and we were like the little brother who never lived up

I kept on hiring top-notch people, and they were building the company. We made it a very employee-oriented company and I challenged my management team to build on that culture. Managers realized that they were not doing any work for their clients—the employees were. Since our managers' biggest clients were their employees, every manager got trained to focus on building up their employees.

Raj Soin

Raj Soin

to the big brother. They were always telling us basically that we never lived up to their expectations. They made about four times their money in less than three years. I don't know. I think that's a pretty good return.

**Modern Technologies Corporation (MTC)
Ohio**

Was it easy or hard to start MTC?
I had wanted to start a business ever since I graduated from college, but it took me about 12 years to quit my job.

With hindsight, home runs like MTC look obvious. But at the time you tested the waters, right?
Initially I started some small-scale businesses on the side while keeping a full-time job. I did not have much success in those ventures because every time I encountered major roadblocks I quit that business and refocused on my full-time job. The commitment level dramatically increases when you know you don't have any belt and suspenders.

It was a question of commitment.
I was committed at two different places. Start-ups require a lot of energy and commitment and that's very difficult to provide on a part-time basis.

What inspired you?
At first I tried to start businesses in areas where I saw other people making money. I really did not get successful until I specialized in engineering. Forming MTC was right down my alley, and it worked.

Yes, well, lots of people form consulting companies. Very few get to an IPO.
We were lucky to have hired excellent people. Our executive team was very strong and focused. The hardest thing was in the beginning of the company.

Trying to establish a name as a consultant was a challenge.

How did you break through all those challenges?
I took a subject that I knew I could be world-class in—productivity improvement—and I approached a seminar company. I made a deal with them. I would present seminars where they could charge the students and keep all the revenue. I would get only $1,000 a day plus expenses and any consulting work coming out of it.

What happened?
First, because we continually distributed fliers announcing our seminars, I was perceived as a specialist on the subject. Second, people who attended the seminars became a good source of consulting contracts.

I don't believe in a particular industry, and I don't believe in technology or product. I believe in people. Give me the right horse and I'll bet on any race.

Raj Soin

That's a great tactic.
People value your opinion and take you a lot more seriously when they're paying to listen to you. The seminars enhanced my credibility.

Did you really start the company with $1,700?
My wife and I started with about $1,700, and that included the value of furniture we moved from home to office.

And within three years you had 200 engineers. By the time it was acquired by BAE, MTC employed 3,000 engineers. How did you do that?
I think that many people have entrepreneurial desires. They want to build a business and succeed, except the majority of them fall into the same

trap I did—they want the security of a paycheck. So we set up a model where we could provide our people with security, but give them an opportunity to be their own entrepreneur. I started what I call our self-funded incubator.

How does the incubator work?
I challenge my engineers and other employees who come up with an idea to present it, and then we fund them to take it to the next level. As they progress, we decide whether or not we will continue to fund it. Over the life span of MTC we spun out 20 additional companies.

What happened to those companies?
We sold some of them to other companies and management teams, but we still have five operating companies in Soin International's portfolio.

What's an example of one of these funded ideas?
There's so much talk about plastics not being biodegradable. It takes 250 million years for it to degrade and it gets dumped into landfills. An engineer developed a method where we could take a little bit of dirty plastic and make a good, useful product out of it, even with 10 to 15 percent contamination.

Great idea. What happened?
After we got the patent we spun out CTC (Composites Technologies Company). It came right out of our consulting company and currently has more than $30 million in revenue.

That's an amazing example of harnessing all of the creativity at the company. You took MTC public

in 2002 when it was at about $100 million revenue. Why go public?
All our companies were self-funded and all our assets were tied up. We did not have much cash, so we decided to generate liquidity out of at least one company.

Belated congratulations on the IPO.
We went against the advice of investment bankers, who told us not to sell personal stock at the time of the IPO. Half of the stock sold in the IPO was my personal stock.

I understand, believe me. Any advice for entrepreneurs on hiring?
For the first three or four years, most of my employees were drawing much higher salaries than I was drawing myself. I kept on hiring top-notch people, and they were a great help

A lot of employers say they expect loyalty from their employees. What they don't realize is that loyalty is a two-way street. If we start being loyal people will respond.

Raj Soin

130

in building the company. We made it a very employee-oriented company. Everything we did was focused around our employees, and I challenged my management team to build on that culture. Managers realized that they were not doing any work for their clients—the employees were. Since our managers' biggest clients were their employees, every manager got trained to focus on building up their employees and, in turn, they expected employees to take care of the customers.

And for you as the leader—
I don't believe in a particular industry, and I don't believe in technology or product. I believe in people. Give me the right horse and I'll bet on any race.

Andrew Carnegie, who dominated the steel industry, said that even if you took away the entire steel industry, he could take his team into any other industry and they would be just as successful.
Exactly. You ask, what is the secret? Every business has problems, but if you have the right team of people and the right motivation, you will find a way to make it a success. If you don't have the right people and you go it alone—I don't care how good the technology is—you will succeed only to the level of your own competence.

Why the focus on defense contracts?
I focused on productivity improvement. What I found was that marketing to individual companies was a very long, drawn-out process, whereas the Department of Defense

(DOD) acquires major systems from large corporations and does not always have the technical strength internally to evaluate those corporations. So I started by working with the Air Force, where I would send people to evaluate major contractors like McDonnell, Lockheed Martin, or Martin Marietta. Also, in service areas, the DOD gave us access to much larger contracts.

Aren't government contracts much harder to win?
Yes. It is a more time-consuming process. It takes a couple of years to get your first contract, but then you get large and long-term contracts, whereas if it's private industry, you generally get smaller and short-term contracts.

And then you build up good momentum.
Once I started that focus, all the engineers I'd been hiring began concentrating on defense and we moved into all types of engineering work. As we expanded our footprint technologically, as well as geographically, we kept growing fast.

Was the Midwest a disadvantage, working in defense?
Interestingly, one of the largest defense acquisition centers is in Dayton, Ohio. Most technical service companies with defense contracts start and build around Washington. I like small cities and I didn't want a two-hour drive to work, so I chose Dayton. It's a great area to raise a family and it was right by the Wright-Patterson Air Force base. Later on we opened

People value your opinion and take you a lot more seriously when they're paying to listen to you.

Raj Soin

a large office in Washington without moving the headquarters there.

What are your thoughts on loyalty?
A lot of employers say they expect loyalty from their employees. What they don't realize is that loyalty is a two-way street. If we start being loyal people will respond.

How so?
Even when the company got big, my wife always made sure on every employee's anniversary date, the spouse received a gift from her and me. If an employee got sick with something like cancer and needed a treatment that insurance wouldn't cover, we sometimes covered it with our own money, not corporate money. Even though we did it quietly, the word got out among the employees, and

it started generating more and more good feelings toward the company.

Raj, what was the biggest crisis that you ever faced?
Making payroll and managing cash flow.

That's the one that keeps entrepreneurs up at night.
We really didn't have money, but I had some credit cards. Quite often I'd end up charging my credit card to make payroll, and hope the payments would come in to pay the credit card later.

How did your partner like that?
My wife has always helped and stood by me in all our endeavors. She used to go to the lockbox every day to see what payments came in. One night

she walked in, tears in her eyes and said, "Raj, we have a problem. Today is payday and no checks have come in and we cannot meet payroll." I told her to charge it to a credit card and she just busted out crying. She said, "Which one? Every one of them is over the limit."

What then?
I got so shook up. You realize the day you miss payroll, that's the day you're done. I told her that I didn't want her to come into work anymore. She used to handle my books. It wasn't 'til months later that I got around to explaining to her what I was going through—that I was scared to the extreme, and the last thing I wanted was to come home to a wife who knows all the details of my problems, making me more scared. So I got her out of the office.

But that didn't—
Interestingly, none of the paychecks bounced.

But what about—
Three months later I walked into the office of one of my engineers, Mike Ward. We were just talking and I happened to see a bunch of paychecks sitting in his desk drawer, which was open. I asked him, "Mike, how come you haven't cashed any of these paychecks?" He said, "Raj, I saw your wife crying in your office. I knew you guys were in financial trouble. My wife is a nurse. I'm paid well. So I thought, I'll cash them when the company has money."

We three signed up as a team, worked as a team, and didn't make a big decision unless we were all in agreement. That was a good strategy because we have very different personalities. For us to agree on something, we generally looked at it from many different angles. It's really powerful to have a diverse team!

Phil Soran

Phil Soran

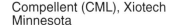

Raj, you just confirmed my faith in entrepreneurs. And I think you justified four years' work on this book. Thank you for being inspiring.
Those types of people stayed with me 'til the end.

Compellent (CML), Xiotech
Minnesota

Phil, you are going to inspire generations of junior high math teachers.
I taught junior high for several years and I really liked that, but I wanted to do something more entrepreneurial. I went to work for IBM back in the '80s. It was the best training ground for what I would end up doing.

Some people wouldn't have left. I mean, it was IBM.
I left for a small data warehousing company, where I learned a lot about raising money. I got a taste for the small company, and acquired skills you don't learn at IBM.

Let's talk about Xiotech, which you took from launch to sale to Seagate in five years for $360 million. Congratulations.
Thank you.

You, John Guider, and Larry Aszmann founded Xiotech in '95. How did that come to be?
It was a little bit of divine intervention. Larry was my next-door neighbor. We were both in the technology industry. Larry hooked the three of us together.

Partnerships don't always work out.
John and Larry had worked together before at several companies. We three signed up as a team, worked as a team, and didn't make a big decision unless we were all in agreement. That was a good strategy because we have very different personalities. For us

to agree on something, we generally looked at it from many different angles. It's really powerful to have a diverse team.

Did you know this intuitively or did you discover it as you got to know each other?
A little of both. People are the result of their histories. You have to understand people's histories and make sure that you really communicate well with one another, which is the hardest thing to do even with people you know well.

So the team came first.
And the idea came second. A lot of people have an idea, then they go find the team. We actually started meeting in my basement. Silicon Valley people may start companies in their garages, but in Minnesota it's too cold to do

People are the result of their histories. To be a good partner, you have to understand people's histories and make sure that you really communicate well with one another, which is the hardest thing to do even with people you know well.

Phil Soran

it in your garage, so you go to the basement.

What happened in the basement?
John and Larry are pure engineers—one has hardware background, one has software background. I was the sales and marketing person. We started brainstorming, wrote the business plan, and raised our first round of angel money—$885,000. Ultimately, the idea ended up being what we now call a storage area network. That term wasn't even around back then. It is now the dominant architecture for data storage.

You were pioneers for storage area networks and eventually raised $28 million in venture capital. You hit on something profound—that storage

needs only grow larger, never smaller.
That's true. Even in a recession you can't quit storing your data. It's going to keep coming at you, and you have to figure out how you're going to handle it.

Xiotech is hardware and software, while Compellent is just software?
On the first endeavor we had to design hardware and software. By the time of Compellent, there were major advancements in industry standard hardware, so we've focused our differentiation on software.

Was there a break between companies?
We kind of retired for about a year. If entrepreneurship is in your blood, you gotta do it again, so we went back

to the basement with another white board. We looked at the market and came up with some new ideas.

Same basement, different white board. Got it.
But this time the basement was finished—no concrete floor—and we actually had a little desk down there rather than a ping-pong table, so we really upgraded.

I would think you could have sprung for an office.
One of our previous venture capitalists offered their offices, so we eventually moved there. We had their secretary as support, access to their research analysts, and a nice office to interview engineers. It was a really classy move by them.

Could you have started funding Xiotech on your own?
We knew that with this big of a thing—that much hardware and software design—we needed significant money, and we didn't have that money. Raising the money was basically up to my network and me. My network wasn't family and friends—it was a real strong angel community in the Twin Cities.

Was raising money hard or easy?
It was a challenge. We were an unproven team. Once we got angel money, we were able to get the VCs interested. But the critical thing was to have a local venture capital lead.

No Silicon Valley VCs for you?
The VCs in California would literally say, "If you're more than 30 minutes

> A lot of people have an idea, then they go find the team. In our case, the team came first and the idea came second. We started meeting in my basement. Silicon Valley people may start companies in their garages, but in Minnesota it's too cold to do it in your garage, so you go to the basement.

Phil Soran

> There tends to be too much emphasis on the business plan. You need to plan and have your strategy written down, but I've seen a lot of entrepreneurs spend too much time doing multiple iterations and minor tweaks on the business plan. Develop a prototype instead of writing a fancy business plan.

Phil Soran

Phil Soran

from my doorstep, I'm not interested in investing in you."

You're not alone, brother.
I think Minnesota is a big advantage over the two coasts. There's a lot of mainframe talent, a good education system, and a real strong engineering base here. We've never used a headhunter to hire anybody. Minnesota talent is more stable and loyal. If employees have been treated well, they tend to stay, as opposed to jumping every six months to the next start-up. And once we found a local VC lead, by the way, we were able to attract VCs from the Valley.

Xiotech employed 420 people, and when you left it had hit $100 million revenue run rate. What was the secret sauce behind Compellent?

We built the right team—founders, employees, and investors; discovered some customer pain points; and developed easy-to-use software that directly addressed the pain.

Why not fund it yourselves?
The opportunity we were going after was very large, and it was complex software we were going to write. We needed significant money and deep pockets.

What was different about Compellent?
Compellent is redefining the way network storage works. It helps manage data more efficiently. For example, if something bad happens, you can roll back time and make the data look like it did before the bad event occurred. By moving inactive

data to lower cost disk drives, you can cut costs by 70 percent. We also have ways to allocate storage, but you don't have to buy it until you actually need it.

You started Compellent in 2002, and the IPO was October 2007. Nice timing.
Timing is a really important skill to have. We were good at just-in-time hiring and just-in-time IPOs. The peak of the market was October 9th. We went public on October 10th.

And then the world went into an economic tailspin.
We went public a little earlier than we had planned, but the market was ripe and we were growing quickly. A lot of people will tell you stories about the pains of being public, but I'm glad

we are. In these economic times, being on the NYSE and having a nice balance sheet with no debt and lots of cash makes you a much safer bet for customers.

Beyond your founding team, any thoughts on hiring and company culture?
We've been able to be pretty picky about hiring people who are "best of breed." When you do that, you create respect among your employees and increase their self-confidence. The second thing is, we're well-known for our culture, which we call "positive-aggressive." We want to be very aggressive in pursuing our goals and objectives, but we always try to do it in a positive manner, which is a combination of ethics, style, attitude,

We went public a little earlier than we had planned, but the market was ripe and we were growing quickly. A lot of people will tell you stories about the pains of being public, but I'm glad we are. In these economic times, being on the NYSE and having a nice balance sheet with no debt and lots of cash makes you a much safer bet for customers.

Phil Soran

and enthusiasm. Being aggressive is all about winning, and positive-aggressive is about how you win.

Do your customers know that?
How you win and lose permeates how you treat your customers, prospects, and vendors. We just had a worldwide user conference and about 50 of our customers came up to me and said, "I don't know what you have your people drinking, but they're just different to talk to. They all like what they do and where they work." They sense the culture.

Any advice for entrepreneurs?
There are three major risks in starting a company: number one is financing. If you don't have the fuel for the engine, it doesn't matter how good your idea is. The second risk is distribution—

how you're going to sell the product. The third risk is technology. Investors and entrepreneurs tend to focus too much on technology and not enough on distribution. How are you going to sell millions of dollars worth of your product? How are you going to convince people to buy it? Technology is hard to develop, but you control the process, whereas the sales environment—you don't control it.

Why did you sell Xiotech to Seagate?
Two reasons. Storage area networks were new, so we had the double whammy of educating our customers on a new architecture and on who our young company was, because we were unknown. That's a hard sale. We felt like this would get a lot more

traction a lot quicker if we had a bigger brand behind us. Timing-wise it turned out fantastic. I'm really glad we did the acquisition versus an IPO at that time.

Because it was 2000.
Maybe, but I kind of had a lightning bolt moment. I called each of the board members, who were all VCs, and asked them what they would sell the company for. I got the exact same answer from everyone save one, and his number was four times higher. He wanted to go public in the worst way. He thought we were going to be a big IPO. We had a late night meeting once where I said, "There's one problem here. Everyone around the table is a millionaire except me." And that VC told me he'd change his attitude on that statement alone.

He could take the risk you couldn't take.
I have four kids, and I didn't know how I was going to get them through college. It wasn't like we were flush with cash. It was a personal thing, but it was also a business decision to do the acquisition.

What's the biggest mistake company founders make?
There tends to be too much emphasis on the business plan. You need to plan and have your strategy written down, but I've seen a lot of entrepreneurs spend too much time doing multiple iterations and minor tweaks. One of the founders of YouTube told me that in the Valley they just build a prototype and show it to people as opposed to spending hours writing a business plan. Do more of that.

There are three major risks in starting a company: number one is financing. If you don't have the fuel for the engine, it doesn't matter how good your idea is. The second risk is distribution—how you're going to sell the product. The third risk is technology. Investors and entrepreneurs tend to focus too much on technology and not enough on distribution. How are you going to sell millions of dollars worth of your product? How are you going to convince people to buy it? Technology is hard to develop, but you control the process, whereas the sales environment—you don't control it.

Phil Soran

Brian Sullivan

That also translates into marketing.
Engineering and technology people have trouble distilling down technical information to something understandable. Marketing your message is really hard to do, but it's really important. The simpler you can make it, the better.

What is the most critical quality an entrepreneur has to have?
Drive. You gotta have drive to succeed and then be able to figure out a way to make it happen regardless of the challenges you run into.

That's a common theme—
There's no doubt there's higher risk, lower pay, and more on the table when you're on your own, but in some ways, it is less stressful because you control your destiny. If something's not

right you can change it. Within a big organization you can't control what's going to happen.

One of the things I admire about you and your partners, Phil, is that you protected your original angel investors.
The angel investors didn't have the same terms as the VCs, so we retroactively gave the angels better terms. It cost us money, but it was the right thing to do. They were the first ones to believe in us and had taken the most risk.

Recovery Engineering
Minnesota

You invented PUR water filters, took your company public, and then eventually sold to P&G for $270 million. It's interesting that one of your professors at Harvard helped you get into business as a relatively fresh college grad.
About a year after I graduated, my thesis advisor told me about a friend whose dad had a patent for a device that could desalinate seawater. My professor's friend didn't really know what to do with it, and my professor knew that I was looking at various business ideas and wanted to start a business. He set up an introduction and the end result was that I bought that patent, which ultimately became

worth about five percent of our revenue as we grew. It allowed me, as a 24-year-old, to start a business, develop an engineering team, get the initial distribution for a niche product, then use that as a foundation to develop our next and subsequently largest product line.

How did you know you wanted to start your own company?
My father was a businessman, so I was exposed to business leaders and I had a sense that I didn't want to work for somebody. I felt I had the ability to be successful on my own. I wasn't interested in doing my time, so to speak, and waiting 10 years.

You also prepared by taking your first job out of college with a

Walmart or Target or Home Depot don't cut you slack just because you might be a young company. They expect you to operate in a way that's consistent with the largest companies in the world. That's a fairly high hurdle for a young company because you have to develop a lot of capabilities very quickly.

Brian Sullivan

company that owned a number of businesses.
I worked for a holding company that parachuted me in to look at their businesses and make recommendations. I thought I'd find one of the companies within this holding company that they'd be willing to sell to me. It was unrealistic, but it gave me exposure to a variety of different businesses.

Any background in water purification?
I had done a paper on the economics of water and was familiar with the explosive growth of the bottled water market. I wasn't dying to start a manual desalination business as much as I thought it could be a platform to build a brand in the drinking water arena.

Good focus on your part.
My real intention from Day One was to use this as a step along the way towards building a drinking water brand and, ultimately, that was what we did.

Tell me about the first product.
We developed manual desalinators that the US Navy, Air Force, Army and other militaries across the world now use in life rafts as emergency water backup. We then developed 12-volt motorized versions for use by offshore cruising sailors. Desalinating seawater is very energy-intensive. Our technology made it possible to desalinate seawater with very low energy requirements, so manual effort or 12-volt battery input would be sufficient. Those were niche markets,

but ones where we were the sole player. We had 100 percent market share.

Ah! That's music to any entrepreneur's ears.
Even though it was small, it became very profitable. We were aggressive in leveraging what we learned. We developed additional technologies for different market segments, and while they had different distribution channels, they had very similar challenges in terms of the technology development, marketing and sales approach.

How many lives did your products save?
There were a few situations where people were, literally, shipwrecked. One couple, the Butlers, was sailing

2,000 miles off the coast of Costa Rica. Their boat was rammed and sunk by whales. They then spent 66 days in a life raft, and survived only because they had our water purification product. They were featured in *People* magazine and became recognized around the world.

That was in 1988, a year after product launch. That's a testimonial.
We had a similar situation off the coast of Africa, so we had a number of survival stories. About the same time the Butlers were rescued, a couple was shipwrecked off the coast of Bermuda, and they didn't have our product. They were discovered five days later, but the man had died and the woman was so sick it took her two months to recover. The Butlers,

I have been given many opportunities, and I realize any success I may have is more a function of having taken full advantage of those opportunities rather than taking credit for them.

Brian Sullivan

There were a few situations where people were shipwrecked. One couple was sailing 2,000 miles off the coast of Costa Rica. They were rammed by whales, spent 66 days in a life raft, and only survived because they had our water purification product.

Brian Sullivan

138

Brian Sullivan

after 66 days at sea with our product, walked off the life raft and took a plane home. They were fine. They didn't spend any time in the hospital.

Did they also have food, or was it just that they had fresh water?
Typically these life rafts have fishing gear, so they were able to catch fish. But fish without water won't sustain you.

Did you raise money to start the company or fund it yourself?
I put in some money and then raised about half a million dollars from angels. That allowed us to get going and survive for about a year, and then we raised $1.2 million more from angels.

How far did the money get you?
It allowed us to get to positive cash flow, and at that point, we had

developed and launched our second product line, drinking water products for campers and military infantrymen. We then had two product lines, we were profitable, and we were growing more than 50 percent a year.

You had a small IPO in 1993. Was that a reverse merger or—
No, it was just one with a local brokerage firm that specialized in helping early stage companies get access to capital. Minnesota had companies like St. Jude Medical and Cardiac Pacemaker that followed a very similar path—angel money was raised, then a small public offering, and, ultimately, the big home run.

At the time of the IPO what was the company valued at?
It was probably $25 million.

Your first money raised was at a dollar, the second round was at $2.50, the first public offering was $7, the second public offering was at $13, the third offering was $15, the fourth offering was $30, and then, ultimately, the sale was at $35.50. What was the secret sauce here? How did you keep on building value?
Often companies will develop products that may fulfill a need, but they're too expensive, which limits their market share. We spent a lot of time trying to understand what the consumer was looking for—what problems they had. We then developed solutions to meet both the customer's functional needs as well as their price expectations.

How did that translate when you launched the PUR line of consumer products?
We identified the three biggest problems customers had with household water filters. First, they didn't have confidence that filters removed the right contaminants, so we developed some very innovative technology that removed more contaminants than any filters available at the time. And, second, they didn't know when to change the filter, so we developed a monitoring technology that would tell them when to replace the filter.

What was the third?
Price. A $200 water filter had a very limited appeal. People can buy a gallon of water for a dollar. We thought that, ultimately, we'd have to offer products

Often companies will develop products that may fulfill a need, but they're too expensive, which limits their market share. We spent a lot of time trying to understand what the consumer was looking for— what problems they had. We then developed solutions to meet both the customer's functional needs as well as their price expectations.

Brian Sullivan

Technology should solve a problem and not be an end in itself.

Brian Sullivan

that would range from $15 to $50 in price and have replacement filters that would result in a cost less than a dime a gallon. We knew if we couldn't develop a product that cost less than $6 to manufacture, the business model wouldn't work. Once we solved those challenges, I felt pretty confident that we had a product with a very significant market potential.

You were solo founder. Was there a key hire for you?
My VP of engineering and I were essentially invention partners and were listed that way on a number of the patents. I always considered him my business partner because we were a very good fit. I had a pretty good sense of the market, how to solve problems and how to leverage technology,

but I wasn't an engineer. Identifying a problem is usually where your opportunities come from.

You are listed as inventor on a handful of patents awarded to the company. Not bad for an econ major.
Well, I had some good help.

There's a lesson in this because so many times people invent interesting technologies that don't result in anything
That's the trap. Technology should solve a problem and not be an end in itself.

Any advice for people starting companies right now?
Be very objective in defining the rationale the customer will use to buy your product, and be very tough about

understanding the true incremental benefits that you're creating relative to the alternatives.

But sometimes you have to have rose-colored glasses to get past barriers.
I see business plans, and oftentimes people come up with a better alternative but the price outweighs the benefit.

What about Minneapolis, a plus or minus for run?
Being located in Minneapolis was a big help because the community has a tremendous entrepreneurial culture. There was a ready investor pool, so I was able to raise money more cheaply from angel investors than I could have in other cities. It also meant that

there were people from Fortune 500 companies who were interested in joining start-ups and taking risks.

Did the company ever face a crisis?
We needed to spend a lot of money to build our brand, which meant that we were spending tens of millions of dollars to advertise. We also had to invest tens of millions of dollars to build out our manufacturing capability. We not only were inventing end-product technologies, but we had to invent manufacturing technologies to produce them. It was a fairly complex and expensive undertaking that had a lot of moving pieces. We had to maintain sales momentum at our retailers so that they would list our new products. The big risk was getting out of rhythm with them and losing shelf space.

When Walmart places an order, you have to deliver your product to their distribution centers within a 12-hour window. If it is not there, they're not going to place another order. They aren't interested in excuses.

Brian Sullivan

Brian Sullivan

It sounds like a lot of plates spinning.
We never hit the wall, but we brushed up against it a couple times. I felt like we were on a knife-edge for about four years as we were building the business.

It's Aristotle: "We are what we repeatedly do. Excellence, then, is not an act, but a habit." You had to introduce product to retailers in the first quarter, then ship in the third quarter?
Right, and if you got off that cycle, then you'd essentially blown a year. And you'd lose your credibility with retailers so your opportunity to launch new products and expand your shelf space would be reduced.

You mentioned the business getting into a rhythm—
As a new consumer products company, it's very important to establish a rhythm with your retailers. Very few new brands get built because the bar you must overcome is set fairly high. Retailers are only interested in products that can sell, so if you launch a product and it doesn't sell through, they're not going to have much interest in your next one. If you launch and don't physically deliver it—after they've set aside shelf space and committed advertising dollars to support it—you will really damage the relationship. When Walmart places an order, you have to deliver your product to their distribution centers within a 12-hour window. If it is not there,

they're not going to place another order. They aren't interested in excuses.

So many entrepreneurs think the world will give them a pass as a start-up.
Walmart or Target or Home Depot don't cut you slack just because you might be a young company. They expect you to operate in a way that's consistent with the largest companies in the world. That's a fairly high hurdle for a young company because you have to develop a lot of capabilities very quickly.

Wasn't the mass market its own challenge?
We first developed distribution outside of mass merchants. We then approached Target to be our

first mass-market retailer, and we partnered with them successfully. We were then able to keep introducing new products and obtain more shelf space at Target, and use that success to win over Kmart and Sears. The last major retailer we went to was Walmart. We did not want to find ourselves in a situation where Walmart controlled our destiny. We had established the market, our product had consumer demand—it was successful. Ultimately Walmart wanted it, and we could work with them from a position of strength.

What's your new company, SterilMed?
We reprocess medical devices so that hospitals can get additional use out of them to reduce their costs and environmental waste. There are only two of us in the industry, and it's

I think here in the Midwest there's a tremendous amount of modesty. Guys over on Sandhill Road in Northern California are out on the PR trail long before a revenue stream is invented. We are the total opposite!

Jeff Surges

Jeff Surges

Extended Care Information Network
Illinois

growing very rapidly. It has grown 40 percent a year for the past six years since I took it over. So far, so good.

And congratulations—as we were going to press we learned you successfully sold SterilMed, rumored to have gone for about $200 million.
It helps to land in the right place. I have been given many opportunities, and I realize any success I may have is more a function of having taken full advantage of those opportunities rather than taking credit for them.

What is the most important quality that a founder should have?
Be a very clear thinker. And be relentless.

We tend to think of entrepreneurs as loners out on the range. But your first and only job interview was with Glen Tullman (see Glen Tullman, page 147) and at one point you worked for Howard Tullman (see Howard A. Tullman, page 152). So it's really more of a connected world.
Yes. I am also connected to several other founders profiled in this book. ECIN (Extended Care Information Network) is the start-up or re-start Glen Tullman, Phil Sheridan (see Phil Sheridan, page 123), John Croghan (see John Croghan, page 26), and I have in common. We took the business

plan, put some money in, then angel funding, then venture funding. Eventually Allscripts acquired ECIN in 2007.

John and Phil were the idea guys, physicians at the core—
Glen and I thought that to do it right, we couldn't just incubate it in the Chicago market only, when the healthcare problem we were trying to solve was nationwide.

You created a way to find nursing homes via an online version of the Yellow Pages.
The idea was to take a hospital case manager off the phone and give them a database they could search for a patient's extended care.

Sounds like a fine idea.
The problem was that it wasn't a business efficiency tool. It added a step to the process. It was more like, "Do everything you always did. Now search this database, find data and then call."

Not so good.
The great idea was to automate a manual process—to make it efficient so people would want to use it in place of what they used to do.

A good problem to take on, because those patients had to move somewhere—to rehab or home care or a nursing home.
These particular patients are about 100 percent of a hospital's length-of-stay problem. If a patient just goes home, it ends. But when these patients

You've got to have a circle of trust. Angels invest in 10 different companies hoping one, two or three make a hit. VC funds are in 10 different investments hoping one, two or three hit. Board members typically serve on 10 different boards hoping one, two or three hit. You have to separate out who's just playing the field, making some bets. How do you define your circle of trust? Ask yourself who's going to be with you on the cloudiest, darkest days.

Jeff Surges

Jeff Surges

leave the hospital to go to a nursing home, there's a new payer, a new reimbursement.

You and Glen Tullman were first at Enterprise Systems, which Glen took public and later sold to HBOC for $235 million. Big wins, but not well known.
I think here in the Midwest there's a tremendous amount of modesty. When I meet with guys on Sandhill Road in Northern California, they are out on the PR trail long before a revenue stream is invented. We are the total opposite.

Opposite and—
There's also a Midwest mentality, which is to bet on the jockey, not on the horse. I really think that's Chicago. There is a community of

successful entrepreneurs here. And when it's done right, you get the Mike Holmgren effect. When he coached the Packers to that Super Bowl, he had 11 assistants. Nine of them are NFL coaches today.

Any advice for entrepreneurs?
You've got to have a circle of trust. Angels invest in 10 different companies hoping one, two or three make a hit. VC funds are in 10 different investments hoping one, two or three hit. Board members typically serve on 10 different boards hoping one, two or three hit. You have to separate out who's just playing the field, making some bets. How do you define your circle of trust? Ask yourself who's going to be with you on the cloudiest, darkest days.

Do you mean the management team or the investors?
The investors are part of the team.

Well—
Every day at ECIN the number one question from investors was, "Are you committed to this, Jeff? Are you and your team committed to it?" My response was, "I'm sticking this out 'til the end even if it costs me a future opportunity. I'm born and raised in Chicago and I don't want to leave here. I'm going to make good for you on this because I'm coming back for another one." That was my mantra the whole time.

Your ambition wasn't that it was a billion-dollar opportunity.
It wasn't a grand slam, but it was pretty good for a first-time

entrepreneur with a business that sputtered initially. I repotted the soil, grew it, and ultimately sold it for close to $100 million.

You went from running your own show to being a part of Allscripts, with thousands of employees.
I think I can be just as entrepreneurial here. There are more toys in the sandbox and I run a nice, big business unit. But I'm taking a breather from having a board of directors, keeping investors happy, and meeting with lawyers and auditors. I read three to four plans a month and give commentary back to friends.

Did you have a mentor?
Glen Tullman, ever since I first interviewed with him. And I reach out

Making money doesn't make you better or smarter, but it does give you choices.

Mark Tebbe

Mark Tebbe

to a couple of other mentors who help teach me. I go in with questions and get sound advice.

Lante Corporation, Answers.com (ANSW) Illinois

Lante had its IPO in 2000, but how did you come to start it in 1984?
I worked for Arthur Andersen & Co. after college, but I was told I couldn't get promoted working on microcomputers. Andersen said they only saw value in minicomputers and mainframes, so I quit because I saw the value of the microcomputer in business.

Ah, impetuous youth. You were young.
I was 23. And I thought I would just do consulting for a while. One thing led to another, so I started hiring part-time people.

Well, did you have—
No. I quit and had nothing in terms of clients or anything.

It sounds like you just had passion driving you.
I really liked how the use of desktop microcomputers could change computing in businesses. I started calling every Chicago corporation, finding out what their plans for microcomputers were, and seeing if there was a project I could do for them.

That's the way to learn!
I learned that what started as Tebbe and Associates quickly became T&A, which is not a good reference for a business. And I looked like I was 18. When I went to meet with people, all I ever heard about was what their kids

were doing in high school or college because they assumed I was the same age as their kids.

Your first strategic problem. What did you do?
I started working with a guy named Andy Langer, who had left Andersen to work on a software program. We became Langer, Tebbe and Associates, which eventually became Lante. He was 38.

He was the gray hair. Did his years help?
Don't underestimate the value of experience. He would sit back and say, "Have you thought about this, have you thought about that?" He was always looking at not just what happened, but why it happened.

You have two eyes, two ears, and one mouth. If you want to be successful, use them in that proportion. Entrepreneurs overemphasize what they are talking about, forget to listen, forget to look.

Mark Tebbe

Mark Tebbe

Sales went from zero to $76 million. That's pretty good for a guy who started dialing for consulting projects.
Yes, but a lot happened in between. The early days were cold-calling for project opportunities during the day and working on those projects at night. Eventually we grew a great team to both sell and work, but I still worked some nights.

You went public in February of 2000, raising $80 million for the company right under the wire, before the market collapsed. Was that just luck or did you know something was coming?
Entirely lucky timing.

So you're sitting there with all that cash and now the market completely tanks. It's like you're in the life raft and everything's okay but—
Sure, we had cash, but at that point we had a thousand employees and nothing for them to do because no one was spending money on IT services. We ended up doing layoffs and closed our Singapore and India offices.

You hired a CEO before the IPO. Why?
I woke up every morning seven days a week thinking about what proposals we had to get out, what contracts had to get signed, what deliverables we had, and who owed us money. After my divorce in 1997, I wanted to work less so I could spend more time with my two kids. I realized that no amount of money could buy back time with them as they were growing up.

How did you grow the company? Did you have venture investors?
Lante grew entirely out of cash flow, but when I made the decision to become a more involved parent (and I owned 97 percent of the stock), I brought in outside investors as well as private equity money. But that was 15 years after I started the company.

Positive cash flow is a good thing.
Yes, but in the early years, every time I ran payroll, I had to look to make sure I had enough money in the bank. Sometimes I needed to make up the difference with my credit card.

That was early on. Then you became the go-to Internet development firm.
We were very fortunate to be one of the early developers of the web. We wrote Dell.com, AmericanExpress.com, Schwab.com, and Microsoft.com. We also wrote many of the early transactional web sites, such as epicurious.com, espn.com, expedia.com, and americanairlines.com (now aa.com).

What put you in that fortunate position?
We were always on the cutting edge of new technology from Microsoft, Netscape, Lotus, and IBM. We were focused on client server systems and microcomputer-based applications, so the Internet was a natural extension of that.

You are the only person I know who can say he has long-standing friendships with both Bill Gates and Michael Dell.
When I met Bill Gates, he had a

One of the best things I ever did in my business was to give employees lots of room to do what they wanted to do.

Mark Tebbe

company with less than 20 employees and I was a high-school kid. And I've known Michael since he had six employees. I've been able to retain my friendships with both because I've never exploited my relationship with them—and never will.

Did you buy Microsoft stock at the opening?
I still have my original "Friends and Family" shares—a thousand shares at $19 a share—before many splits.

Which brings us to Lante's stock. It peaked at $87½ and then dropped to 55 cents. I know people asked you at the time how you felt.
At the high point, my personal holding was worth about $1.25 billion, but I knew it couldn't last. I ended up losing 99.7 percent of my net worth because,

again, paper went up, paper went down. We sold the company for $1.10 a share.

Those are tough decisions.
I knew my number.

What do you mean, your "number"?
Everybody has a number. It's the amount of money you could live on for the rest of your life in a lifestyle that you desire and not have to worry about earning money in a business. For me, my stock cost was less than half a cent a share. We had been trading before the offer for below cash value. SBI paid twice what the stock was worth. It was a good deal for everybody given the challenging environment for tech stocks.

Thus fortunes are made. Congratulations.
Maybe not a "fortune" but enough to allow my family and me a very comfortable lifestyle. I still made a lot more money than I ever thought I'd make in my life.

To be at peace with that is not easy.
The problem for most people is that as soon as they get close to their number, it creeps. They don't want to just go on vacation to Hawaii, they want to stay at the Four Seasons, then at a private home, and soon after, at their own home. And then it's not just flying first class on United Airlines, they want a private jet. I ran a business for 20 years within a budget. I can definitely live within a budget.

Then came Answers.com. How did you think that up?
One of my Lante board members was Mort Meyerson, vice chairman of EDS. We met for dinner with a friend in Israel who wanted to buy a patent and was thinking of starting a company. Mort said, "You know what? I think good ideas are worth a million dollars. Mark and I are gonna buy 30 percent of your good idea for $300,000 and Mark's gonna be on the board." That became GuruNet and then Answers.com.

Your timing was good.
It's December 1998, and by the first quarter of 1999 we had a prototype. We raised $28 million for our software company.

Don't underestimate the value of perspiration for solving a crisis.

Mark Tebbe

Mark Tebbe

That started out as software?
Yes, software designed to work within a corporation. It could look on your PC screen to see what you were working on and quickly look up information within the company or on the web. But the software never took off.

Why not?
The lead venture capital investor wanted to shut the business down in 2004. We weren't going to let that happen. Shortly after that discussion, as I was helping my kids with their homework, I noticed that my son couldn't find relevant information when he was looking stuff up on the web. I thought there had to be a place where people could find information on a topic. Frankly, there wasn't one, so I

thought it would be worthwhile to use our remaining corporate assets to build one.

Great revelation over homework, but with dwindling resources what could you do?
We took a huge step forward when I found the domain name, Answers.com. It was held by a bankruptcy lawyer in Michigan and he was trying to sell it for $250,000. We ended up buying it for $80,000.

New name, new business model. Did it take off then?
Well, a couple things happened. Leveraging our development team in Israel, led by a Chicago-raised CTO, we wrote a prototype in a couple weeks and the actual site in about two months. Shortly after we launched

Answers.com, Walt Mossberg wrote an article about it in the Wall Street Journal. Traffic doubled in a week.

And then Google put you up on their results page?
We were very lucky. Right after launching Answers.com, a Google product manager fell in love with our information format and decided to put a definition link for search terms in the upper right corner of most Google search result pages.

I'm kind of speechless. That's way beyond luck.
We had this customized link to Answers.com for nearly five years, with no contract and just a handshake. But luck happens as a result of hard work in a very connected industry like technology.

In 2009 Google redesigned their results pages and they now point elsewhere.
At one point, that was a lot of our traffic. When the link was removed in December 2009, it was less than five percent.

And then you completed a reverse merger into a public shell. That's not easy.
We needed the currency to convert out some of the VCs who didn't want to remain investors.

Why not a regular IPO?
It cost too much and we didn't have any money. It was kind of a dicey public market at that time in technology. The reverse merger gave us a way to get public without a lot of cost.

Take your revenues, and cut them in half. Take your costs and double them. Now you have a realistic business plan!

— Mark Tebbe.

Glen Tullman

Extended Care Information Network
Illinois

What's the most important quality a company founder should have?
Honesty. Running a business is no different than running your life. I think founders should be honest in their dealings and in their assessments. Look at the facts because facts don't lie.

What facts?
Believe in what you're doing, but keep an eye on what your customers and the markets are telling you. Let's say you're in a service business and you lose nine out of every 10 pitches. You won't win if you're only getting 10 percent. Long term you'll waste so much money trying to get the other nine, you'll never make money off the one you do get. You try to explain why: "Oh, well, they just don't get it." What the founder or CEO has to understand

is that it's not the customer. You didn't solve the problem for them in a cost-effective manner. You didn't mitigate their risk. You have to take a step back and ask the hard questions of why something didn't occur along the way.

But sometimes even knowing cold hard facts isn't enough.
Take Answers.com, for example. We knew we overly depended on search engine optimization from the day we founded the company. We put it as a risk factor, but sometimes forgot how important it was to us—until the day Google changed their algorithm and suddenly some of our traffic disappeared. Then we got it. We got slapped upside the head with the reality.

You grew up in a town of 200 people and moved to Chicago. Wouldn't California have been easier?
I like Chicago. I think people here tend to downplay a little bit of what they've accomplished because it's the right thing to do. You end up with longer-lasting friendships. I'm not even a rounding error in Michael Dell's net worth, but he's been there for me and I was there for him. Hey, you and I—our business paths crossed only a little bit when you were on the board of High Beam, and before that with your magazines. But, you know? We're friends. Anything you need.

Thank you, Mark.
Right back at ya.

Social anthropology isn't a popular way into a career leading technology companies.
I went to Bucknell University and I lived with the Amish. I was fascinated with their culture and even wrote my honors thesis about my experience. Then I went to Oxford for my diploma in social anthropology, which stemmed from my original research on the Amish.

Like the movie *Witness* without the murder?
It's a long story. Short version is, I worked on a professor's farm planting blueberry bushes to help pay for school. When he had a heart attack,

When you're running a smaller company, personal interaction, which is what entrepreneurs are known for, works. It's the relationships and the one-on-one work together. The sacrifices, the disappointments, and, of course, the wins. The larger the company gets, you have to substitute culture and stories for that personal interaction. You want people who know and think like you—who 'get' the culture—and you have to sculpt those people in a way, and it only happens under fire. You can never do it without tension, pressure, and stress.

Glen Tullman

Glen Tullman

his wife called and asked for help. The farm was snowed in, so the first task was to shovel by hand the snow from a mile-and-a-half-long driveway. When I reached the top, I saw a bunch of farm animals. They saw me too, and that's when we realized that this kid from New Jersey didn't know what to do. Then I heard this clickety-clack and saw a carriage. It was the Amish neighbors who had come to help. They milked the cows and then invited me back to eat with them. It was like Star Trek, being beamed back 100 years with no electricity and no connection to the outside world. That's how I ended up writing about the Amish.

You learned business at your brother Howard's start-up, Certified Collateral Corporation (see Howard *A. Tullman, page 152*), then went on to lead Enterprise Systems, and now Allscripts. What do you think drives an entrepreneur?
Part of the reason you're successful is you're hungry. Most entrepreneurs had something that was dysfunctional in their background—either their parents were divorced, they were poor, or they had a hardship of some kind. They almost always have something to prove.

There is a reason why we are not all working for IBM.
Exactly. I think it was Bobby Knight who said, "I would never recruit a kid with grass on his front lawn," because when you're diving for a basketball on asphalt, you have to really want that ball.

You're an American entrepreneur with big operations in India. How does that work?
We have employees in India, and I compare them to kids here. They want what we have and they're willing to do anything to get it. People say you go to India because it costs less. It might have been why you went, but you stay because the employees work harder and are getting smarter, especially in math and science. And they are more appreciative of the jobs. They're driven in a way that you can't teach. American kids have to realize that the world is getting more competitive.

We talk a lot about how inspiring entrepreneurs can be. You inspired one of your company directors to make a movie?

I took one of Allscript's directors, Robert Compton, for his first visit to India and he became fascinated with the Indian education system. We took a lot of photos and videos, visited schools, and learned the culture. He later went back to India and spent $700,000 on a documentary called *Two Million Minutes*. Our visit led to a new career for Bob and appearances on *Good Morning America*. He said to me once, "You told me you were taking me on a trip. You changed my life."

Bob Compton had previously recruited you to Enterprise Systems. His documentary, *Two Million Minutes*, what does that refer to?
Two million minutes is the amount of time kids spend in high school. Compton's premise is that how that

You learn to develop a soft shell but a very hard core. You have to be able to take those hits and survive them. To be resilient. If you make it through, you're unbelievably strong.

Glen Tullman

time is spent will determine the success of a country in 10 years. In the documentary, he compares two top-notch kids in each of three countries: the United States, India, and China.

The conclusion is that we're gonna get our clocks cleaned here?
Well, that's what's happening now. It's about being hungry; it's about this whole entrepreneurial drive their kids have. Bob's like Edward Deming, who tried to warn US auto manufacturers of an impending crisis if they didn't act, but like Deming, he's being ignored. We should listen to him. Now he's doing the same with his latest book, *Win in China*, which speaks to how China puts more value on entrepreneurs than we do.

How do you build a great company?
When you're running a smaller company, personal interaction, which is what entrepreneurs are known for, works. It's the relationships and the one-on-one work together. The sacrifices, the disappointments, and, of course, the wins. The larger the company gets, and we're now close to 3,000 people, you have to substitute culture and stories for that personal interaction. You want people who know and think like you—who "get" the culture—and you have to sculpt those people in a way, and it only happens under fire. You can never do it without tension, pressure, and stress.

Jeff Surges (see *Jeff Surges*, page 141) told us you were his mentor. Did you have a mentor?
I'm honored to be considered Jeff's mentor. I had a great mentor during my time in the government—Howard Messner. Howard was the highest-ranking civil servant when I worked for both the Carter and Reagan administrations. One day Howard asked me, "Glen, can you do me a favor?" I said, "Howard, whatever you need." He asked me to deliver a pizza to a guy named David Stockman, but it was a setup. I delivered the pizza, and David said, "You gonna have a slice with us?" "Sure," I said. The next question was, "Look, we're buried here, can you give us a hand? I'll cover for you with Howard." I didn't leave the office for two days.

Why start in government only to end up an entrepreneur?
I applied for a Truman fellowship because I didn't have a lot of money to pay for college. I wrote an essay about cutting back government, not knowing that the Truman fellowship is judged by government officials. The judges asked me how I knew to make cuts without having worked in government. I ended up not getting the Truman fellowship, but I got an interview with Howard Messner.

What stands out about the mentoring you received?
Both Howard Messner and my older brother Howard Tullman, another key mentor, were unbelievably honest. The only way you really grow is if someone tells you where you have flat spots. And that's tough.

Being an entrepreneur has everything to do with putting every second and every ounce of energy into building your business. No venture guy will ever invest in your business if you say your life is 'in balance.'

Glen Tullman

Glen Tullman

And you are brutally honest with your own teams.
I learned from my brother Howard that when you're growing a company and somebody does something wrong, you can correct him or her individually and then one person learns that lesson. Or you can send an e-mail to the whole company and the whole company learns that lesson. It's a much faster way to learn, but it's very painful for that individual. To survive in that environment, you have to develop a soft shell but a very hard core. You have to be able to take those hits and survive them. If you make it through, you're unbelievably strong.

Can entrepreneurs have balanced lives?
Being an entrepreneur isn't for everybody. It has nothing to do with balance. It has everything to do with putting every second and every ounce of energy into building your business. No venture guy will ever invest in your business if you say your life is "in balance." So the answer is, you try. Billie Jean King said, "No one changes the world who isn't obsessed." I think she had it right.

It sounds like a mixed blessing.
Be careful what you wish for if you think you want to be an entrepreneur. There are good things about it— incredible highs—but there are also challenges, sacrifices, and tough choices you have to make.

It's not only rare to find champion company founders, but two brothers in the same family. Were you competitive?

Yes, hyper-competitive. When Howard and I used to run together, if one of us was breathing hard the other would speed up. We even compete cutting turkey at Thanksgiving. But that's because we know that's how you get better. My mother always promoted high standards and was honest when you didn't achieve them. We knew how to get approval from her and from my dad: be the best.

The expression, "it's just business, it's not personal," doesn't work for you, does it?
Every time you lose, a little piece of you dies, and every time you win, you rebuild that. It's all personal. I was just speaking with our sales team about it. When you're out there selling and somebody buys from someone else,

they're saying, "You suck and your product sucks." And if you take that to the next extreme, "I don't want your kids to be fed." Because guess what? People lose their jobs when they don't sell. That's what they're saying to you—this is the most personal thing somebody could say to you. And the reason entrepreneurs succeed is because it is so personal.

Vince Lombardi did not actually say, "Winning is everything." He said, "The will to prepare to win is everything." Do you agree with that?
Absolutely. This reminds me of an incredible guy named Kevin Carroll, who rose from poverty to become chief energizer at Nike. He talks about the "lonely work," that's the work that you do when no one's looking.

I used to fall in love with everyone I interviewed and I'd say, 'We can make anybody successful' or 'We can find a job for any talented person.' And that's just completely wrong and a really bad idea.

Howard A. Tullman

The hours that winners spend after everyone else has gone home. In our family, it was clear that you might not win, but it would never be because someone outworked you or was more committed. Never!

How do you do that as CEO at Allscripts?
We had a conference at the Trump Tower recently and we gave everybody a bottle of Dling water, which cost us $25 per bottle. That could only happen at Trump. A guy wrote and thanked us and said it was a fun touch. But he said he brought it home and his wife took it. So I sent him a second one and I wrote, "Listen, here's a second bottle. Do not show this to your wife." He wrote me back, "The idea that the CEO would take the time to write personally means the world to me and I've told so many people in my company. That's what we aspire to." That little touch, that's the lonely work, the extra hours that go into differentiating yourself and your company. But that time isn't free. It's a choice.

What could be done to help entrepreneurs succeed in the heartland?
Somebody ought to build a technology triangle, just like they did in North Carolina. That was somebody's vision! This is a fine place to do business and to recruit people, but we haven't maximized our advantages to help entrepreneurs. We have some great academic institutions. We could be a powerhouse if we created kind of a consortium of learning.

Knowing how you are inspired—that's inspiring. Your high school football experience was an enduring lesson?
All of the varsity players at my high school in New Providence coached Pop Warner football, so the average Pop Warner team ended up with many high school senior coaches. Every position had a coach. Kids who otherwise would have been ignored got first-class attention and stayed with the program longer because they had somebody rooting for them and coaching them. That led to a much wider selection and a whole farm system. Plus, those kids and their parents—sometimes a few thousand people—came to watch the games on Sundays, which meant the program was well funded. So, the coaches understood developing a program and that led to winning ... a lot. We were undefeated as seniors and that taught me that if you want it bad enough, anything or any dream is possible.

A lot of people wait for a perfect solution to come along and never get their businesses going. The idea of just getting going and assuming that the right tools, the right systems, and the right people will come along is crucial to the entrepreneurial process.

Howard A. Tullman

Howard A. Tullman

Certified Collateral Corporation (CCC), Original Research II Kendall College, Experiencia, Tribeca Flashpoint Media Arts Academy, The Cobalt Group, Tunes.com
Illinois

You, Scott Jones, and Mahendra Vora are prolific founders. What drives you, Howard?
I've been privileged to be able to pursue so many exciting ideas and create so many different companies. I'd say the greatest driver and the most satisfaction both come from the same idea. I love to build places where people are excited about what they're doing and have a chance to learn, grow, and really create their futures through their own talent and hard work.

CCC was a home run.
I practiced law for 10 years and retired in 1980 to start CCC, which is now about 30 years old. It's a large public company that provides information to the automobile and insurance industries. I took it public in 1983 and sold it in 1987 for $100 million, which was real money back then.

Then you had more home runs.
Well, in the mid-'90s, we launched most of the music sites for the web, including Rollingstone.com, TheSource.com, DownBeatJazz.com, and a little site called Tunes.com. We sold Tunes.com to eMusic for $136 million. I had a great little computer game development company called Imagination Pilots, which is ultimately one of the reasons I started Tribeca Flashpoint Media Arts Academy. And before and after that I've had another four or five businesses and done a couple of turnarounds.

What I find fascinating is that from your self-taught training as a company founder, you took on an underperforming, money-losing college as your next start-up.
Kendall wasn't my first big turnaround. I did a major restructuring in Atlanta and saved maybe a thousand jobs and then sold the business to Reynolds & Reynolds after six months. So I had some practice in the trenches, but Kendall was completely insolvent when I stepped in. We moved the college from Evanston after 75 years there to a brand-new, state-of-the-art culinary facility in downtown Chicago and then sold it about a year later for a whole lot of money to Laureate Education, which is a large, public education corporation.

How's a turnaround different from a start-up?
When you do turnarounds, the conversations are all about problems rather than futures. You're always short on time and money and you've got to find creative and encouraging ways to deliver difficult and unpleasant messages. And, above all, you've got to get everyone to face the facts. It's the rule of frogs: If you've got to eat a bunch of frogs, start with the biggest one first.

The name of the game is not to try to be right all the time. It's to win. You win by always moving forward, making your share of mistakes, and learning from them as you go along.

Howard A. Tullman

It's just wild that a college could be an entrepreneurial success story. What was the challenge at Kendall?

At Kendall, apart from being broke, we had what we called the "lipstick on a pig" problem. When I got there everyone told me, "We need new marketing materials." And I said, "The school sucks. Why would you want more people to come to a school that sucks? Let's fix the school first and then we'll get really good marketing materials." We had a picture of a pig with lipstick on it as a reminder not to spend marketing dollars until there was a real story to tell. The trick and the challenge were to focus on real issues, real solutions, and real change rather than on cosmetic attempts to hide the problems.

And then you launched Experiencia. And then Flashpoint.

Experiencia trained fifth- and sixth-graders to be entrepreneurs and scientists. In Chicago alone, we trained about 20,000 public school students and really changed their lives in important ways. Then in 2007 we started a school right next to city hall called Tribeca Flashpoint Media Arts Academy, a two-year, high-end vocational college for the digital media arts, and it's been a huge success already.

Why such passion about education?

It came from just being disgusted at what a crappy job we're doing building the future for education. It makes me sick when I hear students say that the most boring place they go every day is school. I just don't think it has to be that way.

How can business improve the education system?

The biggest problem is that educators build and work in narrow silos instead of working collaboratively across disciplines. It's all about turf wars and tenure. Schools get stuck with non-technical faculty who don't want to change or further their education. So if you're trying to teach today's workflows or collaborative development across multiple disciplines, the traditional schools just aren't equipped to do that and, frankly, don't want to. The only real change will come from new businesses like Tribeca Flashpoint that are willing to start from scratch and build the systems that will work for tomorrow.

Do you need to be on a coast to succeed?

We're better positioned here because people are more stable and more likely to stay with you. People have one foot out the door in New York and Silicon Valley. The week after you start a new business, half the people in those places are wondering when they can leave and start their own clone. One of the reasons Microsoft succeeded is that Redmond was just far enough away from the Valley so that VC funds couldn't raid it every single day and suck off all the talent for other start-ups. Microsoft managed to keep the main team together for a long, long time.

CEOs shouldn't do any hiring. They just love to talk too much. Thirty seconds into any interview, the CEO is selling a candidate on the company instead of finding out about that person's skill sets or anything else. When they get done, the CEO says, 'I really like that person,' but couldn't tell you a thing about him. What actually happened is that he talked to a good listener who enjoyed his spiel.

Howard A. Tullman

Howard A. Tullman

Your companies have created around 6,000 jobs. Where do you recruit?
We go wherever we can find young people who actually want to work and who appreciate the value of hard work and consider it a virtue. It's just a part of their makeup. A great work ethic is really critical in the early years of a business. It's not a straight line to anywhere. It's a lot of ups and downs. You've got to have people who take their satisfaction from achievement and results, not from looking for quick kills and a desire to make tons of money.

What is the secret element you bring to your businesses?
One of the main tricks is to find industries that are oligopolistic. If you do that, you discover that there are only a few customers and it doesn't

matter what you spend to effectively get your company's story in front of those customers.

This is the complete opposite of entrepreneurs always trying to find the most massive market.
Well, my focus has always been on creating simple process improvements that solve big money problems in industries that have certain structural characteristics. So, in insurance, there are only 12 insurance companies that matter; in automotive, there are only about six increasingly shrinking businesses that matter. It's just math.

How important is marketing in that equation?
It's so expensive now to make noise out there. You have to find situations where the money you spend to reach

the real decision-makers is somehow manageable for a young, under-funded company as most start-ups are. In the auto business, for example, when we started CCC, we couldn't afford to make the kind of brochure these guys saw every single day in their business. If you spent less than a trillion dollars, they would say, "these are crap" and they would throw them away. But, if you only had to make 25 great-looking selling kits, even by hand, you could afford to spend a fortune on each one and they'd look great. This approach was an early key to our credibility with some very conservative customers.

So one secret is to find opportunities in industries structured in a certain way. What's another characteristic of the kinds of businesses you like?

The only kinds of businesses I'm ever really interested in are those that provide services or products that either improve productivity, save time, or reduce costs. If they don't do one of those things fairly convincingly, then I don't think that ultimately they're going to be successful.

And you're a pretty impatient investor, aren't you? That's the Howard Tullman doctrine of F*#!ed or Famous, right?
Well, I do have a whole separate strategy of venture investing. I'll spend any amount of money for six months, but after that point either you make the metrics or you forget it, because going sideways is something no company or investor can afford to do for very long. It's not just money. It's a question of

It's so expensive now to make marketing noise out there. You have to find situations where the money you spend to reach the real decision-makers is somehow manageable for a young, under-funded company as most start-ups are.

Howard A. Tullman

The hardest hire in a young company is the sales manager. That person is going to be the most hated person in the business because, to do his job right, he has to constantly fire the worst performers. That's totally inconsistent with the rest of the business culture.

Howard A. Tullman

opportunity costs as well. You either take your shot and make it, or you move on.

Give me an example of you as investor.
There's a company in Chicago that was marketing services to the real estate industry. I said, "Here's the deal. We'll give you this amount of money, but there are only 12 SMSAs (statistical geographic areas) in the whole country that are large enough to really matter. You either get the main real estate firms in four or five of those areas signed up in the next six months, or you don't get another penny. But if you do, you've got a business."

So many entrepreneurs don't get it right. What's the secret to success?
One secret is to start with what you

have. A lot of people wait for a perfect solution to come along and never get their businesses going. The idea of just getting going and assuming that the right tools, the right systems, and the right people will come along is crucial to the entrepreneurial process. If you don't understand that it's a completely iterative process, and that the name of the game is successive approximation, not postponed perfection, you can easily become paralyzed.

That's a good one. Any more secrets?
It's critical to avoid what I call "lawyer's disease." Lawyers generally aren't great entrepreneurs because they are totally consumed by the need to be right all the time. The name of the game is not to try to be right all the

time. It's to win. You win by always moving forward, making your share of mistakes, and learning from them as you go along.

Are there predictable tough times, like when a start-up is most vulnerable?
At exactly the point where you have to hire your first grownup, you're vulnerable.

What do you mean by "grownup"?
Someone who is added laterally to the organization who wasn't there from the start, but who's crucial to going forward. Typically, this is someone with no original equity and who's got a comp package much different from the young people who've been working like dogs since the beginning. That's the point where your original people

become somewhat vulnerable. They're thinking, you're bringing in these people when you told us that we four guys were always going to each own 25 percent of the company. You have this horrible problem of explaining that growing a business takes both kinds of employees. It takes some grownups who will get paid a lot of money, but whose equity is never going to be worth that of the original young tigers. Of course, you have to also tell them that if the company doesn't build the team it needs to grow, they'll end up with a large piece of a non-existent pie.

What's the toughest challenge as a CEO—hiring?
I don't think CEOs should do any hiring at all.

A big mistake entrepreneurs make is trying to hire too many people like themselves. A successful business needs a whole bunch of different people with different skills. You have to make room for all of them, and a bunch of them aren't going to look remotely like you because, among other things, they're not lunatics.

Howard A. Tullman

Howard A. Tullman

That goes against the entrepreneur-does-it-all mentality, doesn't it?
The CEO is fundamentally a very busy person, typically a great sales guy and fundraiser, but rarely a good listener. CEOs shouldn't do any hiring. They just love to talk too much. Thirty seconds into any interview, the CEO is selling a candidate on the company instead of finding out about that person's skill sets or anything else. When they get done, the CEO says, "I really like that person," but couldn't tell you a thing about him. What actually happened is that he talked to a good listener who enjoyed his spiel. I was even worse. I used to fall in love with everyone I interviewed and I'd say, "We can make anybody successful" or "We can find a job for any talented person." And that's just completely wrong and a really bad

idea. HR people should figure out job descriptions. God forbid I should ever do that.

More mistakes to be avoided?
A big mistake entrepreneurs make is trying to hire too many people like themselves. You need to understand early on that a successful business needs a whole bunch of different people with different skills. You have to make room for all of them, and a bunch of them aren't going to look remotely like you because, among other things, they're not lunatics.

Reserve the lunacy for the founder?
Well, it takes a few loonies to launch a great company and make it successful. But many good, talented people just want a job and the company ultimately

needs them to grow. We can't all be crusaders or all be insane.

It's like a mix of the sane and the insane.
We have actually fired people because we thought they weren't neurotic enough. In the early stages of a company, it's really important to communicate a sense of urgency to the rest of the team. Sometimes that's hard to do if you're too well adjusted.

You're actually serious. What's the hardest position to fill?
The hardest hire in a young company is the sales manager. That person is going to be the most hated person in the business because, to do his job right, he has to constantly fire the worst performers. That's totally

inconsistent with the rest of the business culture.

Why? Isn't this the way companies keep getting better? Raising the bar all the time?
Yes, it is. But in a start-up, you spend all this time talking about a familial organization. Meanwhile, a good sales manager is firing 10 percent of the sales staff every month because they're not performing—but it's built into the job. It's especially hard to find people like this because they're not necessarily people we particularly like. Some might say, "Oh, this guy is bad because he runs a boiler room." Well, guess what? That's what sales is.

High-tech ventures fail 93 percent of the time because they don't know where their money goes. They don't train employees to make decisions like they make at home. Employees might buy a $20 item at Macy's and return it six times until they are happy with it, but at work they'll spend $20,000 for something that doesn't work and they won't fight for it. So how do you create a culture where you aren't cheap, but you are frugal? That's frugality with class.

Mahendra Vora

Mahendra Vora

It sounds gut wrenching.
That's why it's always the hardest hire—to find somebody tough enough to do it and keep doing it. Entrepreneurs are so optimistic they believe in everybody. They're very resistant to getting rid of non-performers. They think they can change them. They're usually wrong and it takes a special person to tell them that.

InterComputer Communications, Pioneer Systems, SecureIT, Intelliseek, Vinimaya, Marshal8e6, Lucrum, Vora Technology Park, iCall, Vora Tech Park II, Vora Data Centers, Bluespring Software, dbaDIRECT, Ascendum, Essentio, TalentNow, Zakta Ohio

You were on a PhD track after receiving your masters degree in computer science from the University of Michigan. What got you started launching companies?
A friend of mine was starting a company in Cincinnati called Intercomputer Communications

Corporation, so I joined him. I got a feeling of entrepreneurship and a little bit of equity. I come from a family that is very entrepreneurial—at least the past seven generations have owned their own businesses. They basically believe that even if you make half as much money, you should work for yourself. You should create jobs and define your own destiny.

That's a common theme for founders.
The whole purpose of coming to the US and finishing my education was to start my own company.

Luckily you and your co-founders did well. ICC grew from four to 250 employees and $25 million in revenue in five years.

We built it, sold it to Digital Communications Associates, now part of Attachmate, and made some money. I took every penny except $1,000 and invested in my second company, Pioneer Systems. I built that and sold it for a few million dollars to Unisys, and then I used about 70 percent of that money to build SecureIT and Intelliseek, and then the fifth, sixth, and seventh companies.

Pioneer was your first win, but Intelliseek was a $100 million winner, selling to ACNielsen.
We sold half at one price, and then a year later we sold the other half at the higher price.

How did SecureIT get started?
Right after selling Pioneer Systems, my partner started SecureIT and I

Pioneer, Intelliseek, and Ascendum worked because of the five people at the top. It's not that the other people are not important, but those five make sure there are 25 people like them reporting to them, and those 25 make sure there are 125 underneath them like that.

Mahendra Vora

Mahendra Vora

started Intelliseek. We both made our first million dollars-plus from Pioneer Systems and decided to hedge our bets and share minority positions in each other's companies. He took the lead in SecureIT and I led Intelliseek.

SecureIT was sold to VeriSign after just two years. Then you focused on Intelliseek, which eventually employed 100 people. What does the company do?
Intelliseek started as a search engine called BullsEye and eventually became a search engine for brand management. Initially, we missed the mark big time because nobody wanted to download a 6MB desktop application, especially with slow speed in those days. We had 3 million users and only $20,000 a month in revenue.

Not a significant revenue model?
We could not charge for the product because search was supposed to be free.

What did you do?
We changed our product offering and business models a few times—until we became successful. We made a server version that would search all enterprise documents, search engines, and network drives, pulling information from multiple sources. That was called Enterprise Search Server. Despite some success in the government sector, we could not charge sufficient dollars. We added a text mining engine extracting sentiment, and started looking at blogs and all that to add some more value.

How did that go?
That is how we got it right. One of the automotive giants had a huge problem with one of its suppliers. They wanted to find out from the Internet what people were saying about the company. We collected unstructured data—millions of postings about what people were saying about a brand, product, or challenge on the Internet—in real-time and developed a brand dashboard.

Great phrase, a brand dashboard.
Another company in Cincinnati had raised $31 million to do the same thing—they called it BrandPulse—but they had no text-mining technology or sales execution capability. We had great technology and execution capabilities with multiple start-up experience, but no marketing. They

were awesome marketing people—some of the best I have ever worked with—Harvard grads who had worked for P&G. They had $10 million left. I was running out of money.

A marriage made in heaven.
Definitely a marriage made in heaven. We took our technology and put it under their product name and sold it to car companies. We were monitoring real-time consumer sentiment on major makes and models. Every month these giant automotive companies would get a report that said, last month there were this many conversations about you on the Internet, on this many blogs, and in this many chat rooms, and this percentage of the people talked about price, body style, service, or dealership. We started extracting

Good entrepreneurs develop 60 percent of their vision in a product, put that product in the hands of their customers, and let customers help them with the remaining 40 percent, especially if the first few are trusted customers.

Mahendra Vora

You want to look for people with ego in business. The question is, what do they have ego about? If they have ego about competition and winning, that's great. If their ego is about themselves only and you cannot tell them anything to improve upon, that's wrong.

Mahendra Vora

market intelligence on any given brand and people just couldn't believe that we could deliver it for $5,000 a month.

And it was automated.
They were spending more money on focus groups with canned questions, and we were giving them unsolicited, real-time, quantified message content for a fraction of the cost.

It's a great conclusion but it couldn't have been easy along the way.
From 1998 to 2006, I went out of business at least seven times.

You went out of business?
My definition of going out of business is no money for payroll, no bridge funding, and VCs not ready to invest more—essentially running out of time to be successful with my vision.

You missed payroll?
I have never delayed or missed payroll in my life.

How did you get by?
One time when I had no money for payroll, the VCs gave us a million-dollar line of credit as a bridge, but they did not allow me to pull it because they had lost confidence in the company. So for three-and-a-half months, I made payroll from my personal savings account.

You originally funded the company with $2 million from the sale of Pioneer, and then raised $6 million from VC funds. Any advice on hiring?
I have a strong belief that A-players hire A-players, B-players hire C-players, and C-players hire F-players.

Your first few hires will have a lot to do with the eventual success of your venture.

Define an A player.
When you're looking for the best people, you have to look at effort, attitude, and values, and then skills, expertise, and experience. They are all important, but the first three are more critical.

Why?
You ask yourself: Can I rely on them? Can I trust them? Do they trust me? Do we share the same vision? Believe in the same cause? Is there a brotherhood or sisterhood or family kind of environment, but still with the utmost focus on professionalism? It's a culture, like when you tell people it's time to go home and they say, "No,

no, no. I gotta get this done." When my developers were working day and night and I couldn't help them, I didn't go home. I stayed and made coffee.

Anything to support them.
Whatever it took. I went and got pizza. I mean, I made sure I worked at least as hard as they did. I was not at a golf course. I just worked alongside my people and got into their hearts. I made sure they knew exactly what our agenda was, what our challenges were.

Everyone's commitment was the key?
Pioneer, Intelliseek, and Ascendum worked because of the five or six people at the top. It's not that the other people are not important, but those five make sure there are 25 people like

You have to have humility with confidence. Nobody wants to work with people who are difficult, but if you're a pushover, it does not work. You have to decide when to show your two percent side, your tough side, and not show it more than two percent of the time.

Mahendra Vora

Mahendra Vora

them reporting to them, and those 25 make sure there are 125 underneath them like that.

That's inspiring.
These people were so committed and caring. They took feedback and had no ego when it came to personal improvement. You want to look for people with ego in business. You don't want egoless people. The question is, what do they have ego about? If they have ego about competition and winning, that's great. If their ego is all about themselves, such that you cannot tell them anything to improve upon, that's wrong. So we had a great fight with the outside world but the enemy was not us.

But as organizations grow, people start protecting their turf.
The best way to fight politics is to not understand it.

Not understand it—
You never acknowledge it. Whatever it is, let's just talk about it. Pretty soon people stop telling you bad things about other people because they know as soon as they tell you, you will go and tell the other person and find out what is happening.

You have a book in the works.
Yes, about the way I have run my ventures. My first message is "aggression with ethics." I am not willing to admit that if you are ethical, you cannot be successful or if you're aggressive, you're dishonest, or that

being unethical—taking shortcuts, for example—is the only way to succeed.

Aggressive means unethical—that's just a stereotype?
I don't know who gave license to this stereotype, but I don't believe it. Second: "creativity with process discipline." If you try to create too much process, measuring, say, the number of times people go to the bathroom, that does not enhance productivity. But you can't say, "I'm an artist and I don't really care whether we make money or not," because it's not a charity. How do you foster creativity while maintaining processes?

I get it. What else?
My third premise is "frugality with class." High-tech ventures fail 93

percent of the time because they don't know where their money goes. They don't train employees to make decisions like they make at home. Employees might buy a $20 item at Macy's and return it six times until they are happy with it, but at work they'll spend $20,000 for something that doesn't work and they won't fight for it. How do you create a culture where you aren't cheap, but you are frugal?

That is a challenge lots of companies struggle with.
The next point is "humility with confidence." Nobody wants to work with people who are difficult, but if you're a pushover, it does not work. You have to decide when to show your two percent side, your tough side, and not show it more than two percent of the time.

In this or any economy what you are selling must be a painkiller. Not just vitamins.

Mahendra Vora

The two percent side?
The tough side!

Oh, that's good. We should have asked all the founders about the required percentage of toughness. Next time.
Next, and extremely important, is "quality with speed." A lot of people tell me if you want quality, it's going to take a very long time. But if you want something done quickly, it will lack quality. Who came up with this? I tell my employees, quality comes with the attitude in which you do everything—it's about putting your name on your work.

That's another great test of assumptions.
The world's best companies are known for this. Google gets it. They get the job done fast and still deliver quality. So does Apple.

How does the founder or leader fit into this? What makes for a great CEO?
My definition of a great CEO is someone who is able to make better and better decisions with less and less information in less and less time, and being more and more correct on those calls they make.

Mahendra, you started with one company, then launched two, three, then—I'll cut to the chase. I'm counting 17 start-ups.
Yes. I currently have 12 companies in my portfolio—all in IT infrastructure, IT services, and online and enterprise software products.

Any advice for company founders?
In this or any economy, what you are selling must be a painkiller. Not just vitamins. Entrepreneurs become narcissists. They fall in love with their product even if it doesn't really relieve much pain for their customers. Good entrepreneurs develop 60 percent of their vision, put the product in the hands of their customers, and let customers help them with the remaining 40 percent, especially if the first few are trusted customers.

Have you had a company fail?
Not yet and I hope it stays that way.

In your industry the success rate is seven percent, and you are accelerating the number of start-ups as you get older?
Brother, that's the only way to be, right? Because you don't know how much time is left.

How We Did It

In January of 2007, as I sat in the SeaTac airport in Seattle waiting to fly home to Chicago, I picked up a book of quotes and started wondering if anyone had ever published something similar with quotes from great company founders. I was curious about how they did it—how they hit their home runs—especially the great company founders around me in the Great Lakes states.

Then I thought about Napoleon Hill, author of *Think and Grow Rich*, who, with introductions from Andrew Carnegie, was able to interview 500 of the leading industrialists, inventors, and bankers of his day, including Henry Ford and Thomas Edison. I decided my goal would be to create a book of quotes that could be read in one sitting. In the attention-deficit world we live in, I couldn't picture a long narrative book but rather something that got right at the "secret sauce" in a founder's own words.

The first step was to research and identify the qualified, inspiring technology/innovative home run hitters. After 18 months' research, we ended up with an impressive list.

Things got interesting when I started thinking out loud about hosting all of these luminaries in one room at one time. At first, the idea sounded outrageous. How was I going to convince dozens of self-made millionaires and billionaires to show up and be recorded? These were all very private individuals who didn't know me or have reason to trust my intentions.

Thanks to help from friends around the region and in the venture capital community, the event was a success—about half the founders appearing in the book showed up that day, September 8, 2008. It was a rare moment, with champion entrepreneurs sitting elbow to elbow, engaged in discussions about their entrepreneurial starts as well as their highs and lows. We captured the occasion with photography and recorded each founder's comments. Essentially, the book was co-authored in 90 minutes.

Over the following two years, I interviewed many additional founders. So much "gold" was uncovered that a simple book of quotes didn't seem sufficient, so we designed a book within a book, to offer either a quick dose of inspiration with large quotes at the top of each page, or the more detailed Q&A from the interviews in smaller print at the bottom.

No matter how you read this book, whether it's just the quotes or the full Q&A, you'll find practical advice and encouragement from all the founders. That's the secret to how I got 45 people responsible for $41 billion in value to participate in this book—to take time to reflect, be thoughtful, and even write out their quotes by hand. We all simply shared the same goal of helping the next generation of entrepreneurs.

There's buried treasure hiding in plain sight here, inspiration that you can take and use right now. Can you find it? You can report on your findings, progress, and more at www.HowTheyDidItbook.com. Join us to share your own experiences and inspiration.

Acknowledgements

How They Did It could not have been created without the support, encouragement, and assistance of many people.

I tested out the idea for this book on some friends in the Chicago venture capital community. Ellen Carnahan, Tom Churchwell, Matt McCall, David Weinstein, Chris Girgenti, Jim O'Connor, Steve Vivian, and Michael Krauss instantly agreed to help. Surprisingly, no one looked at me like I was nuts to think that I could assemble these folks in one room. (I think they reserved their comments about my sanity for a later conversation among themselves.) In fact, they not only validated the idea, but Ellen, Tom, Matt, David, Chris, Jim, Steve and Michael then went to bat to encourage many founders to show up at the authoring event on September 8, 2008.

I also turned to my own mastermind group—Michael Welbel, Dean Klassman, Kris Keller, Chris Turley, Jim Rice, Keith Baker, Lewis Kaplan, Julie Audino, and Mark Ingraham—who helped me think through the idea.

To my sister Lisa Jordan, art director and designer, and marketing whiz Nancy Shaw: our routine visits to Potbelly's Sandwich Shop to discuss how to launch the project were not wasted. Your marketing and design help was the perfect beginning.

The idea became a reality once we began the two-year research process. To Dan Grant at William Blair and Joe Ferraro at Goldman Sachs: thank you for helping research the public companies and founders who were invited to participate. Jessica Canning at Dow Jones' VentureSource: your help was invaluable in identifying private company founders. Interns Aisha Saleem, Maddie DeWitt, and Matthew Movahhed also helped research

companies and founders. My thanks to Dr. Patrick Kavanaugh, author of *The Maverick CEO: Dane Miller and the Story of Biomet*, for allowing us to use one of his quotes and for his wonderful book about Dane Miller.

Once we identified the majority of founders and companies we wanted to include, we needed help with introductions and further identification of private company founders not easily located. To Jason Apple, Anna Belyaev, Buzz Benson, Pam Bishop, Dana Boyle, Jim Carey, Tony Christianson, Jay Cowles, Governor Jim Doyle (state of Wisconsin), Mike Ellwein, Darcy Evon, Rick Federico, Tom Figel, Dan Fleming, Cheryl Gain, Scott Glickson, Erik Greenfield, John Hanak, John Hoesley, Bekah Kent, Brad Lehrman, Rich Meeusen, Patti Moreth, Basil Mundy, John Neis, Jim Pearson, Freya Reeves, Lloyd Shefsky, David Sneider, David Snyder, Ed Spencer, Mark Stiegel, Dave Tolmie, Peter Urbain, Dale Wahlstrom, Scott Wald, Kevin Willer, and Bruce Zivian: thank you for your great ideas and your help, as well as your introductions to friends, resources, and champion founders. John Bergstrom, you saved us in Minnesota, a land that knew me not. Buckley Brinkman, Ron Leaf, Paula Norbom, Rex Lewis, and Chris Mahai: you went out of your way to be helpful and I am in your debt.

Without the existence of the Economic Club of Chicago, under the wonderful leadership of executive director Grace Barry, this book would not have been possible. Chicago benefits from having this powerful institution that includes the CEOs of many of the most successful companies headquartered in the city and suburbs, including technology companies and venture capital funds. Those who volunteered to help evaluate the candidates for this book are almost all members of the Economic Club, as are many of the

Chicago-area founders nominated for the book. This common bond eased the effort of gathering the founders back in September of 2008.

The Strategic Coach program, founded by Dan Sullivan, was my proving ground throughout the process of planning and executing this project, and I am grateful to Adrienne Duffy for her guidance and support and to Dan Sullivan for creating and growing a truly valuable organization.

To design the book, I relied on great advice from Abigail Pogrebin, author of *Stars of David* and *One and the Same*. Friends Bailey Allard and author Marti Barletta (*Marketing to Women*, *PrimeTime Women*) provided invaluable advice on design and naming the book. My good friend Mitch Rogatz, president of Triumph Books, coached me on every issue known to book publishers, a generous act of friendship.

My steadfast editor throughout was Denise Barr, ever cheerful and able to work with a diverse group of entrepreneurs. You see great photos of founders taken by Michael Candee at the kick-off event on September 8, 2008. The wonderful book design is due to Lee Blair, charged with the mission of creating two books in one. I thank my operations manager and RedFlash Press editor, Olivia Wolak, for her continuing excellence in everything she does, supervising every aspect of business with grace and intelligence. Marketing manager and RedFlash Press editor Erin Clement saved this book repeatedly by her attention to detail. My constant friends Dina Temple-Raston, Scott Goodman, Michael Tobin, Marc Ricard, Barbara Holmes, Bobby Yablunsky and Paul Rosenbaum listened through four years of planning and execution.

163

continued on 164

Acknowledgements

continued

To actually launch the book into the world, my thanks go to staff members Elias Crim, Jeff Weinman, and Maxine Weinman, as well as to Ellen Carnahan (again!) for sage advice on design and book launch. Michael Krauss not only helped by moderating the discussion on 9/8/08 but then proved to be the linchpin for making sure the launch event was a success. For publishing advice and for their help in making the November 16, 2010 publication date a great and memorable experience, I thank Arjun Aggarwal, Michael Alter, Karen Barch, Raman Chadha, Kapil Chaudhary, Kelly Cutler, Dana Damyen, Linda Darragh, Tom Figel, Terrance Flanagan, Anne Gilberg, Carl Gulbrandsen, Dave Guttman, Sarah Habansky, Fred Hoch, Ken Hunt, Steve Kaplan, Maria Katris, John Kessler, Ed Longanecker, Jessica Matthews, Spencer Maus, Bret Maxwell, Jim Jay, Catherine McGivney, Nancy Munro, Brad Niedermaier, Maura O'Hara, Mary Paskell, Dorothy Radke, Cindy Richards, John Roberson, Michael Roberts, Rod Shrader, Marty Singer, Spencer Stern, Gaye van den Hombergh, Ted Wallhaus, and Doug Whitley.

Of course this book was not possible without the cooperation and enthusiasm of the remarkable founders who agreed to share their thoughts. I do not take their affirmations lightly. If there is one commonality in the heart of America, it is, on the whole, modesty. More flamboyance would have made this book much bigger, but may have diminished some of these founders in their hard-fought results.

The unsung hero in any start-up is the spouse, the partner who listens to endless ideas and pitches all day and sometimes all night, and remains supportive through thick and thin. Sharon, my love, thank you. Let's hope all this hard work rubs off on Sophie and Eliana.

I did achieve my goal. I've become emboldened by these founders' optimism, good nature, and indomitable spirit. The practical nature of their advice not only helped me plan and complete this book, but pushed me along successfully in my own ventures. I hope their energy jumps off the page and encourages you with passion and determination.

Robert Jordan
Northbrook, Illinois
November 16, 2010

164

The Fine Print

We defined a successful founder as someone who launched, grew, and sold a company for approximately $100 million or more, or took a company public for $300 million or more in market valuation. I made exceptions to my own rule, and chose founders and co-founders based not only on the metrics, but also for their demonstrated ability to inspire. Every statement, statistic, question, and answer in the book should be taken as a matter of opinion from these founders.

We did not attempt to interview every qualified company founder in the region. And, where multiple founders were involved, we usually did not interview co-founders. The emphasis was, and is, on insight and inspiration, qualitative not quantitative. The selection of founders cannot be viewed as rigorous.

The author was a shareholder in InnerWorkings.

One more thing: while these companies experienced extraordinary success, in some cases I can guess that early or late investors did not all have good returns, and we don't mean to imply otherwise.

Thanks to These Organizations

Affinity Capital
Minneapolis, Minnesota

Bell, Boyd & Lloyd
Chicago, Illinois

BioBusiness Alliance
St. Louis Park, Minnesota

BioInitiative
Minneapolis, Minnesota

Cellular Dynamics
International, Inc.
Madison, Wisconsin

Cherry Tree Ventures
Minneapolis, Minnesota

Chicago Booth Business Book
Roundtable
Chicago, Illinois

Chicago Chamber of Commerce
Chicago, Illinois

Chicagoland Entrepreneurial
Center
Chicago, Illinois

Connelly Roberts & McGivney
Chicago, Illinois

DePaul University's Coleman
Entrepreneurship Center
Chicago, Illinois

Dow Jones VentureSource
San Francisco, California

The Economic Club of Chicago
Chicago, Illinois

Edgewater Funds
Chicago, Illinois

Entrepreneurs' Organization
Chicago, Illinois

Goldman Sachs
New York, New York

Google Inc. (Chicago Office)
Chicago, Illinois

i2a
Chicago, Illinois

Illinois Chamber of Commerce
Chicago, Illinois

Illinois Technology Association
Chicago, Illinois

Illinois Venture Capital Association
Chicago, Illinois

Inc. Magazine and Mansueto
Ventures
New York, New York

IvyLife
Chicago, Illinois

Kauffman Foundation
Kansas City, Missouri

Kellogg Alumni Club of Chicago
Chicago, Illinois

Kellogg Venture Community
Chicago, Illinois

Lake Effect Public Relations
Chicago, Illinois

Landmark Education
San Francisco, California

Market Strategy Group
Chicago, Illinois

McGuire Woods
Chicago, Illinois

Midwest Venture Partners
Chicago, Illinois

MIT Enterprise Forum
Chicago, Illinois

MK Capital
Northbook, Illinois

MOJO Minnesota
Minneapolis, Minnesota

MVC Capital, Inc.
Chicago, Illinois

NICO Corporation
Indianapolis, Indiana

The Polsky Center for
Entrepreneurship at Chicago Booth
Chicago, Illinois

Portage Equity Investments
Minneapolis, Minnesota

Portage Venture Partners
Chicago, Illinois

Prism Opportunity Fund
Chicago, Illinois

The Pritzker Group
Chicago, Illinois

Purdue Technology Centers
West Lafayette, Indiana

River Cities Capital Funds
Cincinnati, Ohio

RiverPoint Investments
Minneapolis, Minnesota

Seyen Capital Management
Chicago, Illinois

Southern Minnesota Initiative
Foundation
Mankato, Minnesota

Strategic Coach
Rosemont, Illinois

SurePayroll
Glenview, Illinois

TechAmerica
Naperville, Illinois

TechPoint
Indianapolis, Indiana

Throo Arch Partners
Minneapolis, Minnesota

THRIVE Wisconsin Biotechnology
Initiatives
Madison, Wisconsin

165

continued on 166

Thanks to These Organizations

continued

TiE Detroit
Detroit, Michigan

TiE Midwest
Chicago, Illinois

The UIC Institute for
Entrepreneurial Studies
Chicago, Illinois

University of Illinois
Champaign, Illinois

Wharton Club of Chicago
Chicago, Illinois

William Blair & Company
Chicago, Illinois

Winning Workplaces
Chicago, Illinois

Wisconsin Department of Tourism
Madison, Wisconsin

Wisconsin Investment Partners
Madison, Wisconsin

Contents

167

Index

171

About the Author

Robert Jordan is author of *How They Did It: Billion Dollar Insights from the Heart of America* and president of two companies: RedFlash and interimCEOinterimCFO.

A product of the University of Michigan, Jordan loved Ann Arbor so much he almost didn't come back home to Chicago after graduation. Following two years selling in the computer graphics division of Moore Business Forms, Jordan attended business school at Northwestern University's Kellogg School of Management. Academic life wasn't quite the same after having been allowed by Moore to sell solo in a territory covering New England with a boss 1,000 miles away. And coincidentally an opportunity to launch a company presented itself. In a class on entrepreneurship, Jordan heard a fellow student complain about having bought a brand-new PC with a modem but having not a clue whom to call or what databases to dial up.

Recognizing this as an opportunity, Jordan decided to publish a magazine about online services and commercial databases. With the help of seven fellow MBAs and management professor Stuart Meyer, he wrote a business plan that was awarded $5,000 from Kellogg alums who had formed an in-school venture fund. With that he dropped out to raise more money and launch *Online Access*, the first magazine anywhere in the world to cover the Internet. After a few years of fits and starts, things started to click, eventually landing Jordan on *Inc.* magazine's *Inc. 500* list of fastest-growing companies. Ten years along, the magazine was sold to CMP Media, which merged it into a competitive magazine.

Jordan then launched two companies: RedFlash, a project implementation team; and interimCEOinterimCFO, the worldwide network of interim, contract, and project executives.

The network has thousands of members from 42 countries and serves as a free resource for finding instant, executive talent on demand.

Jordan ran in the Chicago, San Diego, and New York marathons, and completed them very slowly. He eventually finished his degree at Kellogg and enjoys biking, tennis, reading, nature, spiritual study, making art, and spending time with family and friends.